Green Men &
White Swans

The Folklore of
British Pub Names

JACQUELINE SIMPSON

arrow books

Published by Arrow Books 2011

2 4 6 8 10 9 7 5 3 1

Copyright © Jacqueline Simpson 2010

Jacqueline Simpson has asserted her right under the Copyright,
Designs and Patents Act, 1988, to be identified as the author of this work

First published in Great Britain in 2010 by
Random House Books
Random House, 20 Vauxhall Bridge Road,
London SW1V 2SA

www.randomhouse.co.uk

Addresses for companies within The Random House Group Limited can be found
at: www.randomhouse.co.uk/offices.htm

The Random House Group Limited Reg. No. 954009

A CIP catalogue record for this book is available from the British Library

ISBN 9780099520177

The Random House Group Limited supports the Forest Stewardship
Council® (FSC®), the leading international forest certification organisation.
All our titles that are printed on Greenpeace approved FSC® certified paper
carry the FSC® logo. Our paper procurement policy can be found at:
www.randomhouse.co.uk/environment

Printed and bound in Great Britain by
CPI Bookmarque, Croydon, CR0 4TD

Illustrations on pp.155 and 167 are reproduced by kind permission of:
The Bridgeman Art Library: detail from 'King Arthur findeth ye old
Woman in ye hut', illustration from *The Story of King Arthur and his
Knights*, 1903 (litho) by Pyle, Howard (1853-1911) (Private Collection/
The Stapleton Collection); Fortean Picture Library: illustration from
'The Wonderful Legend of the Lambton Worm'.

Contents

Introduction

Before anything else, I must warn readers that this is a book about pub names of the past as well as those still current. Pubs have always been vulnerable to having their names changed when they are taken over by new owners or absorbed into a larger chain with its own favoured naming pattern, or because the landlord wishes them to be more up to date and trendy. Local protests are usually disregarded; when an MP raised the issue in Parliament in July 2000, the Culture Secretary, Chris Smith, sadly admitted that 'it is up to the owners of a business to choose its name', though he hoped the breweries 'would bear in mind the unique historic role that many of our public houses have, and think twice before destroying that'.

Worse still, pubs get closed down, a sad fate which is becoming alarmingly common at the present time. So I cannot guarantee that any pub of which I have written in the present tense will still carry the same name, or even will still exist at all, by the time this book is in the shops a few months hence. Signboards are even more vulnerable; they need to be repainted every few years, and artists often take the opportunity to modernise the image. Anybody wanting to visit a pub because of its attractive name or the description of its signboard given here would do well to check in the phone book before setting out.

As a means of identifying a drinking place, physical objects have a history at least as long as painted images or words. In Roman towns, even though most of the people could read and write, taverns advertised themselves by a wreath of ivy or vine leaves hung from a pole, which was taken as an allusion to Bacchus, the god of wine. It is generally supposed (though documentary proof is lacking) that the taverns of Celtic Britain adopted the Roman custom, and that it eventually developed into the 'garland' or 'bush' which medieval innkeepers were required to display whenever they put a fresh brew on sale. The Romans also used painted tavern signs, while their shopkeepers and craftsmen advertised themselves by the display of actual objects, pictorial signs, and terracotta plaques related to their trade; several examples of which have been found in the ruins of Pompeii and Herculaneum.

This custom too was carried over into medieval times; indeed, objects displayed as tradesmen's signs were common in English towns in the seventeenth and eighteenth centuries, and were still to be seen in London in the middle of the nineteenth. By the late twentieth, however, the only survivors (increasingly rare) were the striped pole of the barber, the glass carboys and ornate jars of the pharmacist, the three brass balls of the pawnshop – and, arguably, the blue lamp of the police station and the notorious red lamp of the brothel.

As towns grew, medieval tavern-keepers found it necessary to identify their premises individually, by adopting some immediately recognisable emblem in addition to the 'bush'; this was either painted on a signboard or made in wood or metal and suspended from the front of the building. This is thought to be the origin of simple signs with strong visual impact, such as the Star, the Half Moon, the Bell, the Globe, the Crown, the

Bull, the Bear, the Mermaid, and so forth. These could of course also be used by theatres, brothels, and later by coffee-houses. More complex images drew upon religious art and symbols; many medieval inns were specifically intended to be hostels for the hundreds of pilgrims travelling to the holy shrines at Canterbury, Walsingham, Glastonbury, and elsewhere, and such inns were generally owned by monastic houses. Despite the Reformation, a few religious names and signs continued in use for centuries – see ANGELS & SAINTS, p. 16. Another major influence which first came into play in medieval times is that of heraldry, both aristocratic and commercial – see p. 248. Jacob Larwood and J. C. Hotten discussed a large number of heraldic pub signs in the fourth and fifth chapters of their *History of Signboards* (1866, revised as *English Inn Signs* in 1951).

As time went on, the range of subjects considered suitable as pub names grew ever broader, more diverse, and more fanciful. This book limits itself to those that relate to folklore. So what are the boundaries of folklore? For present purposes, I have taken it to include legends and traditional jokes about a particular locality (or about the pub itself), nursery rhymes, fairytales, pantomime, ballads and folksongs, superstitions, traditional customs (local or national), legendary heroes, witches and wizards, figures from mythology, supernatural beings such as mermaids and hobgoblins, and imaginary creatures such as dragons. Historical persons as such are excluded, but those who owe their fame more to legend than to fact (King Arthur, Robin Hood and his companions, Dick Turpin) are well represented; similarly if the pub's name refers to a legend about a historical person rather than to the person himself (e.g. Drake's Drum), it is included. Some cases are debatable; many people would claim that the murderous Sawney Bean and Sweeney Todd really existed, but in my view there is no adequate evidence that they were ever anything more than horrific legends, and so they will be found here. There are many references to local traditions about smugglers and highwaymen, usually anonymous. Gruesome tales of murder and suicide are equally common. Wicked innkeepers who murder travellers and hide the bodies; suicidal innkeepers; the unlikely discovery of bones or of buckets of blood – all these, and similar macabre ideas, will be found here as 'explanations' of pub names.

The dividing line between literature and folklore was rather harder to establish. Clearly, anonymous medieval writings such as the romances of Guy of Warwick and of Valentine and Orson can count as folkloric sources. Equally clearly, the novels of Dickens or Scott are literature, so pubs named after their characters must be excluded, but what of the Cheshire Cat, the March Hare, the Owl and the Pussy Cat, and indeed the Hobbit? It seemed to me that the works of Lewis Carroll and Edward Lear are now so thoroughly integrated with the largely anonymous and traditional body of 'things every child knows' that their creations have now become 'folklore' to most of the public, and that the same will eventually be true for Tolkien's hobbits – whose name is in any case related to genuinely folkloric figures, the hobs and hobgoblins. Another borderline category consists of names drawn from Roman mythology, e.g. Atlas, Bacchus, Cupid, or Hercules; a thorough knowledge of classical myth was taken for granted among the educated elite, but the 'folk' too would be aware of the most famous gods. There are some pub names where the allusion to mythology comes at second hand, via a reference to a famous ship or aircraft which had borne that name (e.g. Minerva, Pegasus, Vulcan). Cases of such indirect transmission are included.

The most fascinating names, however, are those drawn directly from traditional British local lore, especially when the pub bearing the name is in the very place to which the story belongs – the Lambton Worm at Chester-le-Street, for instance, the Rattlebone at Sherstone, or the Mother Shipton at Knaresborough. Sadly, such names can fall victim to changes in fashion, or to closure and demolition; I mourn the loss of the unique Flying Monk at Malmesbury and the Treacle Mine Hotel at Tadley. Fortunately there are signs of a counter-trend, with pubs that previously bore commonplace names being given new and individual ones which evoke local associations and landmarks; examples include the Giant Inn at Cerne Abbas, the Giant's Rest at Wilmington, the Camelot at South Cadbury, the Pendle Witch in several Lancashire towns. There is a recently built Treacle Mine at Grays in Essex, and a recently renamed Noose and Monkey at Aberdeen. Hopefully the trend will continue, drawing on the ample resources of local legend and custom.

This book cannot claim to be the final word on this subject. There are sure to be pubs which do have stories attached to their names but which escaped my notice because the fact is not obvious to an outsider. For instance, the Plough, or Plough and Horses, is a common name to which no folktale or belief is normally attached, yet by sheer chance I discovered that the Plough at Beddington does have a story to it – a story involving caves, tunnels, and smugglers, all of which are regular elements in British local folklore. On the other hand, not everything that seems folkloric actually is. Searching through the Cardiff phone book I found the intriguingly named Nine Giants pub. What giants were these, I wondered – characters in some local tale? Possibly a circle of nine standing stones somewhere in Wales?

Not so. When I rang, I discovered that they were nine very large trees which used to stand in a garden behind this pub. But all is not lost; if this pub endures, and keeps its name, perhaps a new legend will develop when the trees are long forgotten, and there really will be giants involved. For that is how folklore often grows, wittingly or unwittingly, by recombining elements of old traditions and adapting them to fit a new site.

The pioneering work on the development and significance of pub names – or rather, of the pictorial signboards from which the names arose – is the classic *History of Signboards* by Jacob Larwood and John Camden Hotten, first published in 1866 and regularly revised and reprinted up to 1907; an abridged and updated version which appeared in 1951 under the title *English Inn Signs* is very useful, but can cause problems over dating, since it is often unclear whether a particular comment belongs to the older or the more recent part of the text. The equally extensive collection of *Pub Names of Britain* by Leslie Dunkling and Gordon Wright limits itself to names which were current when they wrote; it was first published in 1987, and revised in 1994. These two books were my primary resource when seeking names to be included in the present study, supplemented by Eric R. Delderfield's *British Inn Signs and Their Stories* (1965, 1972), Bryant Lillywhite's *London Signs* (1972), Paul Corballis's *Pub Signs* (1988), and much trawling through telephone directories. Searching the Internet sometimes also turned out to be useful in locating present-day examples of a name already known or suspected to exist, but the saying 'absence of evidence is not evidence of absence' applies strongly to this method – only a small minority of pubs have websites, and those that do rarely bother to explain the origin of their name or to show their signboard.

I would like to thank all those who gave me information: Paul Cowdell, John and Hilary Daniels, Mark Handsley, Jeremy Harte, Caroline Oates, Ben Parker, Ron Payne, Bernard Pearson, Dusty Roades, Steve Roud, Keith Shipton, Ron Shuttleworth, Robert Turpin, the Surrey History Centre, and the unknown staff at various pubs who patiently answered phone calls enquiring about their names and signboards.

Adam & Eve

See ANGELS & SAINTS, p. 16

Aladdin's Lamp

A handful of tales from the *Arabian Nights* (also called *The Thousand and One Nights*) have become so popular in children's storybooks and as the basis for pantomimes that their foreign origin is almost forgotten. One such is the story of Aladdin and the magic oil lamp he accidentally acquires; when he rubs it, out comes a huge genie which calls him 'Master' and will fulfil all his wishes. Hence the Aladdin's Lamp pub in Darlaston, Staffordshire.

Anchor & Hope

See ANGELS & SAINTS, p. 16

Angel

See SALUTATION and ANGELS & SAINTS, p. 16

Arms: *Blacksmiths' Arms, Bricklayers' Arms, Butchers' Arms*

See PUNS & OLD JOKES, p. 138

Arms: *Norfolk Arms, Marlborough Arms, Salisbury Arms*

See QUEENS' HEADS & RED LIONS, p. 248

Ashen Faggot

At Northleigh in Devon there is a pub whose name commemorates a festive custom which was once common in farmhouses in that county, and in neighbouring areas of Somerset and Dorset. On Christmas Eve the farmer would gather his family, his servants, and his labourers round the hearth, on which lay a massive faggot made up of sticks of ash-wood bound together by many strips of hazel, withies, or brambles. As the fire took hold the ties would eventually burst, one by one; as each broke, the assembled company would shout and cheer, and take a good drink of cider. By the time all were burnt through, a great deal of liquor had been consumed. The custom is first recorded at the beginning of the nineteenth century, and though it may have developed out of the older and much more widespread custom of burning a Yule Log, it has become a lively drinking game. It is still kept up in some pubs, and probably also in a few homes.

Astolat

The Astolat pub at Peasmarsh, near Guildford (Surrey), is named after a place mentioned in Malory's *Morte d'Arthur* and other Arthurian romances as the home of the unfortunate Elaine who died of unrequited love for Sir Lancelot – see LADY OF SHALOTT.

Atlas

In Greek mythology, Atlas was one of the Titans, a group of powerful giants who made war on the gods, were defeated, and were condemned to bear various punishments for all eternity – his was to carry the whole heavy world on his back. He is represented as stooped or half kneeling, with a globe balanced on his shoulders. In the late seventeenth century, this figure was adopted by Flemish map-makers as their emblem (so giving us the word 'atlas'); it became the international trademark of all who made or sold maps and globes. But since few people nowadays remember the link between atlases and the Titan Atlas, when his name is given to a pub (such as the one in Bath), this is probably more a tribute to mythology than to cartography.

B

Babes in the Wood

The story which inspired this pub name at several places in
Yorkshire – York itself, Dewsbury, Batley, and Hanging Heaton
– is now chiefly known as a pantomime plot, where it has been
elaborated so as to include Robin Hood and Maid Marian as its
leading characters. Originally, however, it was a simple, pathetic
tale of two orphan children whose uncle hires men to murder them, so that he can get their fortune. Instead, the thugs
abandon the children in a lonely wood, and there, after trying
to survive by eating blackberries, they meet their end. In the
words of a ballad which Thomas Percy included in his *Reliques
of Ancient English Poetry* (1765):

> Thus wandered these poor innocents,
>   Till deathe did end their grief,
> In one anothers arms they dyed,
>   As wanting due relief.
>
> No burial these pretty babes
>   Of any man receives,
> Till Robin Redbreast piously
>   Did cover them with leaves.

And now the heavy wrathe of God
   Upon their uncle fell;
Yea, fearful fiends did haunt his house,
   His conscience felt an hell.

His barnes were fired, his goodes consumed,
   His landes were barren made,
His cattle dyed within the field,
   And nothing with him stayed.

And in a voyage to Portugal
   Two of his sons did dye;
And to conclude, himself was brought
   To want and miserye.

This deeply moral tale was not always taken very seriously. In the eighteenth century, 'babes in the wood' was a slang term for criminals who were being punished in the (wooden) pillory

The Babes in the Wood

or stocks. The pub at Hanging Heaton adopted this humorous interpretation for its sign.

Bacchus

Bacchus is the Roman god of wine, corresponding to the Greek Dionysus, who is obviously suitable as the patron of any drinking place. Like other deities from classical mythology, he would have been far more familiar to people in previous generations than to our own; 'Bacchus' and 'Jolly Bacchus' pubs were therefore common. In art Bacchus is normally represented as a young, vigorous and bearded man, crowned with vine leaves and flourishing a goblet of wine, but for some unknown reason signboard-painters of the early eighteenth century preferred to show him as a fat little child, rather like a cupid or a cherub, sitting astride a barrel. Pubs with signs of this type often came to be known as the Boy and Barrel, for example at Selby in West Yorkshire.

Bag o' Nails

This name, once common in London and elsewhere, was shown by Bryant Lillywhite in his *London Signs* (1972) to be a straightforward example of the adoption of a trade emblem – in this case, the emblem of ironmongers. It has been included here because of a widespread and persistent claim that it is really a 'corruption' of the allegedly 'original' name Bacchanals or Bacchanalia, a rowdy Roman festival in honour of the wine-god Bacchus. No evidence has been brought in support of this speculation, which like other such theories is more ingenious than convincing.

Baptist's Head

See ANGELS & SAINTS, p. 16

Bar t'at

The clue to this apparently meaningless name is that it belongs to a pub in Ilkley in Yorkshire, and that this pub was previously called the Ilkley Moor. It alludes to a local folksong which has become known far and wide as the anthem for Yorkshire people wherever they may be, 'On Ilkley Moor baht 'at'. The last two words mean 'without a hat', but their spelling has been distorted in the pub's name, for the sake of a clever pun upon the word 'bar', nowadays a fashionable element in such names.

The song is a gruesome tale of the consequences of wandering hatless on the cold moors. The singer asks, 'Where hast tha been since I saw thee?' and follows up with the accusation, 'Tha's been a-courtin' Mary Jane / On Ilkley Moor baht 'at.' This leads to the warning 'Tha'll go an' catch thy death o' cold /On Ilkley Moor baht 'at', and so to 'We'll have to go and bury thee', 'Then t'worms'll coom and ate thee oop', 'Then t'ducks'll coom and ate oop t'worms', 'Then we shall coom and ate oop t'ducks', and finally:

> So we shall all have etten thee,
> On Ilkley Moor baht 'at,
> On Ilkley Moor baht 'at, on Ilkley Moor baht 'at,
> On Ilkley Moor baht 'at.

Barley Mow, Barley Stack

As a noun, the word 'mow' now seems mysterious, but it was once familiar to English farmers. It means a pile or heap, and a 'barley mow' is a stack of newly harvested barley, which will later be threshed. Since beer is made from barley, it is appropriate for a pub to be called the Barley Mow (as is the case at Chiswick, Tandridge, Oswestry and elsewhere), often with a sign showing reapers happily dancing round the stacked sheaves. There is a traditional drinking song that begins:

> Here's a health to the barley mow, my boys,
> Here's a health to the barley mow,
> We'll drink it out of the jolly brown bowl,
> Here's a health to the barley mow!

The Barley Mow

It continues through many verses, according to how many likely or unlikely vessels the singers can imagine themselves drinking from.

Though the name is still quite common, the fact that it includes an obscure word has suggested one of those exercises in misplaced ingenuity which purport to 'explain' pub names: it has been alleged to 'really' come from the French *bel amour*, 'fair beloved'. But the painter William Hogarth knew quite well what it means, and how it is connected to England's national drink;

in his painting *Beer Street* (1751) – the happy, healthy companion-piece to his sinister *Gin Lane* – the scene includes a prosperous pub of this name, with its sign being repainted.

See also HARVESTERS & WHEATSHEAVES, p. 182

Bear, Bear & Bells

See GAMES & SPORTS, p. 78

Bear & Ragged Staff

This name is found at Berkswell in Warwickshire, Romsey in Hampshire, Crayford in Kent, and elsewhere. It is represented visually by a bear rearing up on its hind legs, chained to a club formed from a tree-trunk whose branches have been roughly lopped, leaving it 'ragged'. This curious term is a distortion of the correct heraldic semi-French name for such an object, a 'staff ragulee'. Some pubs have dropped the 'Ragged', which makes little sense in modern English, while at Bristol it has been changed to 'Rugged'. This image is of heraldic origin; the bear and staff formed the crest of the coat of arms of the Neville family, the earls of Warwick. According to their family traditions, the first earl, who was named Arthgal and lived in the time of King Arthur, once killed a bear by strangling it with his bare hands, while another early ancestor, named Morvidius, slew a giant with a club made from a tree. It need hardly be said that neither the names, nor the dating, nor the feats of strength should be taken as historically plausible. Crests and coats of arms developed in the latter part of the Middle Ages, and gave rise to legends purporting to explain heraldic designs.

See also QUEENS' HEADS & RED LIONS, p. 248

Bel & the Dragon

It would be intriguing to know why a pub at Cookham-on-Thames in Berkshire has adopted the curious and unusual name of Bel and the Dragon. The source is a couple of stories about adventures of the prophet Daniel – he who is best remembered now for being thrown into a lions' den – which were folktales added onto the original account of this colourful figure in some versions of the Old Testament. They have been excluded from most Protestant bibles, but can be found in Roman Catholic ones as Chapter 14 of the Book of Daniel; they were well known in the Middle Ages.

The first story concerns an image of the god Bel in a temple in Babylon. The king of Babylon tried to convince Daniel that this was a real live god, who ate all the offerings of food which were left in the temple every day. Daniel said it was only a statue, and that statues do not eat, so the king ordered the priests of Bel to prove that it was indeed the god who was taking the food. Either they or Daniel would be put to death, according to the outcome. The priests suggested that the temple doors should be sealed overnight, and promised that by next morning the god would have eaten everything. Daniel accepted the test, but scattered ashes over the floor after the priests had left. In the morning, the food had indeed disappeared, though the seals were unbroken; however, a trail of footprints proved that the priests had re-entered by a secret door and carried it away to eat it themselves.

The second story tells how the king then ordered Daniel to worship a dragon which lived in the city, and was a living creature, not a statue. Daniel admitted it was alive but denied that it was a god:

But give me leave, O king, and I will kill this dragon without sword or club. And the king said: I give thee leave.

Then Daniel took pitch and fat and hair, and boiled them together: and he made lumps and put them into the dragon's mouth. And the dragon burst asunder. And he said: Behold him whom you worshipped.

This is an early example of a device often found in folktales, especially local legends, where a clever hero destroys a dragon by giving it something poisonous or explosive to eat.

Bell

There are very many 'Bell' pubs and inns throughout the country, their signs showing either a church bell or a hand-bell – for ringing a set of tuned hand-bells was a skill once widely practised by teams of men. Usually, no further explanation is offered, but occasionally the name is linked to a local legend.

At Bosham, a coastal village in West Sussex, a pub named the Bell overlooks the harbour. The story goes that centuries ago a shipload of Vikings raided the village and sacked its church, carrying away the finest of its bells. As they set sail with their booty, the villagers pealed the remaining bells in thanksgiving that the danger was over. When the stolen bell heard the peal, it broke the ropes that held it, gave one last melodious clang, and crashed through the bottom of the ship. The Vikings were all drowned. As for the bell, it came to rest at a

The Bell

particularly deep part of the harbour channel (now called Bell Hole) and has remained there ever since. The Bosham men did once manage to fix a rope to it and began to draw it towards the shore, using a team of pure white oxen, as a Wise Woman had told them they must; but at the very moment when success seemed certain the rope broke and the bell rolled all the way back – for one ox had a single black hair on its tail. It is said that sometimes, if one stands at a certain spot, one can hear the sunken bell still ringing under water.

Where pubs are named the Six Bells or Eight Bells, this is generally an allusion to the number of bells in the village church.

Bell & Hare

It is usually thought that incongruous and apparently meaningless 'double' names came about because some landlord decided to combine the name of his newly acquired pub with that of his previous one. This could well have been the origin for the Bell and Hare in Tottenham, London, but at some point a sign-painter chose to relate it to themes from folklore. Well into the nineteenth century, there was a common belief in country districts that witches could turn themselves into hares, which no huntsman could catch or wound unless he himself had a magical hound, or used silver bullets. On the other hand, the notion of excommunicating the wicked and exorcising demons, or some other evil force, by 'bell, book and candle' was – and still is – a proverbial commonplace. The sign for this pub therefore shows a black hare fleeing from an open book, a burning candle, and a large hand-bell which is wildly ringing.

See also GAMES & SPORTS, p. 78

Bell & Mackerel

This curious name once belonged to a pub in the Mile End Road, London. The original reason for it is unknown; probably, like Bell and Hare, it is an arbitrary combination. However, a humorous explanation was current in the middle of the twentieth century, as recorded by Martin Thornhill in his *Explorer's England*. It was alleged that there was a foolish young fisherman who caught a mackerel but decided that he wasn't hungry just then, and had better save it for later. So he tied a bell round it and threw it back into the sea, believing that when he wanted it he would find it again by listening for the bell. The same story is told of pubs named the Fish and Bell. It is a good example of a type of joke which used to be very widespread, though now old-fashioned, describing all sorts of silly and futile actions supposedly done by simple-minded fools.

See also PUNS & OLD JOKES, p. 138

Bell-Savage (Belle Sauvage)

One of the oldest and most famous coaching inns in eighteenth-century London was the Belle Sauvage on Ludgate Hill, demolished in the 1870s. The actual origins of this curious name are quite prosaic. It is first recorded in 1452 as 'Savage's Inn' – this being presumably the landlord's name – and it is known to have had 'the Bell on the Hoop' as its sign. Combining the two gives Bell–Savage. According to an essayist in the *Spectator* of 2 April 1710, the signboard at that time showed 'a savage man standing by a bell'. This he found puzzling, and suggested that reference might be to 'an old romance translated out of the French, which gives an account of a very beautiful woman who is found in a wilderness and is called La Belle Sauvage'. The inn soon adopted this feminine form of its name, which in turn gave rise to a popular belief that the famous Pocahontas, the Native American chieftain's daughter who married an Englishman, stayed at this inn in 1616–17; it is almost certain that this is merely a legend based on the inn's unusual name.

Bishop Blaize (Blaise)

There are pubs named for this saint at Richmond in Yorkshire, Andover in Hampshire, and elsewhere. He is thought to have been the bishop of Sebaste in Armenia in the fourth century, and to have died a martyr. His popularity in medieval England was due to his role as patron of the important trade guild of woolcombers, because of the tradition that during his martyrdom he was tortured by having his flesh torn with iron carding combs. His emblem is either a pair of such combs or a pair of candles, the latter referring to a gift of candles he received from a woman whose son he miraculously restored to life when he had choked on a fishbone.

See also ANGELS & SAINTS, p. 16

Black Cap

See MOTHER BLACKCAP

Black Cat

In Britain, since the middle of the nineteenth century, it has been more and more widely believed that a black cat brings good luck, with the result that this image is common nowa-

days on charms, and on cards wishing the recipient luck or success. It is
therefore surprising that it is rare as a
pub name; one example can be found
at Chesham in Buckinghamshire, and
another in Bristol. The reason that it
is not more common may be that at
the same period there was a counter-

The Black Cat

belief (still prevalent in the USA) that black cats were associated with witches and the devil, so to meet one boded evil. Even
in England, traces of this ambiguity remain; among actors, for
instance, it is sometimes said that though it brings good luck to
a theatre to have a resident black cat, it would be bad luck for
the animal to cross the stage during a performance.

Black Dog

A 'Black Dog' pub is not necessarily so called for folkloric reasons; there are after all plenty of hunting dogs, racing dogs,
and pets of various breeds which simply happen to be black.
However, there are many instances where the story-telling
impulse has obviously been at work. In Weymouth, for example, the Black Dog pub boasts that it was named after the very
first dog of that colour ever seen in England. Folklore loves the
idea of something or someone being the first, or the last, of its
kind.

The explanatory tale may involve history, real or supposed,
local or national. Thus the story told at the coastal village of
Yapton in West Sussex to explain the name of its Black Dog
pub (which was changed a few years ago) draws on an alleged
episode of local history, to pathetic effect. It is claimed that after

Angels & Saints

There is no doubt that during the Middle Ages a high proportion of inns and taverns chose names and symbols with religious significance, especially those catering for long-distance travellers on pilgrimage, those on land owned by a monastic order, and those wishing to honour the patron saint of a local church. They would have offered a reassuring implication of peace, security and heavenly protection. However, the Protestant Reformation and the yet more radical Puritanism of Cromwell's time eliminated many of the old names; since they were so closely linked to Catholicism. Only biblical persons and episodes might win their approval – Adam and Eve, RAINBOW & DOVE, Samson and the Lion, David and Goliath, PILLAR OF SALT, Jacob's Ladder, Jacob's Well, the Baptist's Head, and the Good Samaritan were popular names of this type, still occasionally used.

Of the medieval names, probably the most widespread survival is the Angel. It is generally thought that its early versions originated from inns called the SALUTATION whose signboards showed the Archangel Gabriel greeting the Virgin Mary; Protestant objections to the cult of Mary would have caused her figure to be removed, leaving only that of the angel. But there are two more archangels named in the Bible, Michael and Raphael. Michael was famous for doing battle against Satan and driving him out of Heaven (Rev. 12:7–9); if the angel on an inn sign is spearing a dragon, as at Wootton Bassett in Wiltshire and Birch in Suffolk, he is definitely the Archangel Michael. As for Raphael, he is mentioned only in the Book of Tobias, one of the apocryphal books of the Old Testament included in Catholic bibles but not Protestant ones; there, he appears in human form to help the young

Tobias on a dangerous journey. This would make him a suitable patron for travellers, hence for inns, but his name is not recorded in this connection. There are also, of course, many anonymous guardian angels.

As regards saints, Leslie Dunkling and Gordon Wright reckoned that at their time of writing there were 'some seventy different saints mentioned in British pub names', but warned that in many cases this is simply because the pub is echoing the name of the church in whose parish it stands, or of the village or town; it need not imply any real awareness of the saint or his legend. By far the most popular is of course St George (see GEORGE & DRAGON), whose status as England's warlike patron protected him from Protestant disapproval. Others survived the Reformation because they were the patrons of important trade guilds, e.g. BISHOP BLAIZE for woolcombers, St Crispin for shoemakers, St Dunstan for blacksmiths. Two saints were regarded as patrons and protectors of travellers, CHRISTOPHER and Julian; both are probably purely legendary, and their cults died out in Protestant Britain. Their names are only occasionally found attached to a pub.

There are interesting examples where a pub's name reveals knowledge not simply of the saint but of some colourful traditional tale about him or her, e.g. DEVIL & DUNSTAN, DEVIL IN THE BOOT, FISH & RING. It is intriguing, too, that one or two of the pubs called the Quiet/Silent/Headless/Good Woman (see QUIET WOMAN) originally celebrated a female saint who was martyred by beheading, before being reinterpreted as a sexist joke.

Quite often, a pub name which seems on the surface to be either purely realistic or merely fanciful is actually based (probably indirectly) on an image which to the medieval mind symbolised a religious truth. The PELICAN, the PHOENIX, and the UNICORN conveyed theological dogmas or moral lessons. The LAMB & FLAG came from the Agnus Dei, a visual symbol of Christ, while the CROSS KEYS is the heraldic emblem of the Papacy and a reference to St Peter. An anchor is ambiguous; often it simply shows that a pub has some connection with seafaring, but if it is combined with the word 'hope' it is the traditional symbol for one of the three cardinal virtues (Faith, Hope and Charity), because of St Paul's reference to hope as 'a sure and steadfast anchor of the soul' (Heb. 6:19).

a smuggler was killed by revenue men while he was drinking there, his faithful black dog ran constantly up and down the village, searching for him – and that its ghost is still searching. At Southam in Warwickshire there is a Black Dog pub whose signboard seems at first sight quite irrelevant, for it shows a medieval knight in armour watching with satisfaction while another is having his head chopped off on an executioner's block. This is in fact a tribute to a medieval Earl of Warwick whose nickname was Black Dog, and commemorates an incident in 1312 when he captured Piers Gaveston, the widely hated favourite of Edward II, and ordered him to be beheaded. As the prisoner was led away the earl taunted him: 'The Black Dog of Arden is come to keep his oath that you would one day feel his teeth.'

There are also numerous local legends of ghostly and demonic black dogs haunting particular roads or houses, some of which have influenced local names, including those of pubs. Uplyme, on the border of Devon and Dorset, is a case in point. Since the middle of the nineteenth century it has had a Black Dog Inn, incorporating parts of an older farmhouse, itself built on the site of an old mansion destroyed in the Civil War. The road alongside used to be called Dog Lane; it is now Hayes Lane. According to the legend (first published in the 1860s), every evening as the farmer sat by the fire a large black dog would appear from nowhere and lie down on the settle on the opposite side of the hearth. His neighbours reckoned it must be a demon, but he himself did not mind the uncanny beast. One night, however, the farmer came home drunk, and angry because someone had accused him of being too frightened of the strange dog to drive it away. Seeing it by the fire he tried to hit it with the poker, but the dog rushed upstairs, into an attic, and out through the roof. The farmer struck the poker against the spot where the dog had disappeared, and down fell a box full of gold and silver coins from the times of Charles I. The lucky farmer used the money he found to turn the farm into an inn.

A very sinister legend from Elizabethan times tells of a demonic dog at Newgate Prison, in London EC4, which was demolished in 1902 to make way for the Old Bailey; there used to be a Black Dog Tavern nearby, which can hardly be a coincidence. This creature is first mentioned in a poem of 1596 written by a prisoner, Luke Hutton, and seems to be intended as the embodiment of the despair and guilt felt by the inmates. A woodcut on the title-page shows it as a man-sized monster rearing on its hind legs; it wears a spiked collar with a chain dangling from it, snakes sprout from its head, and its belly is open, revealing its heart. The full story is given in a 1638 pamphlet entitled *The Discovery of a London Monster, called the Blacke Dogg of Newgate*. Two men are drinking at the Black Dog, and one tells the other the horrible tale. During the reign of Henry III, he says, there was a famine so severe that the Newgate prisoners were driven by starvation to kill and eat one another.

Amongst many others cast into this Denne of misery, there was a certaine Scholler brought thither upon suspition of Conjuring, and that he by Charmes and devilish Witchcrafts had done much hurt to the King's subjects, which Scholler, mauger [in spite of] his Devils, Furies, Spirits and Goblins, was by the famished prisoners eaten up, and deemed passing good meat. This being done, such an idle conceit possessed the mindes of the poore Prisoners, that they supposed nightly to see the Scholler in the shape of a black Dog walking up and downe the Prison, ready with his ravening Jawes to tear out their Bowels, for his

late human flesh they had so hungerly eaten, and withall they
hourely heard (as they thought) strange groanes and cries, as if it
had been some creature in great paine and torments . . . in which
desperation they killed the Keeper, and so many of them escaped
forth, but yet whither soever they came or went they imagined
a Blacke Dog to follow, and by this means, as I doe thinke, the
name of him began.

But the other drinker calls this 'an idle fiction':

I know it for a truth, that there is no other blacke Dog, that I ever
saw or heard of, but a great blacke stone standing in the dungeon
called *Limbo*, the place where the condemned Prisoners be put
after their Judgement, upon which they set a burning candle
in the night, against which I have heard that a desperate condemned Prisoner dashed out his braines.

Nevertheless, tales about the phantom dog persisted for generations, often asserting that it would appear on the night
before an execution. Even now, though Newgate Prison itself
no longer exists, books about London's ghosts talk of a shape-
less, stinking black form that slithers along the top of a wall in
Amen Court (off Warwick Lane) which was once the boundary of 'Deadman's Walk', an alley leading from the prison to the
place of execution. This, they say, is how the Dog now manifests
itself.

See also GHOSTLY BARMAIDS & HAUNTED CELLARS, p. 278

Black Horse

This is one of the most widespread pub signs, and seems generally to be chosen simply because it makes an attractive picture, or for some practical reason such as there being racing stables nearby. However, it can also become a focus for the creation of a legend about some phantom horse and its ghostly rider. A well-developed example concerns the old Black Horse Inn in Windsor, which was demolished long ago but has left its name to a passageway called Black Horse Yard. It is said that at rare intervals a phantom coach drawn by two unnaturally large black horses has been seen emerging from this alley at full gallop at the dead of night, heading for Windsor Park; it carries the ghost of a doctor who was hastily summoned to the deathbed of Charles II in 1685. This is supposed to be an omen of death for the reigning monarch, and it is said to have been seen in 1910 when Edward VII was dying.

The Black Horse

Black Robin

At Kingston in Kent there is a Black Robin pub which explains its name by reference to what is believed to be local history. It is said to have been the nickname of a highwayman who was active in the district in times past, and who wore a black mask and rode a black horse.

See also HIGHWAYMEN & SMUGGLERS, p. 208

Black Smock

The Black Smock pub in Stathe (Somerset) owes its name to a tale which, though unmistakably flippant in tone, does draw upon elements of older folk belief. According to this legend, a witch who lived in this village always wore a white smock, until one day she was chased up a chimney, and emerged covered in soot. She was then chased across Sedgemoor until she transformed herself into a hare and escaped.

Witches in folklore are quite frequently said to fly up a chimney on their broomsticks, not because they are being chased but because this makes a good story; it is a way, both dramatic and plausible, to explain how they can leave their homes undetected and in spite of locked doors. As for the transformation into a hare, this is one of the most widespread English anecdotes of witchcraft. In its standard form, it goes: There was once a witch who would regularly change into a hare in order to steal milk from her neighbours' cows, and in order to taunt huntsmen who would try in vain to shoot her. The hare always bolted into the witch's cottage, and when the hunters reached it, all they found was the old woman sitting quietly there. But one day a man loaded his gun with a silver bullet and managed

to hit the hare's rump, and next day the witch was limping
badly.

Blackamoor's Head

This name, found in Cambridge, is a variation on SARACEN'S
HEAD and Turk's Head.

Blade Bone

The real reason for this pub name in the East End of London
is unknown, but in their book of 1994 Leslie Dunkling and
Gordon Wright report a bizarre legend about it: that a murdered
man's body had been hidden in the cellar, and that when it was
discovered the landlord persuaded the police to let him keep one
shoulder-blade as a memento, to be displayed for the customers. It makes a good tale, but there could be other explanations.
Perhaps a real but remarkable blade bone of a whale was once on
display, or even that of a dinosaur, as was done at the similarly
named pub at Buckleberry Common near Reading in Berkshire
(also noted by Dunkling and Wright). Or perhaps it was a joke
based on the former popularity of Shoulder of Mutton as a name
for an inn which served food as well as drink, implying that here
the joint was so tasty that only the bone was left.

Bladud Arms, Bladud's Head

Two Somerset villages near Bath, Lower Swainswick and
Larkhall, chose to name their pubs after King Bladud, a legendary personage who – according to medieval and Tudor historians – ruled Britain several generations before the coming of

Julius Caesar. His story first appears in the highly unreliable *History of the Kings of Britain* by Geoffrey of Monmouth, in about 1136. According to Geoffrey, he built the city of Bath and 'fashioned hot baths therein, meet for the needs of men, the which he placed under the guardianship of the goddess Minerva, in whose temple he set fires that could not be quenched'. Bladud was not just a builder but a great magician, who 'fashioned himself wings and tried to travel through the upper levels of the air, but fell onto the temple of Apollo in London, and was dashed to pieces'.

Some time during the sixteenth or seventeenth century a second legend developed about Bladud (it is first mentioned in humorous verses in 1666). This claims that while still a prince he was driven from his father's court because he had caught leprosy, and was reduced to living in poverty as a swineherd. His pigs then caught the disease from him, but were cured as soon as they wallowed in the mud of a hot spring which they had discovered while foraging for food. Seeing this, Bladud rolled in the mud too, and was cured. He returned home, and when he later became king he built the magnificent baths which still house the healing spring, and founded the city of Bath there. It is doubtful whether this story was ever seriously believed, but it certainly was often used as publicity for Bath as a spa. It became even more famous after Charles Dickens gave a comic version of it in chapter 36 of *The Pickwick Papers*.

Blarney Stone Bar

There are a good many pub names in Britain which are in fact based on Irish folklore, not English or Scottish. This usually means that they have, or had, an Irish landlord, or served a high proportion of Irish customers. One such is the Blarney Stone Bar in Glasgow. Built into the outer wall of Blarney Castle near Cork there is an inscribed stone which declares that it was set there by Cormac Mac Carthy, the lord of the castle, in 1446. His descendant of the same name was famous for having delayed the English who besieged him there in 1602 by false promises of surrender, and so it was said in later generations that anyone who could kiss the stone with his name on would have the gift of getting anything he wanted because of his sweet tongue. Since the actual stone is very awkwardly placed and dangerous to reach, tourists are now invited to kiss a replica which is more accessible.

Bleeding Heart

Bleeding Heart Yard, in London's Hatton Garden district, takes its name from a Bleeding Heart Inn which once stood there. Steve Roud in his *London Lore* (2008) and Antony Clayton in *The Folklore of London* (2008) both plausibly suggest that this had originally been one of the medieval Catholic religious names for an inn (similar to the Angel or the Lamb); the allusion would be to the emblem of the Virgin Mary's heart, which is represented as bleeding and pierced by swords when she is honoured as Our Lady of Sorrows.

However, a secular legend to explain the dramatic name has been current since at least the early nineteenth century. It is said that in the time of Elizabeth I Sir Christopher Hatton – the powerful courtier who built Hatton House and after whom Hatton Garden is named – owed his success to the witchcraft of his wife, Lady Elizabeth Hatton, who had pledged herself to the Devil for his sake. And sure enough the Devil came for her, as the Victorian writer Charles Mackay tells in *Extraordinary Popular Delusions and the Madness of Crowds* (1841):

> The room is to be seen where the devil seized her after the expiry of the contract he had made with her, and bore her away bodily to the pit of Tophet; the pump against which he dashed her is still pointed out, and the spot where her heart was found after he had torn it out of her bosom with his iron claws has received the name of Bleeding Heart Yard, in confirmation of the story.

In the latter part of the nineteenth century the folklorist J. P. Emslie was told by local Londoners that 'Lady Hatton, having sold her soul to the devil, knocked out her brains on the pump in that yard ... [and] since then blood will flow out of the spout if anyone will work the pump at midnight'.

See also ANGELS & SAINTS, p. 16

Blind Beggar

This pub, in London's Whitechapel Road, E1, takes its name from a very well-known story, that of the Blind Beggar of Bethnal Green. In its original form the tale goes back to the sixteenth century, but it became famous through a broadside ballad dating from about 1685, the text of which was included by Thomas Percy in his collection *Reliques of Ancient English Poetry* (1765). This tells how Bessie, the beggar's beautiful daughter, goes to work in an inn in Romford, where several men fall in love with her, and four of them ask her to marry them. But when she tells them who her father is – a blind man 'who daily sits begging for charitie' – three out of the four are horrified and withdraw their proposal. The fourth, however, a knight, declares that he cares nothing for rank and wealth. He takes Bessie to meet his family, who are protesting angrily at the idea of such a marriage, when the beggar himself appears and boasts that he can match, and even surpass, their riches. And so he does, throwing two gold coins on the floor for each one that the knight's father can produce, to be Bessie's dowry – of £6,000, 'plus a hundred pounds more to buy her a gown'!

> Thus was fair Bessie matched to the knight,
> And then made a ladye in others' despite;
> A fairer ladye there never was seene
> Than the blind beggar's daughter of Bednall-greene.

Later, the beggar appears at the wedding feast richly dressed, and explains that his name is Momford and that his blindness was due to a wound sustained in battle while fighting for the king of France, from which he almost died. A young woman found him on the battlefield and saved his life, after which they married; returning to England, he disguised himself as a beggar to avoid enemies.

Thomas Percy, however, introduced some verses of his own into the conclusion of the ballad, frankly stating that they are 'a modern attempt to remove the absurdities and inconsistencies which so remarkably prevailed in this part of the song, as it stood before', so that 'the story is rendered more affecting and is reconciled to probability and true history'. Since the name 'Momford' has no particular significance, Percy changed it to the aristocratic 'de Montfort', thus offering an impressive historical identification. According to him, the beggar is Henry de Montfort, eldest son of Simon de Montfort, who led a revolt against Henry III and was killed at the battle of Evesham in

1265; it was in that battle that he was blinded, and rescued by a baron's daughter. To escape their enemies, they disguised themselves as beggars, and lived in hiding at Bethnal Green. This legend became very popular, partly through its romantic appeal and partly because Simon de Montfort was regarded as one of the heroes of England's history, a champion of Parliament against royal power. The idea that the Blind Beggar was his son is firmly fixed in the traditions of Bethnal Green.

Blowing Stone

A house in the village of Kingston Lisle in Berkshire has in its garden a block of sarsen stone with several narrow holes running through it, called the Blowing Stone, because to blow hard through one of them produces a sound like the note of a horn. This stone is a source of local pride, and has given its name to the pub. Originally it stood in the crest of a nearby hill, until it was brought into the village in the eighteenth century. According to legend, King Alfred the Great blew through it to gather his troops for the battle of Ethandune in 878, his decisive victory over the Danes. And that, people say, is why the village itself is called Kingston, i.e. King's Stone.

Boadicea

There are at least two pubs named after Queen Boadicea in London, one in Clerkenwell and one in Charing Cross station. The explanation goes back to the romantic speculations of popular historians in Victorian times. Boadicea (more correctly called Boudicca) was a queen of the British tribe of the Iceni who revolted against Roman rule in AD 60–61; according to the Roman historian Tacitus, she was motivated by personal revenge, having been flogged in punishment for a previous act of rebellion, and her daughters raped. At first she achieved considerable successes, including burning the towns of Colchester, St Albans, and London, but eventually Roman troops ambushed the Britons and massacred them, whereupon Boadicea fled from the battlefield and poisoned herself.

Tacitus does not name the site of this battle; many Essex writers claim that it was at Aymesbury Banks, or on Tiptree Heath, but those from Middlesex say it took place on Stanmore Common. However, the antiquary John Nelson wrote in 1811 in his *History of Islington* that it was 'supposed' that a certain hamlet alongside a small bridge over the river Fleete in London (near the present King's Cross station) had been called Battle Bridge 'from its contiguity to the spot where the celebrated battle was fought between the Roman General Suetonius Paulinus and Boadicea, Queen of the Iceni'. He offered no evidence other than the name itself, and the fact that this site is on a hill close to the outskirts of Roman London. The name survives as that of a nearby street, Battle Bridge Road. In 1937, the writer Lewis Spence adopted Nelson's view in his *Boadicea, Warrior Queen of the Britons*, saying it was supported by tradition and by several of the older antiquaries. Unfortunately for the theory, modern place-name research has shown that the seemingly significant name was only recorded in 1559 – the place was previously known as Bradford Bridge, meaning a bridge over a wide or broad ford.

It is probably due to Spence's book that many Londoners came to regard the queen as a local heroine. At some point, probably in the 1940s, there arose a popular rumour that her grave lies somewhere under King's Cross station – some say under platform 9, others under platform 10. A placard has recently been placed near the station entrance publicising the claim. Spence himself, however, had said that her burial place remained unknown. He felt this was appropriate: 'But what better cenotaph can greatness have than tradition, what shroud more fitting than the web of tradition? Boadicea, whose name is Victory, sleeps in no Pantheon of the visible, but in the spacious and mist-circled cavern of British romance.'

More broadly, it can be said that Boadicea's standing as a high-profile figure in the popular version of our history dates from a dramatic poem by William Cowper, 'Boadicea: An Ode' (1782). He imagines the 'British warrior queen' consulting a Druid before launching her revolt, and receiving the assurance that whether she is victorious or not 'Rome shall perish' and her own people are destined for future glory:

> Then the progeny that springs
>   From the forests of our land,
> Arm'd with thunder, clad with wings,
>   Shall a wider world command.
>
> Regions Caesar never knew
>   Thy posterity shall sway,
> Where his eagles never flew,
>   None invincible as they.

This fictional prophecy of the rise of the British Empire established the image of Boadicea as a patriotic symbol, which became even stronger in the nineteenth century; Victorians also respected her as a defender of outraged womanhood and a prototype for the powerful queens regnant, Elizabeth I and

Victoria herself, while to Spence she was 'a goddess in armour descending to the succour of a folk enslaved' and her voice 'a trumpet calling to a people whose very element is freedom'.

Boar, Blue Boar, White Boar

See QUEENS' HEADS & RED LIONS, p. 248

Bo-Peep

Eric Delderfield, in his *British Inn Signs and their Stories* (1965), states that the Bo-Peep pub in St Leonard's-on-Sea, East Sussex, got its name because it was built on a corner, in such a way that it is half hidden by other buildings and seems to be peeping round them. This would hark back to the basic meaning of the phrase 'to play bo-peep', known from the late Middle Ages onwards, and defined in Dr Johnson's *Dictionary* as 'the act of looking out and then drawing back as if frightened, or with the purpose to frighten some other'. It was – and still is – a simple game played by adults to amuse babies. The phrase may also have once meant playing hide-and-seek, as Iona and Peter Opie suggested in their *Dictionary of Nursery Rhymes*.

However, the pub signboard as described by Leslie Dunkling and Gordon Wright in 1987 is more complicated. On one side it showed a boatload of smugglers coming ashore, implying that they would be playing a teasing game of hide-and-seek with the excise men; this idea suits a coastal town in an area where smuggling was common. On the other side was an illustration of the nursery rhyme:

> Little Bo-Peep has lost her sheep
> And doesn't know where to find them.
> Leave them alone, and they'll come home,
> Bringing their tails behind them.

See also MOTHER GEESE & CATS WITH FIDDLES, p. 46

Brass Monkey

The Brass Monkey pubs in Edinburgh and in Teignmouth (Devon) owe their name to a rough slangy phrase for icy weather, namely that it's 'cold enough to freeze the balls off a brass monkey'. Eric Partridge in his *Dictionary of Slang* (1961) dated this to the late nineteenth century and judged it to be 'mainly Australian', though it has become more common in Britain in recent years. Like much slang, its original inspiration can only be guessed at, but the earliest references (from the 1850s)

The Brass Monkey

all set it in a nautical context. There is a 'respectable' theory which claims that on old warships the cannonballs were stored in piles on brass trays called 'monkeys', and that in very cold weather the trays would contract, causing the balls to roll off. However, as the experts of the *Oxford English Dictionary* point out on their website, there is no evidence that any such trays ever existed, nor does brass contract to such an extent, nor were cannonballs stored on deck. Furthermore, the earliest record of the phrase gives it as 'cold enough to freeze the tail off a brass monkey', while in America there was a parallel but rare expression, 'hot enough to melt the nose off a brass monkey', which occurs in Herman Melville's *Omoo* (1850). The reference is therefore definitely to an animal's anatomy. One possibility is that it alludes to the popular little figures of the Three Wise Monkeys who 'see no evil, hear no evil, speak no evil'; these are often made of brass, and are far too respectable to have any balls. Originally Oriental, they were sold in great quantities to tourists, sailors, and European markets generally.

Brazen Head

There are pubs of this name in Lisson Street, London, and in Cathcart Road in Glasgow. It alludes to a magical artefact which was allegedly made by a learned Franciscan friar in Oxford in the thirteenth century, Roger Bacon – a scientist, philosopher and alchemist who was later thought to have been a magician. According to a legend current in the sixteenth century, Friar Bacon and his friend Friar Bungay had worked for many months to produce this head. If all went well, it would utter prophecies, and impart secret knowledge; he hoped it would tell him how to build a wall of brass all round Britain, to thwart any enemy. However, the spirits had warned him that he must on no account miss the first message the head would utter, for if he did it would never speak again. He waited for hours, and when he felt he could no longer keep awake he told his assistant Miles to take over the vigil. While Bacon slept and Miles kept guard, the head suddenly spoke: 'Time is.' Miles thought this was too stupid a message to be worth waking his master for, and ignored it. A little later, the head said: 'Time was', but Miles ignored it again. Finally it said: 'Time is past', burst into flames, and destroyed itself.

Bridge on Wool

According to local tradition (as given by Leslie Dunkling and Gordon Wright in their *Pub Names of Britain*), the fifteenth-century bridge across the river Camel at Wadebridge in Cornwall was quite literally built upon a foundation of sacks of wool sunk into the river bed, at the suggestion of the village priest, Parson Lovibund. Hence the name of the pub there, and its sign which shows the priest and his bishop riding across the bridge. Those who find it hard to believe in this alleged method of establishing firm foundations will probably prefer the alternative explanation that when it is said that a bridge (or a church) was 'built upon woolsacks', what is meant is that it was paid for by someone who had grown rich as a wool merchant.

Brockley Jack

There is a pub of this name in Brockley Road, London SE4. According to the main local tradition, it was named after a notorious landlord in the eighteenth century, Jack Camp, who was also a highwayman, and hanged himself rather than be caught. It is unclear how much historical basis there is for the tale, but it fits well with the tendency to romanticise the memory of highwaymen – once this particular type of robber had died out. It is also sometimes said that the 'Jack' in question was Jack Shepherd, a notoriously bold robber, hanged at Tyburn in 1724, who was famous for his many daring escapes from prison; in Victorian times, his adventures were celebrated in cheap serial novels and in pantomimes. A third version claims that the pub got its name from the legendary Spring-Heeled Jack, rumoured to prowl the streets of London and elsewhere from the 1830s onwards; he was said to terrify people after dark by suddenly appearing in some grotesque disguise, and then to rush away at great speed, bounding over walls by means of springs hidden in his boots.

See also HIGHWAYMEN & SMUGGLERS, p. 208

Bucket of Blood

In their survey of pub names Leslie Dunkling and Gordon Wright noted that in 1980 what had previously been a conventionally named New Inn at Phillack in Cornwall was rechristened the Bucket of Blood. This name brings to mind the once popular joking 'swear-word', 'Hell's bells and buckets of blood', but the authors were told that there is a story behind it. This tale – which they kindly reassure readers is untrue – is that a former landlord had once gone to draw water from his well, and that his bucket had come up filled with blood, because a murdered and mutilated corpse had been dumped in the well overnight. Further details were given by Andrew Grundon, the painter who created a sign to match the new name; according to the story he was told, the corpse was that of a revenue man, killed by a gang of smugglers who used the pub as their meeting place. Gruesome 'explanations' for pub names seem to be a popular form of humour.

See also HIGHWAYMEN & SMUGGLERS, p. 208

Bull & Mouth

Two old London pubs, one in Aldgate and one in St Martin's le Grand, have this rather strange name, illustrated in their signs by the image of a bull alongside a huge, gaping mouth. It may simply have arisen by the amalgamation of two pubs, one called the Bull and one the Mouth. However, Bryant Lillywhite, in his *London Signs* (1972) explains it by reference to what was apparently once a popular rhyme:

> Milo the Crotonian
> An ox slew with his fist,
> And ate it up at one meal,
> Ye gods, what a glorious twist.

This Milo was a real person, a famous Greek athlete of the late sixth century BC whose strength was proverbial. Various anecdotes were told of him, some more credible than others –

The Bull & Mouth

that he killed an ox with one blow of his fist, or that he carried a cow on his shoulders through the Olympic stadium, and in both cases that he then ate the whole animal at a single meal. He is said to have died as a result of trying to tear an oak tree in half; he managed to make the beginnings of a cleft in it, but the two halves closed in on him, trapping his hands so firmly that he was unable to pull himself free, and while he was helpless a pack of wolves arrived and ate him.

Some commentators have tried to explain the pub name as a misunderstanding of 'Boulogne Mouth', meaning the harbour of that town, and supposedly commemorating a British victory in a sea battle there in the reign of Henry VIII. Like most theories based on the notion of words misunderstood, this is both unlikely and unnecessary. The idea of a gigantic mouth guzzling a meal of beef is quite appropriate to an inn serving food.

See also PUZZLING PAIRS, p. 112

Byard's Leap

It seems strange that a pub in Sheffield should have this name, for the story to which it refers is located many miles away, at Byard's Leap Farm near Cranwell in Lincolnshire. It concerns a horse named Byard.

The term 'bayard' for a bay-coloured horse goes back to the Middle Ages, and is particularly famous in medieval French romances of adventure as the name of a wondrous steed belonging to the hero Renaud de Montauban and his brothers the Four Sons of Aymon – it could magically extend its back so that all five could ride on it at once. However, the Lincolnshire story has nothing in common with the old romances, apart from the horse's name. It tells of a horse that made an amazing leap, in shock at having a witch riding on his back. He is said to have covered sixty feet (twenty metres) in a single bound, the limits of which are now marked by large horseshoes set in blocks of stone, set up by a Victorian owner of Byard's Leap Farm to replace previous 'hoof-prints' in the ground which were getting hard to see.

There are various versions of how the witch came to be on Byard's back. One account tells of a farmer who consulted a Cunning Man on how to get rid of the village witch. The advice he got was to take his horses to drink at a pond, and watch to see which looked up first when a stone was thrown into the water. Then he must ride this horse to the witch's hut and offer her the chance to ride pillion behind him, but keep a knife ready to cut her arm as soon as she does so. The first horse to lift its head was a blind one called Byard, but the farmer kept to the plan, and rode off on Byard. When he offered the witch a ride, she leaped up on the horse's back, digging her long sharp nails into him so painfully that he too gave a great leap, and she fell off. She tried a second time, and the same thing happened. But the third time she clung on, despite Byard's third leap, and the farmer succeeded in cutting her arm, and so she lost all her power, as witches do when one draws their blood. In another version, the witch is stabbed as soon as she mounts, and in her dying agony drives her nails into the horse's back; the horse makes only a single leap, but it is a huge one.

Camelot

The Camelot is a pub in the village of South Cadbury, near Yeovil (Somerset), at the foot of Cadbury Castle, a hill with an Iron Age hill-fort on it; it has an attractive Celtic interlace design on its signboard, and in the bar there is a display of prehistoric items found during excavations at the fort. For over four hundred years there has been a belief that Cadbury Castle was the true site of King Arthur's Camelot (though Malory's *Morte D'Arthur* clearly identifies it with Winchester). The claim was first made in 1542 by the antiquarian John Leland in his *Itinerary of England and Wales*:

> At the very South Ende of the Church of South-Cadbyri standeth Camallate, sometyme a famose Town or Castelle ... Much Gold, Sylver, and Copper of the Romayne Coynes hath been found ther yn plowing ... Ther was found in *hominum memoria* [within living memory] a Horse Shoe of Sylver at Camallotte. The people can tell nothing ther but that they have herd say that Arture much resorted to Camalat.

Later in the sixteenth century, the Welsh chronicler Elias Gruffudd came upon a more elaborate folk belief about 'a hill near Glastonbury', though he unfortunately does not say whether he means Cadbury or Glastonbury Tor:

[The English] talk much more about [Arthur] than we do, for they say and strongly believe that he will rise again to be king. In their opinion he is sleeping in a cave under a hill near Glastonbury, and indeed if one could give credence to many diverse people from that district he appeared and conversed with many people in many strange ways three hundred years ago.

This is an instance of a legend known in several European countries, telling of some famous king who lies asleep inside a mountain, surrounded by his warriors. In some cases it is promised that he will awake in the hour of his country's greatest need, and return to save his people; in others, it is said that when he wakes it will mean that the End of the World is near. In Britain, where the story is found in several places, the sleeping hero is King Arthur, and the implication is national salvation, not an apocalypse.

In Somerset, these stories persisted. In the 1890s, folklorists recorded a tradition that Cadbury Castle is hollow, and Arthur and his court sit inside it; on the nights of the full moon they emerge to ride round the hill on horses shod with silver – a detail probably inspired by Leland's account – and water their horses at Arthur's Well, a spring among the earthworks of the fort. Also, that one can briefly glimpse Arthur on Midsummer Eve, when the magical iron (or golden) gates in the hillside open for an instant. Victorian archaeologists working on the hill were once asked by an old man whether they had come to take the king away.

Cannard's Grave

At a crossroads just south of the village of Shepton Mallet in Somerset stands an inn called Cannard's Grave, with a sign showing a dead man swinging from a gallows. The macabre name and image are explained by a grim local tale, which exists in two versions. The first is that Cannard was a sheep-stealer who was hanged for this crime; this is the one adopted on the signboard (shown in Delderfield's *British Inn Signs*), showing the corpse swinging on the gallows above an open grave, with a border of sheep above and below.

The second version tells how, at some time in the eighteenth century, the inn was kept by one Giles Cannard, who grew mysteriously rich; some said that he was in league with highwaymen and smugglers, others that he made his customers drunk and then robbed or even murdered them. Some versions of the story say that he was caught, tried, and hanged; others, that when he knew his crimes were discovered he chose to hang himself rather than stand trial. Either way, his grave would quite likely have been at the crossroads where the pub stands, as is implied by its name. Up to 1823 it was normal for judges to order that suicides and criminals who had been executed should be buried beside a road, or actually under it – often, but not always, at a crossroads. This was a sign of their disgraced and outcast status, and was thought to ensure that their punishment would continue in the afterlife by denying them burial in consecrated ground. There may once have been some visible mound which local tradition claimed was the wicked innkeeper's grave, but if so it has long disappeared. But some say his ghost still haunts the area.

See also GHOSTLY BARMAIDS & HAUNTED CELLARS, p. 278

Case is Altered

This strange phrase is legal jargon, meaning that some unexpected fact has come to light and entirely changes the situation; it occurs in various jokes against lawyers and judges from the sixteenth century onwards. As a pub name it was surprisingly popular in the nineteenth century – especially, according to Larwood and Hotten, in Hertfordshire and Middlesex. Sometimes it is simply a popular nickname for a pub whose official title is different, for instance the Weaver's Arms at Banbury in Oxfordshire. There, tradition claims that local weavers were regularly attacked by gangs of other weavers from Bloxham, who almost always won; however, there came a day when the Banbury men completely routed their rivals, crying triumphantly, 'The case is altered now!' and thus renaming their pub. Another, on the road from Woodbridge to Ipswich, is said to have been originally called the Duke of York; the story goes that it flourished during the Napoleonic Wars because so many soldiers were quartered in those towns, but when peace came trade collapsed, and the impoverished landlord took down the old sign and renamed it the Case is Altered.

As so often, people have suggested explanations based on 'misunderstanding' – e.g. of Spanish *casa alta*, 'high house', supposedly used by soldiers returning from the Peninsular War for a house on a hill. The Woodbridge pub already mentioned has an alternative tale attached to it – that Father Casey, a persecuted Catholic priest deprived of his church, set up an altar in one of its rooms, after which it was known as 'Casey's Altar'. And at Cowgate near Dover there is a pub with the variant name the Cause is Altered for which Dunkling and Wright were given the delightfully punning theory that 'herdsmen on their way to market would call in at the pub saying "The cows 'as 'alted, woi shouldn't oi?"'

Castleton's Oak

In his *British Inn Signs* (1965) Eric Delderfield noted the story connected with the pub of this name at Biddenden in Kent. A local man, a carpenter named Castleton, was distressed to hear that a fine old oak in the village had been destroyed by lightning on the very day of his seventieth birthday, and took it as a personal portent. He at once bought some of the timber and made a coffin from it, which he intended for his own use, and kept always in his house. But it was thirty years before it was needed, since the carpenter lived to be a hundred. 'The sign,' says Delderfield, 'shows the old chap sitting in his coffin.'

Cat & Fiddle

This name, which is quite common, lends itself to various visual interpretations. The most widespread, and certainly the original, shows the cat itself playing a fiddle. Sometimes this was rendered fairly realistically, as at Clyst St Mary (Devon) and Bodmin (Cornwall). Sometimes it was in cartoon style, as on the former sign of a pub on the road from Ilkeston to Derby; a more recent sign here has opted for a plausibly realistic interpretation, for it shows a cat sitting quietly at the feet of an old fiddler. A Cheshire pub, on the road from Macclesfield to

Buxton, has on its current sign a ginger cat cautiously inspecting a fiddle lying on the floor, but it also has an older pictorial panel on the wall which shows a cat actually playing a fiddle; this is known to date from before the First World War. At East Rudham (Norfolk), in the 1970s, there used to be a cartoon-style grinning cat who was 'on the fiddle', i.e. stealing from the till, but this has been replaced by the more traditional image of the feline musician.

It seems certain that this image comes from the very well-known nursery rhyme:

> Hey diddle diddle,
> The cat and the fiddle,
> The cow jumped over the moon

even though the rhyme was first recorded in print in about 1765 and London had Cat and Fiddle pubs as early as the beginning of the sixteenth century, as Bryant Lillywhite says. The rhyme could easily have existed orally for several generations before reaching print, and there are in any case medieval visual precedents for the comic but rather cruel theme of a cat-musician playing an instrument strung with cat-gut – a misericord in Hereford Cathedral, for example, shows a cat on his hind legs playing a viol, in a duet with a lute-playing goat.

Suggestions that 'fiddle' is a corruption of the French word *fidèle*, 'faithful', and that there is some historical allusion, e.g. to Catharine of Aragon, faithful wife to Henry VIII, are over-ingenious and should be disregarded.

See also MOTHER GEESE & CATS WITH FIDDLES, p. 46

Cat i' the Well

This unusual name is found in Halifax. It presumably refers to a rhyme first recorded in 1580, to be sung as a round:

> Jacke boy, ho boy, newes!
>   The cat is in the well,
> Let us ring now for her knell,
>   Ding dong ding dong bell.

The more familiar form, dating from the eighteenth century, is the nursery rhyme:

> Ding dong bell,
> Pussy's in the well.
> Who put her in?
> Little Johnny Thin.
> Who pulled her out?
> Little Tommy Stout.
> What a naughty boy was that,
> To try to drown poor pussy cat,
> Who never did him any harm,
> But killed the mice in his father's barn.

See also MOTHER GEESE & CATS WITH FIDDLES, p. 46

Cauld Lad

This pub at Hylton in Sunderland (County Durham) takes its unique name from a famous local legend set at Hilton or Hylton Castle, a fifteenth-century tower house. The story is told in

Mother Geese & Cats with Fiddles

It is good strategy for pubs to adopt names from nursery rhymes and fairytales. They will be familiar to everyone, they call up warm memories of childhood, they are amusing, and they lend themselves well to the sign-painter's art. The same is true for those taken from the classics of children's literature, such as *Alice in Wonderland* and the nonsense verses of Edward Lear. Plenty of examples will be found in these pages – the CAT & FIDDLE, SIMPLE SIMON, COCK ROBIN, JACK & JILL, LITTLE JACK HORNER, BO-PEEP, the MAN IN THE MOON, MOTHER HUBBARD, Old King Cole (see KING COEL), the OWL & PUSSY CAT, the MAD HATTER, the MARCH HARE, etc.

Many nursery rhymes are of uncertain age and authorship, since for several generations they were simply remembered and passed on by word of mouth from mothers and nurses to young children. Some, however, were not originally created as juvenile entertainments but are fragments of adult art forms such as folksongs, street ballads and songs from plays. They began to get into print in cheap publications of the middle of the eighteenth century; more extensive anthologies appeared in Victorian Britain and in America; there, they are known as Mother Goose rhymes, from the title of an early collection. All can now be found, with full commentary, in *The Oxford Dictionary of Nursery Rhymes* by Iona and Peter Opie, first published in 1959.

One obvious attraction of nursery rhymes is their colourful 'nonsense', a surreal humour based on ridiculously impossible situations like a cat with a fiddle, a cradle on a treetop, a pig going to market. Many people, however, find this unsatisfactory, and insist on discovering some hidden meaning to 'explain' the rhyme in a more adult manner. One popular strategy is to hunt for historical allusions and political references, cunningly disguised. The most thorough-going work of this kind was a book produced almost eighty years ago by the American writer Katherine Elwes Thomas, *The Real Personages of Mother Goose* (1930); her proposed identifications are with kings, queens and eminent personages of Tudor and Stuart times. For instance, she points out that in a version of 'Jack and Jill' from about 1765 it is clear from the illustration that 'Jill' is not a girl but a boy (i.e. 'Gill'), and deduces that they represent Cardinal Wolsey and Bishop Tarbes travelling to France to try to arrange a marriage between young Mary Tudor and the king of France. The hill symbolises their difficult task, the bucket holds holy water to represent a Papal blessing, and the failure of their mission contributed to the political downfall of both men. This interpretation would not please the present inhabitants of Kilmersden in Somerset, who claim that Jack and Jill were unmarried lovers who lived there in the reign of Henry VIII and used to meet at a hilltop well; Jack, they say, was killed by a falling boulder in a quarry, and Jill died shortly after in childbirth.

There are occasions when a speculative 'explanation' of some piece of folklore takes the fancy of the public (and especially of journalists) to such an extent that it becomes traditional itself, however mistaken it may be. Such is the case with RING O' ROSES, which many people nowadays are convinced is a coded reference to the Plague; this splendidly melodramatic interpretation has been popular among journalists and fiction-writers over the past forty or fifty years, but medically and historically it is quite implausible.

Another rhyme for which a historical basis has been claimed is LITTLE JACK HORNER, adopted as the name for several pubs. There was a certain Thomas Horner who lived in the reign of Henry VIII, and obtained from the king the Manor of Mells, which had belonged to Glastonbury Abbey. That much is factually true, and the Opies, though generally sceptical of historical identifications, concede that 'there is no objection' to the rhyme having originally referred to Thomas Horner. But they add: 'It must be stressed, however, that the legend which has now become so firmly attached to the rhyme has not been found in print before the nineteenth century.' So far the pub at Mells (the Talbot) has not felt it necessary to change its name to match the tale.

several nineteenth-century sources, the earliest being Robert Surtees, *The History and Antiquities of the County Palatinate of Durham* (1816–40; vol. 3, 1820). The Cauld (= Cold) Lad was said to have been a mischievous but basically good-hearted goblin which had haunted the castle for years, seldom seen but heard every night rummaging about in the kitchens. If the servants had left them untidy, he would clear everything away most efficiently; but if they had put things in good order before going to bed, the Cauld Lad would be heard tossing the pots and pans about and breaking the plates. In the end they got rid of him. They left a suit of clothes for him in the kitchen, and watched when he arrived at midnight, put them on, frisked about in delight, and disappeared at dawn, crying:

> Here's a cloak, and here's a hood,
> The Cauld Lad of Hilton will do no more good.

This, as Surtees knew, is an old widespread traditional anecdote about how a household fairy vanishes for ever when given clothing, usually as a kindly but mistaken gesture of thanks from the humans he has been helping, though in this case, Surtees implies, the servants knew quite well what would happen, and the banishing was deliberate. The situation is further complicated by the fact that the Cauld Lad's noisy and destructive behaviour is more like that of a poltergeist than a brownie, and Surtees notes that some people believed he was indeed a ghost – that of a young servant boy who had allegedly been murdered by a hot-tempered laird of Hilton in 1609, and his body thrown into a pond.

In 1843, another writer, M. A. Richardson, was told that the Cauld Lad had not been properly laid to rest; he still haunted the house, wailing dolefully:

Wae's me, wae's me,
The acorn is not yet
Fallen from the tree
That's to grow the wood
That's to make the cradle
That's to rock the bairn
That's to grow to a man
That's to lay me!

Cheese Rollers

The pub of this name at Shurdington in Gloucestershire celebrates a much-loved local custom held on the Spring Bank
Holiday (formerly, on Whit Monday) at Cooper's Hill, between
Brockworth and Painswick. A large round Gloucester cheese is
sent rolling down the very steep hillside, and tough young men
rush off in pursuit; within a few steps most of them have fallen
over, and are rolling too. The cheese goes too fast to be caught,
but the first man to reach the foot of the hill wins it. This sport
was once a common feature of country fairs in hilly districts; a
Whit Monday Fair was held on Cooper's Hill in the nineteenth
century. In recent years the cheese-rolling has been criticised as
dangerous (minor injuries are common, and occasionally bones
are broken); it was even briefly banned in 1999, at which point
two or three local men went to the hill at dawn and carried
out the custom in secret, so that tradition should not be broken. The following year the ban was lifted. The custom is now
well publicised and remains highly popular. The pub sign shows
three men hurtling downhill.

Cheshire Cat

Several pubs have named themselves after this famous character in Lewis Carroll's *Alice in Wonderland*. The one at Ellesmere Port (Cheshire) has a sign based upon Tenniel's illustration for the original book, showing Alice looking up at the tree branch on which the grinning cat is perched. However, at Christleton (also Cheshire) the cat alone is enough.

To 'grin like a Cheshire cat' was a common phrase in Carroll's time, though its origin is unknown. Two theories were proposed in the journal *Notes and Queries* in the 1850s. One was that it is actually derived from inn signs; there was supposed to have once been a sign-painter in Cheshire who was so bad at drawing lions that they ended up looking like toothy cats. The other suggestion was that at one time Cheshire cheeses were made in moulds shaped like a grinning cat. No example of such a mould, or of such an inn sign, has been produced as evidence.

Chevy Chase

The Chevy Chase pub in Leytonstone Road, London E15, takes its name from one of the best-known traditional ballads of the English/Scottish borders, about a bloody clash between Earl Percy of Northumberland and Earl Douglas in which both these lords, and many of their followers, were killed. The cause, according to the ballad, was a rash vow by Earl Percy that he would cross the border into Scotland to hunt deer on the Cheviot Hills:

> In despite of doughty Douglas
> And all that e'er with him be.

When Douglas heard of this, he in turn swore to stop the hunt. Cross-border raiding was of course commonplace in medieval times, but it is most unlikely that an event leading to the deaths of such eminent men would remain unrecorded in history, so the story has to be taken as an undatable legend summing up and glorifying generations of conflict, not sober fact.

The ballad shows both men, and their troops, as valiant and honourable fighters. As soon as Earl Douglas arrives and finds the English preparing to carry off the deer they have killed, he proposes to settle the matter by single combat:

> 'Yet to kill all these guiltless men,
>   Alas, it were great pitye!
> But, Percy, thou art a lord of land,
>   I an earl in my countrye –
> Let our men on a party stand,
>   And do battle of thee and me.'

Percy immediately agrees, but a Northumbrian squire called Richard Witherington protests:

> 'I wot you bin great lordès two,
>   I am a poor squire of land;
> Yet I'll ne'er see my captain fight on field,
>   And myself to look and stand.
> But while that I may my weapon wield
>   I'll not fail, both heart and hand.'

So battle is joined. The two leaders eventually meet in hand-to-hand combat, equally matched. Douglas offers Percy high honours at the Scottish court if he will yield; Percy refuses, and a moment later an arrow from an unknown Englishman kills Douglas. Percy mourns for him:

> Then Percy leaned upon his sword
>   And saw the Douglas dee;
> He took the dead man by the hand,
>   And said 'Woe is me for thee!
>
> To have saved thy life I'd have parted with
>   My lands for yeares three,
> For a better man of heart nor hand
>   Was not in the north countrye.'

A Scottish knight then kills Earl Percy, and is killed in turn by an English archer, and so the fight continues till nightfall, and even by the light of the moon, till at last:

> Of fifteen hundred archers of England
>   Went away but seventy-and-three;
> Of twenty hundred spearmen of Scotland
>   But even five-and-fifty.

The Elizabethan poet and courtier Sir Philip Sidney paid tribute to the power of this ballad in his *Defence of Poesy* (1579–80), though living as he did in a society where polished rhetorical poetry was admired, he felt he had to apologise for his 'barbarous', i.e. uneducated, tastes:

Certainly I must confess mine own barbarousness, I never heard the old song of Percie and Douglas, that I found not my heart moved more than with a trumpet; and yet it is sung but by some blind crowder [fiddler] with no rougher voice than rude style; which being so evill apparelled in the dust and cobweb of that uncivill age, what would it work if trimmed in the gorgeous eloquence of a Pindar!

Childe of Hale

Hale is a village which was formerly part of Cheshire, but is now reckoned to be incorporated into Liverpool. The 'Childe of Hale' commemorated by its pub was a real person, John Middleton, who was born there in 1578, and became locally famous for his huge size and strength. Not only is he shown on the signboard, but there is a large mosaic of him in the bar.

According to the inscription on John Middleton's gravestone in the local churchyard, he was 9 feet 3 inches – a somewhat incredible figure, showing that legend has been at work. The grave plot is unusually large, like the one at Hathersage where Little John is said to lie. Legend also claims that Middleton's growth was sudden and miraculous. One day, when still a normal-sized boy, he amused himself by drawing the outline of a very large figure in the sand on the banks of the Mersey, and then fell asleep lying within this outline; when he woke, he found he had grown big enough to fit it. From then on, he was too tall to fit into his bedroom, and had to stick his feet out of the window. The local squire, who became his patron, took him on a visit to his own Oxford college, Brasenose, which still has a painting of him and an outline of his huge hand. He was also taken to the court of James I, where he defeated the king's champion wrestler and was given a prize of £20, though it is said that it was stolen from him on the homeward journey; it is sometimes said that he became the king's bodyguard, but this once again is a legendary elaboration of the facts.

The title 'Childe' is meant as a joke. He was neither a 'child' in the normal sense of the word nor a 'young man of noble birth', which is what the term meant in medieval and Elizabethan poetry.

Chimney Boy

A pub of this name in Faversham (Kent) commemorates the 'chimney boys' or 'climbing boys' of the eighteenth and early nineteenth centuries. These were children employed by sweeps to climb up the inside of chimneys and clear the soot from awkward flues which brushes could not reach. It was painful and dangerous work, and public opinion gradually forced Parliament to legislate against the practice; in 1834, a law was passed fixing the minimum age for sweeps' apprentices as ten years old, which in 1840 was raised to sixteen. It was largely ignored, however. A Commission on Children's Employment reported that there were still 'at least two thousand climbing-boys' in 1863; the practice eventually stopped after an eleven-year-old boy was suffocated inside a chimney in 1875.

There was one folk custom in which chimney boys played a conspicuous part. On May Day they always took part in the sweeps' holiday parade through the

The Chimney Boy

streets, accompanying the Jack-in-the-Green and loudly clat-
tering their brooms and shovels. It was commonly believed in
the nineteenth century that this was to celebrate a remarkable
event. It was said that there had once been a little boy, the son
of wealthy parents, who was kidnapped by chimney sweeps and
put to the trade, but that one day he happened to be working in
the very house where his family lived, and either saw a portrait
of his mother in one room or was himself seen and recognised
by her. Either way, there was a happy reunion, and from then on
the mother paid for a yearly feast for every sweep in London,
on May Day. There actually was such a feast, donated by Mrs
Elizabeth Montague of Montague House, Portland Square,
who died in 1800, and so this story is sometimes attached to
her name.

The reason the sweeps are particularly commemorated in
Faversham may be because in 1895 a group of them from that
town had what could well have been a serious accident when
visiting Whitstable, some six miles away. Their leader, who
took the role of the Jack, was encased in the usual pyramid of
greenery, which he accidentally set on fire while smoking a pipe.
Thanks to the greenery, only his whiskers were burnt. His son
was less lucky; while he was trying to put out the flames his
own paper costume caught fire, so that his face, neck and hands
were badly burnt, and had to be dressed with 'cotton wool and
oil'. 'Quite an exciting scene', as the *Whitstable Times* remarked
(4 May 1895).

Christopher

There are pubs called Christopher at Bath and at Eton. The role of St Christopher as the patron saint who ensures the safety of travellers arose because the legendary account of his life described him as a heathen giant who received the grace of faith after agreeing to carry a little boy – who was really Jesus – across a dangerous river, and later devoted his life to helping travellers. This was originally a perfectly serious part of Christianity, and could still be so for a Catholic. But for many people nowadays a Christopher medal is simply a lucky charm to be hung in a car.

See also ANGELS & SAINTS, p. 16

Cock, Fighting Cock

There are very many pubs called the Cock, and the name could carry various meanings. One is folkloric, in that it refers to the once popular sport of cockfighting, which was banned in 1849. Many inns had cockpits on the premises; sometimes a pub is actually called the Cockpit, e.g. at St Andrew's Hill, London EC4, which has fighting cocks on the sign. On the other hand, 'cock' also means a tap or spigot, so pubs could call themselves the Cock and Bottle to show they sold both beer on tap and bottled beer. Furthermore, the possibility of a sexual double entendre can never be entirely ruled out, especially for premises calling themselves the Cock Inn.

See also GAMES & SPORTS, p. 78

Cock Horse

There are pubs named the Cock Horse at Banbury in Oxfordshire, at Maidstone in Kent, and elsewhere. It is of course Banbury which has the best claim on the name, since it alludes to a well-known nursery rhyme:

> Ride a cock-horse to Banbury Cross
> To see a fine lady upon a white horse;
> Rings on her fingers and bells on her toes,
> She shall have music wherever she goes.

A cock-horse is, properly speaking, a toy consisting of a wooden horse-head on a stick, which a child would hold between his legs and pretend to ride. However, the rhyme is mainly used by an adult jigging a child up and down on his or her knee in imitation of a trotting horse. In their *Oxford Dictionary of Nursery Rhymes* (1951), Iona and Peter Opie noted that there are some variations recorded in the eighteenth and nineteenth centuries. Sometimes the rider is an old woman in a bonnet of straw; or she is going to Coventry Cross, not Banbury, and may be thought of as Lady Godiva; or the rider intends to buy a treat for the child:

> Ride a cock-horse to Banbury Cross
> To buy little Johnny a galloping horse,
> It trots behind and it ambles before,
> And Johnny shall ride till he can ride no more.

Or:

> Ride a cock-horse to Banbury Cross
> To see what Tommy can buy;
> A penny white loaf, a penny white cake,
> And a two-penny apple pie.

The present Banbury Cross is modern, for the original was destroyed, as a Jesuit noted in 1601: 'The inhabitants of Banbury being far gone in Puritanism, in a furious zeal and tumultuously assailed the Cross that stood in the market-place, and so defaced it that they scarcely left one stone upon another.'
See also MOTHER GEESE & CATS WITH FIDDLES, p. 46

Cock Robin

Another nursery rhyme provides the name for Cock Robin pubs at Sale in Cheshire and Swindon in Wiltshire. It is a long and gloomy poem which was first recorded in the 1740s and became very popular in the nineteenth century. Only the first two verses are now generally remembered:

> Who killed Cock Robin?
> I, said the sparrow,
> With my bow and arrow,
> I killed Cock Robin.

> Who saw him die?
> I, said the Fly,
> With my little eye,
> I saw him die.

The poem then proceeds to allocate roles in the funeral to various creatures, almost all birds. For instance:

> Who'll be the parson?
> I, said the Rook,
> With my little book,
> I'll be the parson…

> Who'll be chief mourner?
> I, said the Dove,
> I mourn for my love,
> I'll be chief mourner.

The last verse is:

> All the birds of the air
> Fell a-sighing and a-sobbing
> When they heard the bell toll
> For poor Cock Robin.

See also MOTHER GEESE & CATS WITH FIDDLES, p. 46

Cockatrice

Bryant Lillywhite, writing in 1972, already noted that pubs called the Cockatrice were rare (at least one such, at Norton Subcourse in Norfolk, has since closed down); even so, the folklore behind the name is so curious that it deserves a mention.

In heraldry, a cockatrice is a small but highly dangerous monster, having the head, upper body and legs of a cock, but a lower body which tapers away to a reptilian tail, like that of a dragon.

The Cockatrice

Its bite is venomous, but more remarkable is the deadly power of its eyes, for it can kill people simply by staring at them. Strangest of all is its birth: it comes from an egg laid on a dunghill not by a hen but by an elderly cock, and hatched out by a snake or a toad. Traditionally, the way to destroy a cockatrice is to trick it into turning its fatal glance upon its own reflection; this can be done either by placing a mirror at the entrance to its den or by wearing glass armour when going to fight it. Writing in 1608, the naturalist Edward Topsell mocked the legend:

> I cannot without laughing remember the old wives' tales of the vulgar cockatrices that have been in England, for I have oftentimes heard it confidently related, that once our nation was full of cockatrices, and that a certain man did destroy them by going up and down in glasse, whereby their own shapes were reflected upon their own faces, and so they died.

Corn Dolly

This is the name of a pub in Bradford (West Yorkshire), and also – with obvious appropriateness – of one in the *Corn*market in Oxford. Although in the 1990s the latter had a sign representing a pretty girl with ears of wheat in her hair, the term 'corn dolly' more correctly refers to ornaments made by plaiting straw into various shapes, e.g. bells, cages, and stylised human figures.

They became popular in the 1950s, as a handicraft hobby which deliberately revived (and greatly elaborated) an old rural custom which is first recorded in the 1590s. It had been well known in the nineteenth century but died out early in the twentieth, as harvesting became mechanised. As the reapers came to the end of their task they would twist and tie an armful of corn into some form of ornament. This could be something as simple as a cross or a plait, or it could be a human figure, often adorned with ribbons, or even given a dress. This was called a 'corn baby' or 'corn maiden'. Whatever the form of the ornament, making it was a way of celebrating the successful completion of the harvest; it would be carried in triumph with the last load, after which it might be displayed at the harvest supper, or hung up for a year in the barn for luck, or taken to church for the harvest festival.

See also HARVESTERS & WHEATSHEAVES, p. 182

Crispin (and Crispianus)

The brothers Crispin and Crispianus were early Christians, probably Romans, who are said to have gone as missionaries into Gaul, and to have been martyred there around AD 285. It is also said that they earned their living as shoemakers rather than take alms from their converts, for which reason they were chosen as patron saints for shoemakers' guilds in many parts of Europe. In England after the Reformation they were still remembered for patriotic reasons, because Henry V's great victory at Agincourt in 1415 took place on their feast day, 25 October (as Shakespeare stresses). Till late in the nineteenth century, cobblers still kept this date as their annual holiday.

The Crispin Inn at Ashover in Derbyshire and the Crispin and Crispianus at Strood near Rochester in Kent owe their names to

Crispin and Crispianus

a traditional belief that they were founded by a soldier who had fought at Agincourt – at Ashover, this was Sir Thomas Babington, Lord of the Manor. At Stafford, however, the pub sign shows St Crispin himself working at a cobbler's last. There is also a Jolly Crispin in Dudley in Worcestershire.

See also ANGELS & SAINTS, p. 16

Crock of Gold

This name, given to a pub in the London borough of Brent, symbolises good luck and unexpected wealth – for, as everybody knows, there is a crock (or pot) of gold buried at the foot of every rainbow, and it is yours for the taking if you can reach the spot before the rainbow fades. There is also an Irish tradition that the type of small goblin called a leprechaun always has a crock of gold hidden somewhere, but nobody has yet managed to trick or force him into giving it up. Many English people know about this at second hand, although it has never been part of native English folklore.

Crocodile

The local explanation for the presence of a Crocodile pub at Dane Hill in West Sussex relies upon those popular heroes of tradition, the smugglers of the eighteenth century. It is said that they used to hide their contraband in nearby marshland, and retrieve it by means of a large pair of tongs which they called a 'crocodile', presumably because it resembled crocodile jaws.

Cross-in-Hand

This is not only the name of a pub but that of the village in which it stands, which is near Heathfield in East Sussex. It is first recorded there in 1547 in Latin, as the name of a road (*via cruce manus*), and then in 1597 as the village name, Crosse atte Hand. The local belief is that it refers back to the time of the Crusades, and means that Crusaders met here on the way to Rye for embarkation to the Holy Land. The signboard shows a hand grasping a standard with a red cross on a white ground.

An alternative explanation is a story about murderers being pursued by a mob escaping their immediate vengeance by grasping a crucifix and turning to face them. This very implausible idea earned the scorn of Leslie Dunkling and Gordon Wright, who comment: 'The inventor of that tale was probably slightly befuddled at the time and had recently been watching a film about vampires.'

Cross Keys, Crossed Keys

This name is found at Aldeburgh in Suffolk, Lydford-on-Fosse in Somerset, and elsewhere. Crossed keys are the emblem of the Papacy, for Jesus promised Peter that he would give him 'the keys of the kingdom of heaven' (Matt. 16:19), which later generations saw as a symbol of the authority of the Popes, successors to Peter. In popular belief, St Peter is imagined as standing at the gates of heaven with his keys, ready to let in – or to exclude – the souls of the dead. Surprisingly, despite these very Catholic associations, Cross (or Crossed) Keys survived the Reformation as a name for taverns, probably because the emblem had also been adopted into the coats of arms of various bishoprics and abbeys, including Glastonbury.

See also ANGELS & SAINTS, p. 16

Crossed Scythes

See HARVESTERS & WHEATSHEAVES, p. 182

Crumpled Horn

Nursery rhymes are a useful source for unusual and amusing pub names. The Crumpled Horn at Swindon in Wiltshire must surely refer to a line about halfway through the cumulative jingle about 'The House That Jack Built', first printed in the middle of the eighteenth century, but probably older:

> This is the cow with the crumpled horn
> That tossed the dog
> That worried the cat
> That killed the rat
> That ate the malt
> That lay in the house that Jack built.

See also MOTHER GEESE & CATS WITH FIDDLES, p. 46

Cuckoo Bush

The name and sign of this pub at Gotham (Nottinghamshire) celebrate the best-known joke about the best-known group of village fools in English folklore, the Wise Men of Gotham. Having noticed that cuckoos arrive when summer begins and that soon after they have disappeared the summer too is past its best, they deduced that if only they could stop the bird from leaving, winter would never come. So when they saw a cuckoo settling on a bush they hurriedly built a fence to pen it in – and were quite amazed when it simply skimmed over the top of the fence and flew away. 'If only we'd built it a foot or two higher we'd have got her!' they cried.

Stories about the foolishness of Gotham men were already known in the fifteenth century, and went on being told and printed well into the nineteenth. But, as often happens in such cases, there was an alternative version to show that they were far from stupid. According to Robert Thoroton's *History of Nottinghamshire* (1797), the tale as told at that time was that the men of Gotham had offended King John by preventing him and his retinue from riding across certain meadows (which

The Cuckoo Bush

would have made these meadows a public road for evermore). Knowing he would send men to punish them, they started acting like complete idiots – some tried to drown an eel in the village pond, others rolled cheeses downhill so that they could make their own way to market, 'and some were employed in hedging in a cuckoo which had perched upon an old bush'. Seeing this, the king's men just laughed at them and went away.

The current signboard shows the villagers cutting stakes and beginning to raise the fence, while the cuckoo looks on from a tree; and an earlier version showed the moment when it astonishes them by flying away.

Cuckoo Oak

The story which accounts for this pub name at Madeley in Shropshire is the same as for the Cuckoo Bush at Gotham. The villagers, ironically called 'the wise men of Madeley', were so sad to think that the cuckoo would fly away and take the summer with it that they decided to keep it imprisoned. So they waited till it settled on an oak tree, and then held hands in a circle round it. Their neighbours thought they were behaving madly.

Cuckoo's Nest

At Gawcutt in Buckinghamshire is the pub called the Cuckoo's Nest. Now, as everyone knows, cuckoos never build nests, so this might simply be nonsense talk, as exemplified by the children's rhyme:

> One flew east, one flew west,
> One flew over the cuckoo's nest.

Or it might hint at the traditional piece of bawdy symbolism seen in an old song still popular with folk singers. The first known version, dating from the middle of the seventeenth century, begins:

> As I was a-walking one morning in May,
> I met a pretty maid and unto her I did say,
> I'll tell you me mind, it's to love I'm inclined,
> And me inclination lies in your cuckoo's nest.

> Some like a girl who is pretty in the face,
> And some like a girl who is slender in the waist,
> But give me a girl who will wriggle and will twist,
> At the bottom of the belly lies the cuckoo's nest.

In this version the singer promises to wed the girl, and, rather surprisingly, we learn from the last verse that he does. In another, however, the singer boasts: 'And I left her with the makings of a young cuckoo.'

Cupid

Of all gods in Roman mythology, Cupid, the god of love, is probably the most instantly recognisable, and the only one who still plays an active part in popular imagery. The village of Cupid's Green in Hertfordshire once had a pub called the Cupid, with a striking triple sign described by Leslie Dunkling and Gordon Wright: 'In the first [sign] he is frowning at a couple who have quarrelled; in the second he fires his traditional arrows at their hearts; in the third he gives a thumbs-up sign as the couple embrace.'

Cupid

Cutty Sark

Most pubs of this name are commemorating a famous sailing ship, the fastest ocean clipper of the nineteenth century, which is now kept in dry dock at Greenwich. Naturally, there is a Cutty Sark pub only a few minutes walk along the river. But the ship took its name from a poem by Robert Burns, which was itself based on a humorous folk legend, 'Tam o' Shanter'. This tells of a drunken farmer who happens to see a group of witches dancing wildly, and spies on them. The youngest and prettiest is wearing only a 'cutty sark', i.e. a shirt that has been cut short. Tam is so thrilled at the display that he loudly cheers her, and has to flee for his life from the angry witches. When a Cutty Sark pub is found in Scotland (e.g. in Dundee and Dumbarton), the allusion will probably be to Burns rather than to the ship; inspection of the signboard will settle the matter.

D

David & Goliath

See ANGELS & SAINTS, p. 16

Davy's Locker

This unusual name was chosen for a pub at Millendreath, near Looe in Cornwall, and is certainly appropriate for a region where fishing and seafaring were such an important way of life. Since the eighteenth century, 'going to Davy Jones's locker' has been a jocular term for being drowned. The locker is the sea itself, considered as a place full of the bodies of drowned seamen, wrecked ships, and things lost overboard; 'Davy Jones' is imagined as a kind of sea-ogre, a malevolent counterpart to Neptune. It is sometimes suggested that there was once a real human Davy, possibly a pirate, whom popular imagination transformed into a supernatural figure, but no evidence for this has been found. Certainly the first description in print, which comes in Tobias Smollett's novel *The Adventures of Peregrine Pickle* (1751), is of a definitely demonic creature:

This same Davy Jones, according to the mythology of sailors, is the fiend that presides over all the evil spirits of the deep, and is often seen in various shapes, perching among the rigging on the eve of hurricanes, shipwrecks and other disasters to which a seafaring life is exposed.

In the novel, a young prankster frightens a commodore on board ship by dressing up as 'Davy'; he wraps himself in an oxhide and wears a mask of shark's jaws covered in leather, with eyes made of drinking glasses with candles in them. Wearing this, he chases the commodore, bellowing like a bull and letting off a firework. The commodore faints. The episode is presented as comic, and the many references to Davy Jones in later sources are humorous too.

Derby Tup

Usually when the name of a pub is changed, traditional associations are sadly lost. So it is pleasant to note that the opposite process can occur: in 1983 the Brunswick Hotel in Chesterfield (Derbyshire) was renamed the Derby Tup, in honour of a powerful symbol of regional pride and local humour.

A tup is a ram, and a ram has been, since medieval times, the heraldic emblem of the Worshipful Company of Clothworkers and, more generally, of companies associated with the wool trade. However, the Derby Tup (or Ram) is altogether more remarkable – a legendary creature of gigantic proportions, celebrated in a folksong which dates back at least to the eighteenth century. There are several versions. One begins:

As I went out in Derby, 'twas in the month of May,
I spied the biggest ram, me lads, that ever fed on hay.
  And it's true, me lads, it's true, me lads,
  I've never been known to lie;
  If you'd ha' been in Derby,
  You'd ha' seen it the same as I.

The wool on this ram's back, me lads, it reached up
    to the moon;
A little boy went up in May, and didn't come down
    till June.
  And it's true, me lads (etc.)

The song celebrates the slaughter of the tup, and what use was
made of the carcass:

All the women in Derby are asking for his ears,
To make them leather aprons to last them forty years.

And all the boys in Derby are asking for his eyes,
To make them leather footballs to last them all their lives.

There are opportunities for bawdy references; one version ends:

It took all the boys in Derby to bear away his bones,
It took all the girls in Derby to roll away his stones.

In Chesterfield itself, and in many other places in north
Derbyshire and southern Yorkshire, there was a Christmas
custom in which a team of men went from house to house
leading the 'Old Tup' – i.e. one of them would be hunched

up and hidden under a sheepskin or a sack, and carrying a wooden sheep's head mounted on a short pole, so as to look like a grotesque animal. The head would have horns and a hinged, clacking jaw. Another of the team would dress as a butcher. Knocking on the door, they would sing:

> We've brought the Tup from Derby and he's standing at
>   your door,
> And if you let him in, he'll please you all the more.

Once in, they sang the rest of the song, while the Butcher sharpened his knife and the Tup kicked and struggled till he was 'killed' – and, very soon, revived. The team would be given beer and money for this entertainment.

Like many old folk performances, this died out in the early years of the twentieth century, but has been revived by Morris Men and others in recent times.

Devil & Dunstan

Bryant Lillywhite says that there was formerly a pub of this name at Temple Bar in Fleet Street, in London. The reference is to an amusing legend about how St Dunstan (909–88), a learned monk at Glastonbury Abbey who later became Archbishop of Canterbury, got the better of the Devil. Dunstan was a fine craftsman in metalwork. The story goes that one evening when he was busy in his smithy, the Devil, in the form of a young man, looked in at the window and tried to distract him with bawdy and blasphemous talk. Dunstan simply ignored him, so the Devil changed his appearance to that of a sexy, seductive girl. But Dunstan was neither deceived nor distracted; he kept on working at his forge till his tongs were red-hot, then snatched them from the fire, grabbed the Devil by the nose, and held on tight. When he at last let go, the Devil flew off as fast as he could.

See also ANGELS & SAINTS, p. 16

Devil in the Boot

This curious name, found at Winslow in Buckinghamshire, seems at first sight to be one of those arbitrary, nonsensical combinations chosen for humorous effect. But not so. It alludes to the legend of a once-famous medieval cleric, Sir John Schorne, who was rector of North Marston in the same county from 1290 till his death in 1314. After his death he was revered as a saint and miracle-worker; North Marston became a popular pilgrimage centre, with a shrine holding his relics, and a holy well. He would very likely have been officially canonised if the Reformation had not intervened. The most famous story about him was that he had once forced the Devil into a boot – presumably as a ritual of exorcism, though the details of his exploit are now forgotten. A few images of him survive in church carvings and windows; he can be recognised by the fact that he holds up this boot, with the Devil peeping out of the top of it.

Devil's Stone

On the village green of Shebbear in Devon, just outside the church and at the foot of an oak, there lies a very large boulder allegedly weighing a ton, which legend claims was thrown or dropped by the Devil himself, in an attempt to destroy the church. Some local folk, however, claim that it is simply his

The Devil's Stone

gravestone. He died of cold, they say, Hell being far warmer than Devon. Consequently the pub, which also faces the green, is named the Devil's Stone, and its sign bears the picture of a red, cross-legged demon. On 5 November, Guy Fawkes Night, the village bell-ringers gather to ring a peal (as was once widely done on this date); having done so, they go to the boulder and turn it over with crowbars, to make sure the Devil never returns.

Dew Drop Inn

See PUNS & OLD JOKES, p. 138

Dick Turpin

There is a pub named after this famous highwayman in East Finchley (London N2), which is appropriate since it is close to Hampstead Heath, scene of some of his crimes; also one in York, where he was hanged; and in several other towns. Furthermore, the Spaniards Inn in Spaniards Road, on the edge of Hampstead Heath, claims that he was born there, later used it as a base for his robberies, and is now haunted by his ghost. It displays many supposed relics of his career, and a notice declaring:

It is believed by some that the notorious highwayman Dick Turpin was born at the Spaniards Inn on the 21st September 1705. Whether this be true or not, we know that his father was a previous landlord in the early eighteenth century and that young Dick Turpin allegedly watched passing coaches full of wealthy ladies and gentlemen from the upstairs windows. It is in these very rooms that Dick Turpin's life of crime began.

This legend is quite unhistorical; it must have arisen by confusion with Hempstead in Essex, his true birthplace, where his father was indeed an innkeeper. Turpin is also recalled in the pub names Turpin's Tavern at Sutton-on-Derwent and Turpin's Cave at High Beach Hill in Epping Forest; the latter refers to a cave where he is supposed to have hidden. There are also a good many pubs, especially in London, Essex, and along the road to York, where tradition alleges that he used to drink, though they have not renamed themselves in his honour. The historian James Sharpe, in his *Dick Turpin: The Myth of the English Highwayman* (2004), comments acidly: 'There are indeed so many pubs alleging Turpin connections that if all their claims were true, the career of England's most famous highwayman would have been passed in a combination of perpetual motion and a permanent alcoholic haze.'

The true facts of Turpin's life are well documented. He was born in Hempstead in Essex in 1705. In 1734 he joined a gang of violent robbers operating on the outskirts of London; their method was to break into a house and beat up, threaten, and even burn the occupants until they handed over their money and valuables. Within a year most of the gang had been caught and hanged or transported, but not Turpin, who turned instead to highway robbery and horse stealing – at first

in or near London, later in Essex, Lincolnshire, and Yorkshire.
He was eventually arrested under a false name, recognised by
sheer chance, and hanged at York in 1739. He faced death
boldly, drinking and joking with friends who visited him in
prison, and bowing to the crowd as he was driven in a cart to
the gallows.

Turpin's contemporaries did not see him as a romantic figure.
This idea originated in a best-selling novel written almost a
hundred years after his death, Harrison Ainsworth's *Rookwood*
(1834). Ainsworth described highwaymen in general, and Turpin
in particular, as dashing adventurers, fearless, yet always gentle-
manly. He also invented the famous episode of Turpin's non-stop
ride from London to York to establish an alibi, and the pathetic
death of his mare Black Bess at the gates of the city. Here, he
was adapting a story which had been told much earlier about a
different highwayman, a certain 'Swift Nick' Nevison, hanged
in 1684 (see NEVISON'S LEAP). Readers mistook Ainsworth's
fiction for fact, and the Turpin legend was born.

See also HIGHWAYMEN & SMUGGLERS, p. 208

Dick Whittington

Pubs named after Dick Whittington are found in several parts
of the country, whether or not the area has any connection with
the real-life Whittington (c.1350–1423), a rich London merchant who served three times as Lord Mayor and was a substantial benefactor to the city. In the legendary version of his
life (first recorded at the beginning of the seventeenth century),
Dick is alleged to have arrived in London as a penniless orphan,
and become a servant in a merchant's house. A strange stroke of
luck changed his fortunes:

n when sending out a ship

something in it, in order

lessing. Dick Whittington

he had bought for a penny

et; but the vessel happen-

he Barbary coast, the King

errun with rats and mice,

an all the freight besides.

bullied by a cook in the

t as he sat gloomily on a

d Bow Bells in the City of

Turn again, Whittington,
thrice Lord Mayor of London.' So he returned, and soon afterwards received news of his fortune. The story probably dates
from Elizabethan times, and has parallels in other countries; it
is still well known through pantomimes.

Later versions often say that Dick had had his cat with him
from the start, bringing it with him when he came to London;
there may be some confusion here with the story of Puss in
Boots. Some pub signs adopt this idea, showing Dick walking along the road, with a bundle over his shoulder and the
cat following closely; others, notably the Whittington Stone on
Highgate Hill, have him sitting or standing by a milestone, with
the cat in his arms. Also on Highgate Hill is the Whittington
and Cat, which has a remarkable feature described by Antony
Clayton in his *The Folklore of London* (2008):

Behind the uninviting nicotine-stained curtains is a boozer
from another era. I found, towards the rear of the pub, the reason for my visit, the black leathery body of a long-deceased cat.

Games & Sports

Regrettably, many pubs were once the venue for blood sports, eventually banned in Acts of 1835 and 1849. Although there are various other reasons (especially heraldic ones) why a pub is called the Bull, Bear, Cock, or Dog, there is always a good possibility that bull-baiting, bear-baiting, cockfighting, and dogfighting took place in or near its premises. Some names put the matter beyond doubt; there is a Bull Ring pub at Ludlow, and Fighting Cock(s) at St Albans, Oakham in Rutland, Ecclesfield in South Yorkshire and elsewhere. The suppression of bull- and bear-baiting seems to have been effective, such events being conspicuous, but the relative privacy of a pub and its outbuildings gave opportunity for secret cockfighting and dogfighting, and for cock-shying. In the latter, men competed in throwing short heavy sticks at a tethered cock; whoever killed the bird got it as his prize. Performing animals trained by travelling showmen explain the seventeenth-century pub name Dancing Dogs at Battlebridge in Northamptonshire, and probably the more recent Bear and Bells at Beccles in Suffolk.

Currently, the only games which are likely to be played in pubs are darts, billiards, and dominoes. The range was once much greater. In the 1950s, Martin Thornhill in his *Explorer's England* lamented their gradual disappearance. He first mentions skittle-board, also known as 'devil among the tailors', still common then in the west of England; people at Potterne (near Devizes) claimed that their version was 'almost identical with the original game, which it seems was a favourite off-duty relaxation of the Romans who garrisoned Britain'. He then describes 'ringing the bull', in which a player had to jerk a ring hanging from the ceiling in such a way that it is caught on a hook in the wall behind him. Shove-ha'penny originated in the Middle Ages under the name shove-groat; the object of the game was to flip a coin at a given mark, the winner being the closest. In Elizabethan times it was sometimes played on a shovel-board thirty feet (9 metres) long; later pub boards were of course much smaller. In bat-and-trap a short wooden rod would be propelled from a trap, and players had to hit it in mid-air with a bat, knocking it as far as possible. Tip-cat was similar, except that the 'cat', a piece of wood with tapered ends, was not propelled from a trap but struck on one end to make it shoot into the air. Then there was the Spinning Jenny, a circular board marked with numbered segments and fixed to the ceiling, with a free-moving arrow below it; players would set the arrow spinning and bet on which segment it would be on when it stopped. Indeed, the interest of all these games could be increased by betting, or at least agreeing that the loser would buy a round of drinks. Marbles could be played in the yard outside.

A unique competition is described in Bob Pegg's *Rites and Riots* (1981):

> Close to Hebden Bridge, in quite a small area west of Halifax, the sport of Lark Singing took place in the years before World War I. These contests took place in pubs and were attended by the local Lark Men, who brought with them, in special 'dark-boxes', the lark they had taken from the nest, reared, and trained to sing. Each lark was exposed to the light in turn, when, as at dawn, it would give song, and the birds were judged on the length and musical quality of their song.

Sometimes a pub-based contest blossoms into a nationally or even internationally celebrated event. One such is the annual World Marbles Championship held every Good Friday outside the Greyhound at Tinsley Green on the Sussex/Surrey border. Local people claim that it has been played there regularly since Elizabethan times, when two young men (one from Surrey and one from Sussex) fell in love with the same girl, and decided which of them should woo her by playing marbles for her hand. Another is the World Conkers Championship held every October at the Chequered Skipper pub in Ashton in Northamptonshire. This began one day in 1965 when a few friends who had meant to go fishing were prevented by bad weather, and decided to play conkers instead. By now, hundreds take part, many in fancy dress and wearing strings of conkers attached to their clothes and hats; entries come from as far afield as Mexico and Australia.

The barman told me that it had been there for many years and was supposed to be the remains of Dick Whittington's feline friend. From its mouth hangs a similarly mummified mouse.

The names Whittington and Cat and Whittington Cat are also found outside London, e.g. in Hull and at Whitehaven in Cumberland. An amusing variation is at Ye Olde Boot Inn, opposite Whittington Castle in Shropshire; here a footsore Dick is massaging his feet, while his fine white cat is resting on his discarded boots.

Dirty Dick's

Since 1985 this pub, at 202–4 Bishopsgate, London EC2, no longer lives up to its celebrated name, having been forced by modern laws on Health and Safety to clear away the filthy accumulation of cobweb-covered tankards and jugs, mummified cats and rats, which could be seen on shelves behind the bar up to the early 1980s. Where they came from and why they were kept there is explained, somewhat cynically, by Jacob Larwood and J. C. Hotten in their seminal book on *The History of Signboards* (1866):

The name of Dirty Dick's, which graces a house in Bishopsgate St., E.C., otherwise known as the Gates of Jerusalem, and the Old Port Wine House, was transferred to it from the once famous Dirty Warehouse formerly in Leadenhall Street. This was a hardware shop kept at the end of the 18th century by Richard Bentley alias Dirty Dick . . . It is commonly supposed that Bentley was an eccentric character, the son of a wealthy merchant who had formerly kept his carriage and lived in great style, [who] earned his nickname by his conduct after he had been 'crossed in love'. Actually his behaviour seems to have been an original (and very successful) advertisement. The outside of his house was as dirty as the inside, to the great annoyance of his neighbours, who repeatedly offered Bentley to have the place cleaned, painted and repaired at their expense. He would not hear of this, for his dirt had given him celebrity, and his house was known in the Levant and the East and West Indies by no other denomination than the 'Dirty Warehouse in Leadenhall St'.

The writers add that nobody knows just how the name, and the dirt, came to be transferred to the pub in Bishopsgate Street; either this too belonged to Bentley, or when Bentley died its landlord bought the contents of Bentley's room at the warehouse 'to form a unique attraction at his own premises'.

Be that as it may, generations of drinkers at Dirty Dick's have been told the sad, romantic tale to which Larwood and Hotten refer so briefly; in some versions, Bentley's Christian name is given as Nathaniel, not Richard. The story goes that he had been an active, elegant man until tragedy turned him into a melancholic recluse. His fiancée died the day before their marriage, and on hearing the news he locked himself in the room where the wedding breakfast was laid, and never came out again. Nor would he let anyone in. He was fond of cats, and when any of his pets died he simply kept the corpses with him. It was claimed that the dust-covered litter in the pub consisted of items found in his room when he died, some fifty years after the tragedy. Newcomers used to be invited to stroke one of the mummified cats 'for luck', and would get a shock when a hidden spring made it give a very life-like leap.

Currently, the sign shows a shabbily dressed man in a battered top hat, looking rather crazy though not particularly dirty. Two mummified cats still remain on the premises, but hidden away in the vaults, in an enclosed area by the back stairs.

For another pub displaying mummified cats, see the NUT-SHELL.

Dogs, Dancing Dogs

See GAMES & SPORTS, p. 78

Dolphin

See QUEENS' HEADS & RED LIONS, p. 248

Donkey & Buskins

This curiously combined name is that of a pub at Layer-de-la-Haye, near Colchester in Essex. It is recorded by Leslie Dunkling and Gordon Wright, with the explanation that:

> a local farmer who patronised the inn one evening had the considerate idea of transferring his buskins [leather leggings] to the forelegs of his donkey, in order to protect the animal from thorns as it took his master home across the common. The incident became a local legend and has been perpetuated in the inn name and sign.

This anecdote fits one traditional type of joke about idiotic behaviour, in which a man puts himself to inconvenience in order to spare his animal – he may, for example, load his horse onto a cart and drag the cart himself, because he thinks the horse looks tired.

Dove & Rainbow

See RAINBOW & DOVE

Dragon

See GREEN DRAGON *or* RED DRAGON, pp. 118 and 247

Drake's Drum

Pubs of this name celebrate the great Elizabethan buccaneer Sir Francis Drake, who is famous for his role in defeating the Spanish Armada. It is particularly fitting that there should be one at Plymouth, in view of the anecdote which claims that he was playing bowls on Plymouth Hoe when news was brought that the Armada had been sighted. Unperturbed, he went on bowling, saying: 'There is time enough to finish the game, and beat the Spaniard too.' After Drake died off Panama in 1595 various mementos were brought back to Buckland Abbey, his Devonshire home, including a drum which later became the focus for a famous legend. The first hint of it comes in the 1860s, when the folklorist Robert Hunt notes that a retired housekeeper at Buckland Abbey told him that 'if the old warrior hears the drum which hangs in the hall of the abbey, and which accompanied him round the world, he rises and holds a revel'.

This simple belief acquired patriotic significance in Sir Henry Newbolt's vivid poem 'Drake's Drum', written in 1895 for the tercentenary of the hero's death. According to Newbolt, Drake on his deathbed promised that the sound of the drum would call his spirit back to defend England in any hour of danger:

> Take my drum to England, hang it by the shore,
> Strike it when your powder's running low;
> If the Dons sight Devon, I'll quit the port of Heaven,
> And drum them up the Channel, as we drummed
> them long ago.

In 1916 another writer, Alfred Noyes, developed the legend further, as a morale-booster for a nation at war. Writing about submarine warfare in *The Times* on 28 August 1916, he claimed that fishermen at Brixham in Devon believed that Drake's Drum had been heard as Nelson sailed up the channel to confront the French navy at Trafalgar, and again in that very year, 1916, before the naval Battle of Jutland. It hardly matters now whether the fishermen really told Noyes this, or whether he invented the tale himself, for it now has a firm place in tradition – the drum, 'they say', was heard at the evacuation of Dunkirk.

Druid, Druid's Arms, Druid's Head

The Druids were the priestly class in the Celtic tribes of Gaul and Britain at the period when the Romans were trying to conquer these lands. As such, they were discussed by several classical writers, none of whom can be regarded as unbiased; some described them as noble and learned, while others (notably Julius Caesar) alleged that their religion was a barbarous one, centred on human sacrifices. Among the Welsh, these Celtic forebears are remembered as heroic figures, inspiring their people to resist Roman imperialism and to preserve their national identity, their liberty, and their simple natural life-style. It is therefore fitting that there should be a Druid Inn at Goginan, near Aberystwyth.

The theory that prehistoric structures such as the stone circles at Avebury and Stonehenge had been built by the Druids of Celtic Britain for their religious ceremonies was first suggested by the antiquary John Aubrey in the 1660s, and became generally accepted in the 1740s thanks to the books of William Stukeley. Even after archaeologists had realised that the monuments actually came from a much earlier period, they were still often popularly thought to be Druidic well into the twentieth century.

This association accounts for the Druid's Arms at Stanton Drew (Somerset), which lies within the boundaries of a very impressive group of stones forming a circle with various outliers – some being actually in the pub garden. This circle has a legend of its own, about a wedding party who were turned to stone as punishment for their wickedness in dancing on a Sunday, but it does not involve any Druids. Instead, the picture on the pub's signboard is based on the melodramatic image which Druids often had in nineteenth-century literature and art, as priests of a cruel bloodthirsty religion. This was partly drawn from Ancient Roman writers, who condemned them for practising human sacrifice, usually of criminals or captives; but the Victorians went further, claiming they regularly slaughtered infants and young maidens. And so the sign of the Druid's Arms shows a priest at his stone altar, about to slay a victim.

It is a little surprising that most pubs with 'Druid' in their names are in towns, far from any stone circle – the Druid's Head in Brighton, for example, the Druid's Arms in Loughborough and in Bristol, and the Ancient Druid(s) in Cambridge and elsewhere. The reference is probably not directly to the Druids of history but to a social and benevolent organisation called the Ancient Order of Druids, founded in 1783 and still existing, or to its offshoot, the United Ancient Order of Druids, founded in 1833 but dissolved in the 1990s. Lodges of both Orders sometimes used pubs as a meeting place.

Dun Cow

The earliest record of a 'Dun Cow' pub comes from Dunchurch in Warwickshire in 1655. The name is particularly appropriate in Warwick itself; it is popular throughout the Midland counties, and can also be found further afield, e.g. in Bedlington (Northumberland), and in London. It refers to a monstrously huge cow with blazing red eyes which supposedly roamed Dunsmore Heath, terrorising the neighbourhood, till it was killed by the legendary Sir Guy of Warwick towards the end of the tenth century. Tragically, she had originally been a kindly creature with supernatural powers; she could fill a pail with milk for anyone who came. Unfortunately, one cruel woman decided to test the cow's power by milking her not into a pail but into a sieve, and after a while this did cause her to run dry. Maddened with pain and anger, the placid beast became a raging monster. The story of Guy himself goes back to about 1200, but did not at first include a cow among the monsters he is credited with killing; she first appears in the middle of the fourteenth century. This tale, together with other exploits of Sir Guy, later became widely known through cheap printed chapbooks.

In the sixteenth century, visitors to Warwick used to be shown an enormous skull and vertebrae in the castle, a rib more than six feet (2 metres) long in a chapel at Guy's Cliffe, and a shoulder-blade, five feet long and three feet broad (1.6 by 0.9 metres), hanging over one of the gates of Coventry. All were claimed to be remains of Sir Guy's Dun Cow, though in fact they must have been whale bones. Since Sir Guy's story was so well known, it is strange that Bryant Lillywhite in his *London Signs* judges it 'most improbable' that Dun Cow pubs refer to it; instead, he makes the suggestion (which one might feel is even more improbable) that they got their name 'from a dark and gloomy looking cow living on or near the premises adopting the sign'.

In their *English Inn Signs* (rev. edn), Larwood and Hotten noted that the Dun Cow at Swainsthorpe in Norfolk invited potential customers with the rhyme:

> Walk in, gentlemen, I trust you'll find
> The Dun Cow's milk is to your mind.

They also suggested that a pub of the same name which formerly stood on the main road from York to Durham referred to the cow in a very different story. When the Priory of Lindisfarne was destroyed by Vikings in 875, a group of monks carried away the body of the former Prior, St Cuthbert, who had died almost two hundred years previously. For over a hundred years this important relic was transferred from one place to another, until in 995 it found a permanent safe refuge in Durham Cathedral. According to legend, as recounted in the *Rites of Durham* (1593), a holy man told the monks carrying the relic that he had dreamt they should take it to Dunholme – unfortunately, neither he nor they knew where this place might be. But then as they drew near Durham they happened to hear one woman ask another if she had seen her straying cow, to which the second woman answered, 'Yes, she is in Dunholme.' Thus they knew they had reached the end of their wanderings. Although this source does not mention any colour, by the nineteenth century there was a strong local belief that it had been a dun cow; probably this simply echoes the place name *Dun*holme.

E

Eagle & Child

This pub name is quite widespread, probably the best-known example being the one in Oxford, where J. R. R. Tolkien and his friends used to drink (and familiarly known to them as the Bird and Baby; to others as the Buzzard and Bastard). It is of heraldic origin, being derived from the coat of arms of the Stanley family (including the earls of Derby), who owned estates in several parts of England. Their crest shows an eagle perched on a nest which contains a baby, sometimes in a cradle or a basket – an image going back to medieval times, for it can be seen carved in the woodwork of the Dean's stall in Manchester Cathedral, where one of the Stanleys was Dean from 1485 to 1506. The Stanleys had inherited much of their land (through marriage) from the Lathom family, who had also used the eagle-and-child crest,

The Eagle & Child

and the legend purporting to explain it relates to a Sir Thomas Lathom in the fourteenth century.

According to this, Sir Thomas's elderly wife had been able to give him only one child, a daughter, and he was desperate for a son. His young mistress, however, had just born him an illegitimate son. So, he got a servant to take the baby boy into his park and lay it at the foot of a tree where there was an eagle's nest, and then he took his wife for a stroll in the park, and made sure that she heard the baby wailing. He convinced her that it was Providence which had guided the eagle and kept the baby safe, so that he could adopt it as his heir. And so he did, but years later he repented and told the truth on his deathbed; the estates therefore passed to his daughter, who had married a Stanley.

See also QUEENS' HEADS & RED LIONS, p. 248

Elephant & Castle

The most famous pub of this name has long been demolished, but the area of London where it once stood is still known as the Elephant. Other examples can be found in Acton and Southwark (both being London districts), at Trowbridge (Wiltshire), Banbury (Oxfordshire), and elsewhere. One London example, which formerly stood in King's Road, Camden Town, was thought to take its name from what is alleged to have been a real discovery in the 1690s – though archaeologists may be inclined to doubt the accuracy of the interpretation. According to Samuel Palmer's *St Pancras* (1870):

> Mr John Conyers, an apothecary of Fleet Street, who was an enthusiastic local antiquarian, and who made it his chief business to collect local antiquities ... was one day digging in a field near

to the Fleet Brook and Battle Bridge, and not far from St Pancras workhouse, when he discovered the remains of an elephant, an animal totally unknown to the ancient Britons. Near the same spot was also found an ancient British spear, consisting of the head of a flint fastened into a shaft of considerable length. It is from this curious fact that the public-house called the Elephant and Castle derives its name.

Some people have assumed that Elephant and Castle is an incongruous, even nonsensical, name, and have accepted the 'explanation' that it arose from a stupid mistake – the original name, they believe, was 'Infanta de Castille' and referred to Eleanor of Castille, the Spanish wife of Edward I. There is no supporting evidence for this, and like other 'explanations' relying on alleged verbal misunderstandings it says more for the misplaced ingenuity of the inventor than for the facts of history. Others, more plausibly, have suggested that the sign was popularised by a brewery which supplied ale to the British army in India in Victorian times, and that the image of an elephant carrying a small tower on its back alludes to the howdah carried by Indian elephants. Finally, there is a heraldic link with the Cutlers' Company, whose crest is the same image, probably alluding to the use of ivory for the handles of high-quality cutlery.

The Elephant & Castle

Elephants have been used in battle for many centuries, carrying fighting men in a wooden 'castle' on their backs. This fact was well known in Roman times, and featured in entertainments; at Julius Caesar's Games in 46 BC some forty elephants were displayed in the arena, carrying 'castles' from which armed men fought one another. In the Middle Ages the elephant was regularly linked with the 'castle' both in the written descriptions in Bestiaries and in visual art, e.g. in church carvings.

See also QUEENS' HEADS & RED LIONS, p. 248

Essex Serpent

In the middle of the eighteenth century there were two London pubs called the Essex Serpent, one being in King Street, Covent Garden, and the other in Charles Street, Westminster. The first still exists, but the other has long since gone. They got their name from a sensational creature described in an anonymous pamphlet printed in London in 1669, entitled *A True Relation of a Monstrous Serpent seen at Henham on the Mount in Saffron Walden*. If the pamphlet is to be believed, a serpent had been seen several times in Henham in May that year; it was allegedly eight or nine feet long (2.4 – 2.7 metres), as thick as a man's leg, with big eyes and fierce fangs, and a pair of tiny wings which implied that it was in fact a dragon. Dramatic tales of this type were staple fare in the cheap publications of the period, always claiming to be totally true. This one was taken up by the popular annual *Poor Robin's Almanac*, which for several years kept the story going by anniversary entries such as '1672: Four years since the serpent flew at Henham', and '1674: On 30 May a fair is held at Henham for the sale of Flying Serpents' – these presumably being fairground figurines of dragons, or possibly biscuits baked in that shape. Even in those days, people knew how to cash in on a local sensation.

F

Fair Rosamund

There is no doubt that the lady from whom the Fair Rosamund pub at Botley near Oxford takes its name was a real person, Rosamund Clifford. She was the mistress of Henry II and the mother of two of his children, but after some years she withdrew to a convent at Godstow, where she died in 1177, aged about thirty-seven. What made her famous, however, was the romantic and quite unhistorical legend that grew up about her in the later Middle Ages and the Tudor period. It was said that the king had had a house specially built for her at Woodstock, surrounded by a garden maze so intricate that he alone knew the way through it. Nevertheless, his wife, Queen Eleanor, who was bitterly jealous, did discover the secret way by following a thread which had unravelled from Rosamund's embroidery, because it had become caught up by the king's spur, and had been dragged to the exit of the maze when he left. Confronting her rival, Queen Eleanor offered her a choice: to die by poison, or by the dagger. Rosamund chose the poison.

Farmer's Boy

See HARVESTERS & WHEATSHEAVES, p. 182

Feathers, Three Feathers, Prince of Wales' Feathers

See QUEENS' HEADS & RED LIONS, p. 248

Fiddlers Three

At Bradford there is a pub of this name, which is taken from a nursery rhyme dating from around 1700. Its cheerful conviviality makes it a good choice:

> Old King Cole was a merry old soul,
> And a merry old soul was he;
> He called for his pipe and he called for his bowl,
> And he called for his fiddlers three.

See also MOTHER GEESE & CATS WITH FIDDLES, p. 46

Finn McCoul's

The name of this pub in High Wycombe (Buckinghamshire) must surely have been chosen by a Scottish or Irish landlord, for it honours a great hero in Celtic legend who was a warrior, hunter, and seer; his name is variously spelled as Fionn mac Cumhaill or Finn MacCool. Tales about him have been popular for over twelve hundred years in Ireland, and almost equally long in Scotland. Some are fairly plausible, making him the chieftain of a band of wild young men who lived by hunting deer and wild boar, fighting, cattle-raiding and robbing. Others, especially in later folklore, give him supernatural adventures; he visits Otherworld realms, combats or outwits giants, and sometimes is described as a giant himself.

Finnegan's Wake

There is a pub of this name in Edinburgh and two in London, one in Gloucester Road and one in George Street; there may well be others elsewhere. The reference is to a lively Irish folksong which celebrates the power of drink, and so is well suited to a pub. It tells the tale of one Tim Finnegan, a bricklayer, who fell from his ladder when drunk, and was carried home and laid out on his bed, ready for burial. His wife gathered all his friends for a wake, with 'pipes, tobacco and whiskey punch', but a quarrel broke out, 'and a row and a ruction soon began' as the men started fighting and throwing things.

> Then Mickey Maloney raised his head
> When a noggin of whiskey flew at him,
> It missed, and falling upon the bed
> The liquor scatters over Tim.
> Bedad, he revives, see how he rises,
> And Timothy rising from the bed
> Says, 'Whirl your liquor around like blazes,
> The name o' the dhoul, d'ye think I'm dead?'

Fish & Bell

See BELL & MACKEREL

Fish & Ring

One of the recurrent 'tall stories' found in folktales and legends is the one about a ring being thrown into the sea and unexpectedly recovered, sometimes years later, from the belly of a fish which had swallowed it. The painted signboard of the Fish and Ring pub in Whitehorse Road, London E1, shows not only a fish with a ring in its mouth but also a saint holding up a cross, which makes it clear that in this particular case the reference is to the legend of St Kentigern (aka Mungo), a monk and bishop who died in 612. He is the patron saint of Glasgow. It is said that the Queen of Strathclyde was unfaithful to her husband, whose suspicions grew to certainty when he noticed her lover wearing a ring, which he recognised as one he himself had once given her. Furious, the king confiscated the ring and hurled it into the river Clyde. He then confronted his wife and demanded that she show him the ring (knowing perfectly well that this was impossible), and telling her that he would only believe her innocent if she could find it and bring it back to him within three days, on pain of death. She begged St Kentigern to help her, and he told her not to be afraid, for one of his monks had just caught a salmon in the Clyde, and when he gutted it he found that very ring inside it.

Five Alls

In origin, the Five Alls (or the Four Alls) was a medieval comment about social classes. Inns of this name displayed a sign showing the faces of a king, a knight, a monk, and a farmer, each with his appropriate motto: 'I rule all', 'I fight for all', 'I pray for all', and 'I work for all'. Nowadays, the monk is either

I PRAY FOR ALL   I PLEAD FOR ALL   I MAINTAIN ALL   I FIGHT FOR ALL   I TAKE ALL

The Five Alls

omitted or replaced by a parson, and there are variations that include a lawyer ('I plead for all'), a John Bull figure ('I pay for all'), or even the Devil or Death ('I take all'). If all these figures are present the pub, naturally, becomes the Six Alls. Eric Delderfield's book includes a picture of the sign of the Five Alls at Cheltenham where the faces (of king, parson, lawyer, soldier and farmer) are realistically rendered and may well be intended as portraits of individuals; certainly the king looks very like George VI.

Fleece

See GOLDEN FLEECE

Flitch of Bacon

There is only one pub of this name, at Little Dunmow in Essex, for it celebrates the unusual and genuinely ancient ceremony for which this village and its neighbour Great Dunmow are famous. Originally it was an annual one, but nowadays is held only in leap years, on Whit Monday. Couples who have been married for more than a year and a day attend a mock court, complete with judge, jury, and counsel, and swear that they have never had a cross word with one another, nor ever regretted having married. Those taking part need not be local people. If they can stand up to cross-examination and convince the court that they are speaking the truth, they are awarded a flitch – i.e. a whole side – of bacon as prize, and are carried in procession.

The custom is first mentioned in Langland's poem *Piers Ploughman* (1377) as something already well known; there is no evidence to show how much older it may be. At first it was a serious affair, not a comic display; applicants would go to the Priory of Little Dunmow and take an oath, on their knees, that they were telling the truth about their marriage; if convinced, the monks gave them the flitch. When the monasteries were closed down at the Reformation the local Lord of the Manor took on the responsibility for this generosity. He and his successors kept it up till the 1750s, when the current Lord refused to carry it on any longer, and the custom lapsed. However, in 1854 the best-selling novelist Harrison Ainsworth wrote an enthusiastic description, *The Flitch of Bacon, or the Custom of Dunmow*, which created much interest; this inspired a revival the following year in which Ainsworth himself acted as judge at a public hearing of the type that still continues.

Unusually, the pub sign is a three-dimensional one – a carved wooden flitch, painted gold, and set up on the opposite side of the road. Over the pub door, a notice reads:

> Painted in gold ye Flitch behold,
> Of famed Dunmow ye boaste.
> Then here should call fond couples all,
> And pledge it in a toast.

See also THE YEAR'S MERRY ROUND, p. 310

Flying Dutchman

There are pubs of this name in Halifax and Harrogate. It refers to the sinister legend of a phantom sailing ship which is said to have haunted the ocean for generations, especially round the Cape of Good Hope. In most versions, it is the ship itself which is called *The Flying Dutchman*, though sometimes this is said to be the nickname of its (Dutch) captain. The ghostly ship appears only during great storms, and to see it is an almost certain omen of shipwreck and death. It never docks in any port, though the sailors on board do sometimes hail those on real ships and send messages to their loved ones ashore – who invariably turn out to have been long dead. The story goes that the captain and crew can never rest, nor can the ship cease its wanderings: this is the punishment for the captain's sin of blasphemy. Once, long ago, he set out to round the Cape during one of the gales to which those seas are very liable; his crew urged him to abandon the attempt and take refuge in a bay till the seas were calmer, but he replied: 'May I be eternally damned if I do that, though I should beat about here until the Day of Judgement.' He got his way – the ship did round the Cape, despite the storm, but since then has never ceased to sail.

The legend is probably of Dutch origin. There is a brief reference to a sighting of the phantom ship in George Barrington's *A Voyage to Botany Bay* (1795), but the full story first appears in English in *Blackwood's Magazine* for May 1921, after which it became very well known. Richard Wagner's opera on the theme dates from 1843.

Flying Horse

See PEGASUS

Flying Monk

Sadly, the pub at Malmesbury in Wiltshire which was given this unique name in 1965 was demolished in the 1970s to make way for a supermarket. It had commemorated, however briefly, a remarkable piece of local history.

According to the medieval historian William of Malmesbury's *Gesta Regum Anglorum* (*c.*1125), a monk named Elmer who lived at Malmesbury Abbey at the time of the Norman Conquest had attempted a remarkable feat:

He was a man of good learning for those times, of mature age, and in his youth had hazarded an attempt of singular temerity. He had by some contrivance fastened wings to his hands and feet, in order that, looking upon the fable as true, he might fly like [the ancient Greek hero] Daedalus; and collecting the air upon a tower [of the abbey], had flown for more than the distance of a furlong, but, agitated by the violence of the wind and the current of air, he fell and was lame ever after. He used to relate as the cause of his failure, his forgetting to provide himself with a tail.

Some scholars have wondered whether William was wrong to take the story as a literal truth; perhaps it was a moral fable about a magician's impious attempt to do something beyond human power, and his well-deserved downfall. However, what William describes is not so different from modern hang-gliding, so Elmer's experiment might indeed have taken place.

The inn had an attractive sign, showing Elmer plunging down from the tower; it is reproduced in Eric Delderfield's *British Inn Signs and their Stories* on p. 12. A more dignified picture of Elmer, holding a miniature version of his flying kit, can be seen in one of the stained-glass windows of Malmesbury Abbey church.

Flying Saucer

Whether one should include Flying Saucer in a collection of names based on folklore is, quite obviously, a highly debatable issue. In doing so, I am thinking of a category of tales technically termed 'memorates', where the teller describes a startling and unexplained experience (e.g. glimpsing a figure which abruptly vanishes) and interprets it in terms of a pre-existing communal belief in some supernatural entities (ghosts, fairies, demons). Since the 1950s, there have been many reported sightings of lights and forms in the sky which the viewers found similarly inexplicable; they are labelled unidentified flying objects, or more popularly flying saucers, and many have interpreted them as craft containing alien beings from outer space.

There have been several pubs that took their name from them – at Chatham (Kent), Gillingham (Norfolk), and Lutterworth (Leicestershire). The latter later renamed itself after something less mysterious, the Royal Air Force's aerobatic jet planes, the Red Arrows.

Four-Leafed Clover

It is obviously no coincidence that the pub so named is to be found on Clover Hill, near Norwich. A sprig of clover with four leaves, as against the normal three, is one of the best-known symbols of good luck, and has been known as such at least since the sixteenth century. To find one is still supposed to bring prosperity and success; in earlier times, there was also an idea that anyone who wore or carried it would be safe from witchcraft and the evil eye, and immune to magical illusions.

Fox & Grapes

At first glance one might think that this name for a pub, which is found at Preston in Lancashire, in London, and elsewhere, is an example of the fanciful linking of two incongruous objects, for what can a fox have to do with a bunch of grapes? In fact, though, it refers to one of Aesop's animal fables from Ancient Greece. There was once a very hungry fox who noticed some grapes hanging from a vine which had grown up a tree, but they were so high up that he could not reach them, however hard he tried. So off he went, saying: 'They're unripe – they're too sour for me.' In the same way, some people who have failed to get what they want will pretend it was not worth wanting anyway – an attitude known as 'sour grapes'.

The Fox & Grapes

Friar Bacon

This name, given to a pub in Oxford and also to one in the nearby town of New Marston, is a tribute to Roger Bacon (*c.* 1214–92), a Franciscan friar who was one of the finest mathematicians and philosophers of his time, and who studied at the universities of Oxford and Paris. Like several other learned men in the medieval and Renaissance periods, he was suspected by later generations (and possibly also by contemporaries) of having been a magician; he was certainly an alchemist. The magical feats ascribed to him and another Oxford Franciscan, Friar Bungay, form the subject of a sixteenth-century chapbook and of a play by Robert Green (1594). The most famous legend about him is that of the Brazen Head, described above in connection with a pub of that name.

Friar Tuck

According to the Robin Hood legend, the outlaws in Sherwood Forest were joined by a fat and jolly friar who became their chaplain – though he was more than willing to join in their fighting too. There are various references to him from the fifteenth century onwards, and since jokes about the greed, drunkenness and laziness of monks and friars have long been popular, Friar Tuck soon became a standard figure in the story.

Besides pubs explicitly named after him (e.g. at Arnold near Nottingham and Wakefield in Yorkshire), there is also a Jolly Friar at Blidworth, not far from Sherwood Forest. At Cheltenham he has been given a pseudo-antique spelling Fryer Tuck. At Bramcote near Nottingham there is the cleverly named Tuck's Habit – all friars wore habits, but Friar Tuck's personal habit was his love of food and drink, and sure enough the signboard shows him tucking in to a good meal.

Frying Pan & Drum

See PUZZLING PAIRS, p. 112

◈ G ◈

George & Dragon

Pubs of this name can be found in most parts of England, thanks to the popularity of St George as the patron saint of this land. He was a Christian soldier, martyred in AD 303 at Lydda (Palestine); he was much venerated in the Greek Orthodox Church as a warrior saint granting victory in battle. His fame spread westwards after the First Crusade, because at a moment of great danger during the siege of Antioch in 1098 the Crusaders saw a vision of him leading heavenly warriors to help them against the Muslims. A military and aristocratic cult rapidly developed, and was introduced into England by Richard the Lionheart, who ordered his knights to choose St George as their special patron. His feast day (23 April) was made a holiday in 1222; Edward III made him the patron of the Order of the Garter in the 1340s, with the St George Chapel at Windsor as its headquarters; Henry V invoked him at Agincourt; by the close of the Middle Ages he had replaced the pre-Conquest royal saints, Edward the Confessor and Edmund of East Anglia, as the patron saint of England.

Originally, stories about St George simply stressed his courage under appalling tortures and death; there was no mention of his fight with a dragon, which is now the only thing people know about him. This story first appears as one episode of his career as given in *The Golden Legend*, a collection of saints' lives compiled in the late thirteenth century. It tells how George came to a pagan city where people had to send one girl every day to be eaten by a dragon from a nearby lake, and the lot had fallen on the king's daughter; George wounded the monster, bound it with the princess's girdle, and led it into the city like a dog before beheading it, on condition that the king and all his people should become Christians. In religious terms, this is an allegory of how a true Christian can defeat the Devil, but it also has a strong appeal simply as an adventure story.

After the Reformation, people were forbidden to celebrate any saints not actually mentioned in the Bible, but St George had acquired too much importance as a patriotic symbol to be casually discarded. Instead, his legend was remodelled to suit the Protestant ethos. This was done by Richard Johnson in *The Famous Historie of the Seven Champions of Christendom* (1596), by stripping out the martyrdom and other religious elements and replacing them by chivalric and magical adventures imitated from medieval romances. In this version, George is born in Coventry to noble English parents, but stolen soon after birth by an enchantress whose power he eventually outwits. He saves Sabra, the king of Egypt's daughter, from a dragon, and has many further adventures; eventually he encounters a second dragon and kills it, but dies from its poison, and is buried in Windsor Chapel. This story proved immensely popular, and ensured George's status in Protestant England and his enduring fame.

Since the 1990s, there has been a considerable revival of interest in St George as a symbol of Englishness, especially in connection with international sporting events, during which many pubs display his flag, a red cross on a white ground, whether or not they actually bear his name. This is also done on his feast day, 23 April.

See also ANGELS & SAINTS, p. 16

Giant Inn

This is a pub in Cerne Abbas (Dorset) which until fairly recently simply carried the not very original name of the Red Lion, but has been appropriately rechristened as a tribute to the famous local landmark, the naked club-wielding Cerne Abbas Giant, carved on a chalk hillside beside the village. The age of the figure is a matter for argument, since there are no references to it in any charters or other documents until 1694, at which date the churchwardens of the local church paid out the substantial sum of three shillings to have it 'repaired', i.e. scrubbed clean of grass and weeds. Many assume it to be pre-Christian, possibly a Romano-British representation of Hercules, who was generally shown with a club; others accept the information of an eighteenth-century local historian, who called it 'a modern thing' dating only from the middle of the seventeenth century. What is quite indisputable is that the Giant owes his fame to his huge erect penis, twenty-four feet (7.2 metres) long. It is said that a couple wanting children should make love on this spot.

Giant's Rest

Another pleasing example of a pub being renamed in honour of local folklore is that the former White Horse at Wilmington (East Sussex) has for some years now been called the Giant's

Rest. It faces the steep northern slope of Windover Hill, upon which is carved one of England's only two surviving turf-cut giants, the Long Man of Wilmington. He is 229 feet (70 metres) tall, and holds a staff even taller than himself in each hand; when seen close up or from the air he looks unnaturally thin and lanky, but the proportions become correct if the figure is viewed from the flat land to the north of the Downs, at a distance of a mile or so. From there, he is an impressive guardian of his territory.

The first documentary evidence of the Long Man's existence is a sketch in a map made in 1710, but it is generally thought that he is considerably older. Small fragments of Roman tiles found under the outline of the figure prove that it was made after the Roman occupation, though there is no material evidence to prove whether this was in Celtic or Anglo-Saxon times, or even in some medieval period. When Leslie Dunkling and Gordon Wright were compiling their *Pub Names of Britain* in the 1970s, they were told that 'it is thought to be the Saxon King Harold, and to have been created by those who lived in the now-ruined twelfth-century abbey'. This theory was probably suggested by the fact that Hastings, where Harold died, is not many miles away.

By the nineteenth century, the figure was so badly overgrown with turf and weeds that it almost disappeared, but in 1874 it was restored and given a permanent outline of white bricks. One clue to the original date might be the pose of the figure, which is rather like certain naked spear-carrying warriors in horned helmets, shown on Scandinavian and Anglo-Saxon helmets and buckles from the sixth and seventh centuries, and thought to represent the war-god Odin/Woden or his devotees. Maybe one day scientific tests will settle the question.

According to local stories shortly before the First World War, the Giant had once lived on top of Windover Hill, but had been killed – some said in a quarrel with a rival giant living three miles away on Firle Beacon, in which the two hurled boulders or hammers at one another; or, said others, by a local shepherd who flung an extremely hard lump of bread and cheese at him; or again, perhaps he was simply so clumsy that he tripped over his own feet, tumbled down the hill, and broke his neck. Either way, it was said the villagers drew round his outline as he lay dead on the slope, to prove that he had been the tallest person who ever lived. Modern story-tellers prefer to think that he was just asleep on the hillside – hence the name of the pub.

Gipsy Queen

There is a widespread, but mistaken, popular belief that Gipsies necessarily belong to particular 'tribes' which are headed by a Gipsy king or queen. They themselves have at times encouraged the notion as being good publicity. The Gipsy Queen pub in Norwood High Street, London SE27, was most likely inspired by the celebrated Margaret Finch, 'Queen of the Norwood Gipsies', who died in 1740, being allegedly 108 years old, and so bent and doubled up that she had to be buried in a square box. For generations there were Gipsy encampments in the woods of Norwood, on the southern outskirts of London, until the common began to be enclosed in the 1820s. They were famous as fortune-tellers.

Goat & Compasses

See PUZZLING PAIRS, p. 112

Gog & Magog

There used to be a pub in Manchester called the Gog and Magog, and in London the Vino Veritas in Russia Row, EC2 (now demolished), had originally been named the Magog; it used to have two figures of giants at the door, and two others that struck the bell of the clock in its bar. Currently, London has a New Gog at Canning Town, E16.

Gog and Magog are two mysterious figures named in the Bible as allies of the Antichrist who make war on God's People but are defeated; in the Middle Ages they were generally assumed to be giants, and their names were sometimes run together as Gogmagog. They became important in British folklore because Geoffrey of Monmouth claimed in his *History of the Kings of Britain* (*c.*1136) that when Brutus of Troy first came to settle this land he found it full of giants, the worst being a Cornish one called 'Goemagot', whom his follower Corineus killed in a wrestling match. Tudor historians changed the tale, saying there were two giants, Gog and Magog, and that they were not killed but captured and taken to London, where they served as guards at the gates of Brutus's palace.

From medieval times onwards, many large towns used to stage Midsummer pageants and parades, often featuring 'giants' which were constructed round a wickerwork frame and moved by men walking inside them. One surviving English example can be seen in Salisbury Museum, and there are many on the Continent. They were sometimes thought of as the town's mascots or symbols. In London, from the sixteenth century to the eighteenth, successive pairs of processional Gog and Magog figures were regularly paraded on royal and civic occasions, and were kept in the Guildhall when not in use. Also in the

Puzzling Pairs

As was noted in the introduction, medieval inns and taverns used plain single names and images, and this remained the normal custom well into the seventeenth century. Jacob Larwood and J. C. Hotten quote two pamphlets and one poem listing London inns of this period, which between them record some fifty names, of which only four are 'pairs'. Two are heraldic, the BEAR & RAGGED STAFF and the EAGLE & CHILD; the other two, seemingly purely arbitrary, are the Bear and Harrow and the Bear and Dolphin. The latter was sufficiently popular to be used by several inns.

By the eighteenth century, fashions had changed. In 1708 one writer complained of 'the variety and contradictory language of the signs', citing the BULL & MOUTH, the Whale and Cow, the Shovel and Boot, the Bible and Swan, and the Frying Pan and Drum. An essayist in the *Spectator* in 1710 took up the theme, mocking the Bell and Neat's Tongue and the Dog and Gridiron, though willing to accept the CAT & FIDDLE; he also demanded that trades signs should be appropriate – 'What can be more inconsistent than to see a bawd at the sign of the Angel, or a tailor at the Lion?'

One simple explanation for double names is that innkeepers (and other tradesmen) sometimes shifted their business to other premises which already had a name, and that two inns sometimes came under the same ownership; in such cases the two names would be combined, giving pairs such as the Crown and Angel, or the Dolphin and Anchor. Other combinations are obviously harmonious in their symbolism and emotional appeal, even if logically peculiar; the Rose and Crown, for instance, joins two powerful emblems of England's national identity. Yet there remain many which are so puzzling that they have invited all kinds of ingenious but implausible suggestions.

The most popular idea is that the name was 'corrupted' through the ignorance and mispronunciations of the common folk (as opposed, presumably, to the educated drinkers who are theorising about it). Examples repeatedly cited are the CAT & FIDDLE (allegedly a corruption of Catherine la Fidèle, in reference to Catharine of Aragon); ELEPHANT & CASTLE (Infanta de Castille); and PIG & WHISTLE (peg and *wæs hæl*) – but no evidence is offered that the proposed 'original' form was ever recorded. As is explained elsewhere, these three could be better explained as survivals of medieval visual imagery, two of them being probably transmitted through humorous church carvings and one through heraldry.

More perplexing are the BULL & MOUTH (allegedly, Boulogne Mouth) and the Goat and Compasses. The first of these is likely to be a mere combination of two popular names. One can find Bulls all over the country, and though Mouth has become obsolete it was well known in the seventeenth century, when it gave rise to various jokes, e.g. that it was the right inn for 'oyster-wives', fishwives being notorious for hot tempers and foul language, or that a man with no money in his purse should 'dine at the sign of the Mouth', i.e. go hungry. In view of this, it seems both unnecessary and unconvincing to argue that the name is a mispronunciation of 'Boulogne Mouth' and commemorates the capture of the harbour there by Henry VIII.

As for the Goat and Compasses, this is almost certainly distorted heraldry. The Worshipful Company of Cordwainers had three goats' heads on their coat of arms, because in medieval times the finest boots were made from imported goatskins from Cordova; these heads were arranged round a chevron, an inverted V-shape which does indeed look rather like a compass. But Anthony Trollope in his novel *Framley Parsonage* (1861) asserted that in Cromwell's time one pious Puritan landlord had called his inn 'God encompasseth us', which later generations had misunderstood. E. R. Delderfield accepts this theory; Larwood and Hotten, however, put a question mark against it, and Dunkling and Wright say there is no indication that Puritans ever used religious phrases as pub names. Heraldry, either misunderstood or deliberately mocked, must remain the likeliest explanation.

In view of this long history of double names, traditionalists will probably have to learn to love the recent fashion for meaningless combinations involving slugs, toads, parrots or firkins.

Guildhall there was a very fine pair of wooden statues of the giants, carved in 1708 but sadly destroyed in the Blitz in 1940; their current successors were made in 1953 for the Festival of Britain, and are permanently displayed in the west gallery. In recent decades inflatable or wickerwork giants have been used in pageants such as the Lord Mayor's Show.

Golden Farmer

This was the original name of a pub at Bagshot in Surrey, but in the latter part of the twentieth century it was changed to the more familiar Jolly Farmer, presumably because the local story which had inspired it was no longer well known – or, perhaps, was considered too gruesome. It appears to be historically true that one of the many highwaymen who preyed on travellers crossing Bagshot Heath was a certain William Davis. He was well known in the district as a respectable and wealthy farmer; indeed, his neighbours noticed that he was making more money than anyone else, and so they nicknamed him the Golden Farmer. The secret of his wealth was simple; he led a double life, farming by day and robbery by night. He was caught in the end, when one man he attacked managed to shoot him in the back, and he was tried and hanged in 1689 or 1690.

There is an unproven tradition that this was no ordinary hanging but 'hanging in chains', i.e. being gibbeted alive at the place where his crimes were committed. This was a form of slow execution in which the criminal would be trussed up alive in a framework of bars and chains such as was normally used for displaying corpses on a gibbet, and left hanging there to die of hunger and thirst. It was abolished by Elizabeth I, who judged it to be excessive because 'much torture distracted a dying man from prayer'. But if legend can be trusted, it was still practised, occasionally and unofficially, in Surrey in the seventeenth century.

See also HIGHWAYMEN & SMUGGLERS, p. 208

Golden Fleece

The wool trade was so important to England's prosperity for several centuries that it is no surprise to find pubs named the Fleece, or the Golden Fleece, especially in sheep-rearing districts – Huddersfield has one of each, and Halifax too has a Golden Fleece. The latter name alludes to a Greek legend about the quest of the hero Jason and his companions, the Argonauts, so called because their ship was the *Argo*. They sailed northwards from Greece through the Hellespont and into the Black Sea to the land of Colchis, to steal the fleece of a ram with golden wool, which hung from a tree in a sacred grove, and was guarded day and night by a huge immortal dragon which never slept. Jason would never have managed to get it if Medea, the daughter of the king of Colchis, had not fallen in love with him and offered to help. Being a powerful witch, she sprinkled a magic potion over the dragon, which sent it to sleep.

Many commentators, both in ancient and in modern times, have suggested that there is some truth behind the legend, in that it could refer to trading voyages from Greece to the Black Sea, probably in search of amber; it is even possible that the 'golden fleece' refers to a method of panning for gold by laying a fleece in the water of a stream.

Good Woman

See QUIET WOMAN

Gospel Oak

There is a Gospel Oak pub in Birmingham, and this was also
the original name of a pub in the Kentish Town district of
London, which has since been renamed the Old Oak; it referred
to an oak tree that stood exactly on the boundary between
Highgate and Hampstead, in the early nineteenth century. The
change of name is regrettable, since 'Gospel Oak' alludes to
an old and interesting custom formerly common throughout
Britain which had both a religious and an administrative function, the Beating of the Parish Bounds. Once a year, usually at
Rogationtide (the three days preceding Ascension Day), the
rector or vicar of a parish would lead a procession all round its
boundaries, pausing for prayer and a scripture reading at this
or that notable landmark along the route; thus a tree where

The Gospel Oak

some passage from the gospels was always read would become known as the Gospel Oak. The original purpose of the custom – which was part of Catholic liturgy all over Europe – was to pray for God's blessing on the crops of the parish. However, it was also very important that everyone should know just where the boundary ran between one parish and the next, e.g. to allot responsibility for the upkeep of roads and bridges, care of paupers, payment of tithes, and so forth.

Green Bottle

The name of the Green Bottle Hotel at Knottingley in Yorkshire comes from a cheerful traditional song which can be used both as a drinking song and as a sort of tongue-twister, since it involves counting backwards as the song accelerates – a tricky feat, after a few drinks:

> Ten green bottles hanging on the wall,
> Ten green bottles hanging on the wall,
> And if one green bottle should accident'ly fall,
> There'll be nine green bottles hanging on the wall.
>
> Nine green bottles hanging on the wall …

Etcetera, until when the last bottle has fallen:

> There's nobbut the smell left hanging on the wall.

Green Dragon

There is no particular reason in myth or folktale why dragons should be conventionally represented as green or red (rather than blue, yellow or black), but such is almost invariably the case. The Green Dragon is a very common name for English pubs, thought to have originally referred to the heraldic arms of the earls of Pembroke; those called George and Dragon also generally show the monster as green.

The symbolism of dragons is paradoxical, reflecting their long and complicated history in myth, religion, legend, and fairytale throughout European, Jewish, and Near Eastern traditions. In the Christian religious context, the dragon represents (or at least is closely associated with) God's adversary the Devil, notably in the Apocalypse (Book of Revelation), the last book of the Bible.

> There was war in Heaven; Michael and his angels fought against the dragon, and the dragon fought, and his angels, and prevailed not, neither was their place found any more in Heaven. And the great dragon was cast out, that old serpent, called the Devil, and Satan, which deceiveth the whole world; he was cast out into the earth, and his angels were cast out with him.

In medieval times, the same symbolism was used to represent the triumph of holy men and women over temptations and the power of the Devil; there are said to be over forty saints in West European Catholic tradition who, according to the legendary accounts of their lives, slew or banished a dragon. St George is simply the one who, by an accident of history, has been adopted as England's patron.

On the other hand, there was also a secular tradition, essentially aristocratic and chivalrous, in which a dragon – far from being the embodiment of all evil – stood for the courage and ferocity so necessary and admirable in a fighting man. This goes back at least to the time of the Roman army, whose cohorts (subdivisions of a legion) carried dragon standards as their emblems. Similarly, Viking warships often had a dragon or serpent as a figurehead. One medieval historian, Geoffrey of Monmouth, claimed that Uther Pendragon (King Arthur's father) had a dragon standard made of gold 'to carry about with him in the wars', and medieval heralds declared that his arms had been two green dragons, back to back. Uther was of course legendary, not a historical person as Geoffrey supposed, and elaborate coats of arms had not been invented at the period when he was alleged to have lived. But as heraldry developed throughout the later medieval and Tudor periods, four-legged dragons and their two-legged relatives the wyverns were widely used as emblems of valour. It is from heraldry that the Green Dragon entered the repertoire of English pub names.
See also QUEENS' HEADS & RED LIONS, p. 248

Green Man

The majority of pub names have been understood in much the same way in most places and over many years. Not so the Green Man. The interpretation of this name has undergone several sharp changes, which can be seen in the various ways it is represented on signboards, past and present. It can of course be rendered simply as a man dressed in green holding a tankard, or standing beside a beer barrel, but landlords and artists generally prefer to exploit some aspect of its complex history.

The Green Man

The term 'green man' dates from Tudor and Stuart times, when it was used (interchangeably with the older 'wild man' and 'savage') to mean a type of giant who symbolised the brutishness of untamed nature. Such creatures were often represented in courtly masques and civic pageants by tall, strong men dressed in leaves or moss and armed with clubs; they featured regularly in London's Lord Mayor's shows, where their function was to clear the way for the rest of the procession. Similarly, in Chester on St George's Day in 1610 the parade was led by two 'green men' with ivy garlands on their 'huge black shaggy hair' and ivy leaves stitched to their clothes, and carrying massive clubs. An illustration in Joseph Strutt's *The Sports and Pastimes of the English People* (1801) shows a Green Man in pageants who is normally dressed, but crowned with a heavy wreath of leaves and grapes, and wielding a sort of syringe for squirting water at the crowds; this image has inspired the sign of the Green Man at Cold Brayfield in Bedfordshire.

The naked, savage 'green' or 'wild' man was also used in heraldry; the Distillers' Company had a pair as supporters for their coat of arms, which is why they became a symbol for inns – presumably originally those licensed to sell spirits as well as beer – with the name Green Man and Still. John Aubrey, writing in the 1680s, noted that the Wild Man or Green Man sign was 'not uncommon in London', and was drawn as 'a kind of Hercules with a green club and green leaves about his pudenda and head'. A version can still be seen at the Green Man in Berwick Street (London W1). The Green Man on the corner of Plashet Grove and Katherine Road (London E6) shows a 'wild man' figure carrying a tankard and standing next to a barrel, while the one in the Euston Road (London NW1) shows a leaf-clad head and torso, with tankard. There is a fine pair of club-bearing Wild/ Green Men on the heraldic sign of the Woodstock Arms in Oxford.

Besides distillers, herbalists also used the figure as a sign of their trade, and were themselves sometimes nicknamed 'green men'. It is said that the Green Man pub in the Edgware Road (London W2) took its name from a herbalist who had lived on that site in the seventeenth century because of its spring, which had marvellous healing properties. He was particularly famous for an eye lotion made from its waters, and all subsequent landlords had to sign a clause in the lease obliging them to go on offering it to customers, free of charge, in his memory. As recently as 1954 Stanley Coleman wrote in his *Treasury of Folklore: London* that 'you may ask [at the bar] for eye lotion and the publican will measure you out an ounce or two', though it no longer came from the well in the cellar, which had dried up when the Underground was built.

In the eighteenth and nineteenth centuries, however, this sense of Green Man had become obsolete. Writing in the 1860s, Larwood and Hotten could state that the great majority of Green Man inns had replaced the leafy giant with the very popular figure of Robin Hood (dressed, naturally, in a jerkin of green cloth), or with some person who wore green because of his work – a forester, a gamekeeper, an axe-wielding wood-man. Good examples of the latter are at Great Wymondley in Hertfordshire and Wimborne in Dorset. The sport of wild-fowling supplied another interpretation, as seen at Ashbourne in Derbyshire. Here, a hanging board shows a man in green tweeds and wearing a green hat; on one side he is carrying a gun, and on the other he is shooting waterfowl. Another huntsman with gun occurs at Easthampstead in Hampshire. In Essex, the Green Man at Bradwell displays a sign showing Robin Hood, while at Brentwood Robin Hood was replaced about ten years ago by a sign of the 'foliate head' type (see below).

In the late nineteenth century and throughout the twentieth there has been a growing interest in traditional folk customs, which in the case of the Green Man brought a new associa-tion, this time with May Day festivals. He could, for instance, be identified with the Jack-in-the-Green, a May Day figure who will be described below, under that heading. Or the club-wielding leafy giant might be shown alongside a maypole on a village green, as at the pub in Berwick Street, London wi. At Hurst in Berkshire the Green Man appears as a slender figure in a tight-fitting leafy costume, carrying a slender branch over his shoulder and jigging up and down as he watches maypole dancers in the distance.

The latest and most striking innovation is to represent a Green Man simply as a face with leaves sprouting from its mouth and eyes, or peering through leaves – a powerful and pleasing design, based upon a type of ornamental carving very common in medieval churches, the 'foliate head'. Such carvings have been given unusual importance in the public mind because of a theory that they carry a secret pagan message, celebrat-ing the renewal of nature's fertility in spring. The theory first appeared in 1939 but only became widely known in the 1960s and '70s. There have since been several books lavishly illustrated with photographs of beautiful foliate heads from Britain's churches and cathedrals. Some Green Man pubs now display some version of the foliate head as their sign. The earliest was probably a fine example at Rackheath in Norfolk, painted in the 1950s; it has since been replaced by a more modern rendering of the same image. There used to be an impressive one at Oakley in Suffolk; when that pub closed, the sign was taken to the Fat Cat in Norwich to be displayed there. Others can be seen at Scamblesby in Lincolnshire, at Little Snoring in Norfolk, and at Partridge Green in Sussex. This interpretation looks set to become increasingly popular.

An intriguing compromise can be seen at the Famous Green Man at Ewell Village (Surrey). The sign here used to be an unambiguous forester, but in recent years it has been repainted to show the face of a man wearing a large green hat trimmed with leaves; two or three more leaves frame the face, but do not actually sprout from it. Though he looks human, he has a slightly mocking expression, suitable for an elusive woodland spirit.

Gremlin

A gremlin is a very fitting patron for a pub, since (if tradition can be trusted) the name of this goblin species was first revealed to an English air force officer as he sat drinking his pint of Fremlin's beer while reading Grimm's fairytales. Some say he actually saw the creature swimming in the beer and grinning at him. This would probably have been during the First World War, for there is evidence that British airmen stationed in Malta and the Middle East in the 1920s knew a good deal about gremlins; by 1929 they had got into print, in a poem in the journal *Aeroplane* on 10 April. During the Second World War they became very well known indeed, not only to airmen but to the general public; later, in 1984 and 1990, they starred in the American films *Gremlins* and *Gremlins II*. It is therefore surprising that there is apparently only one pub that has adopted their name, at Brecon in Wales.

Perhaps it is the reputation of gremlins as troublemakers which deters landlords, for they are notorious for the mischief they get up to when anywhere near machinery. Admittedly, one would never suspect this from the cheerful, innocent looks of the little pixy-like creature sitting on a toadstool who adorns the signboard in Brecon, but he is surely in disguise. Originally, gremlins specialised in creating mayhem on board aircraft – causing inexplicable malfunctions in the engines, short-circuiting the electrics, altering figures on the dials, drinking the petrol, shifting the position of airfields. Nowadays they have discovered how to tamper with absolutely any apparatus, the more advanced the better, up to and including the finest computers.

Greyfriars Bobby

Edinburgh has long cherished the memory of a small Skye terrier named Bobby as a shining example of doggy devotion. A drinking fountain with a statue of him stands in Candlemaker Row, near the entrance to Greyfriars Kirkyard, and facing this there is a pub named after him. Bobby belonged to a nightwatchman named John (or Jock) Gray who used to come regularly to Traill's Dining Rooms in Candlemaker Row for his midday meal just as the cannon at Edinburgh Castle was fired to mark one o'clock, bringing his dog with him. Gray died in 1858 and was buried in Greyfriars. But Bobby continued to come to Traill's day after day, precisely at one o'clock, and beg for the bun or bone which his master used to give him. It was noticed that he did not eat it on the spot but carried it to the cemetery, where he spent the rest of his time lying on his master's grave. Nobody could induce him to leave. This went on for no less than fourteen years, during which various well-wishers ensured that Bobby was regularly fed and that a kennel was placed for him near the grave, for shelter in cold weather. When he died in 1872 he was buried in a flowerbed near the entrance of the Kirkyard and Traill's was renamed in his honour; the following year the drinking fountain with the statue was donated by Baroness Burdett-Coutts. In 1912, an American writer, Eleanor Atkinson, published a fictionalised version of Bobby's story, which has become a children's classic. His statue, his gravestone, and that of John Gray are now major tourist attractions.

Guy Fawkes Arms

Guy Fawkes was born in York in 1570, but his father died when he was nine, and a few years later his mother took as her second husband a man who lived in Scotton, near Harrogate, so this became Guy's home – which is why there is a Guy Fawkes Arms in that village. Nowadays, he is famous for his part in the Gunpowder Plot of 1605, which if it had succeeded would have been by far the most impressive act of terrorism in history, for it would have meant the death not simply of King James but of most members of both Houses of Parliament, wiping out a large part of the ruling class of the country. To contemporaries, however, and for several generations afterwards, Guy Fawkes was far from being the most famous figure among the conspirators, even though he was the one chosen to enter the cellars where the gunpowder had been stashed, and set it off. In his recent study *Remember, Remember the Fifth of November* (2005), Professor James Sharpe writes:

Unlike Catesby [the actual leader of the plot] and Garnett [a Catholic priest involved in it], Fawkes was hardly ever mentioned in eighteenth-century Gunpowder Treason sermons, while his name does not appear to have figured in books and tracts published before 1800. But such works began to be published in the early nineteenth century, while by that time references to effigies of Fawkes being burnt were becoming more numerous. But in these literary works Guy Fawkes became in large measure a reinvented figure. Nowhere was this more true than in the popular theatre of the period.

Obviously, the moment when Fawkes is discovered in the cellars and arrested just in time to prevent the explosion is the dramatic climax of the affair. Professor Sharpe argues convincingly that it was the use made of this in plays and in historical novels which turned him into the central figure in popular celebrations of what is variously known as Guy Fawkes Night or Bonfire Night, one of the best-loved and most lively folk festivals of England, traditionally held on 5 November, though now often transferred to the nearest Saturday. It also made 'guy' the term for an ugly, ill-dressed effigy which is destined to be thrown on the bonfire.

Guy of Warwick

The legend of Sir Guy, Earl of Warwick, is commemorated not only in pubs that bear his name (e.g. at Welling in Kent), but in the rather more numerous ones called the DUN COW. The earliest form of the story is a poem written in Norman French in about 1200; later versions include an English prose text printed by Wynkyn de Worde early in the sixteenth century, and several ballads and chapbooks of the seventeenth. Guy is alleged to have been born in Warwick in the reign of King Athelstan (i.e. before 939) and to have led the defence of Winchester against a Danish attack in 993, but he is not in fact a historical figure. He is credited with adventures quite typical of medieval romance, in the course of which he killed numerous Saracens, Frenchmen, monstrous boars, dragons, and giants, so as to earn glory and win the hand of his beloved Phyllis. Soon after their marriage, he went on pilgrimage to the Holy Land, where he remained for many years. He eventually returned to Warwick, but lived incognito as a hermit in a cave, begging for bread at the castle gates. Only when dying did he send a message to Phyllis to tell her who he was, showing her a ring as proof. She too then died of grief, and they were buried in the one grave.

Guy of Warwick

Later versions give great emphasis to Guy's role as a monster-slayer, and cite various supposed relics of his achievements. For instance, in Richard Lloyd's *Brief Discourse of the Nine Worthies* (1584), Guy boasts:

> In Windsor forest I did kill a Boar of passing strength,
> Whose like in England never was for highness, breadth and
>   length.
> Some of his bones in Warwicke yet, within the castle lie;
> One of his tusks vnto this daie doth hang in Couentrie.
> I slew also in Dunsmore heath a monsterous wild beast
> Cald the Dun Cow of Dunsmore, which manie men opprest;
> Hir bones also in Warwicke lie yet, for a monument,
> Which unto euerie looker on a wonder may present.

Chapbooks celebrating Guy's prowess often had a woodcut showing him riding in triumph with an enormous boar's head held aloft on his spear, and this image was sometimes chosen for pub signs; he is also sometimes shown with a lion he had overcome and tamed, or riding a wild cow.

H

Half Brick

There are three explanations for the name of this pub in Worthing (West Sussex), which existed until recently at the southern end of Ham Road, close to the coastal road; the first is probably true, the second is plausible, but the third is a local legend elaborating upon a historical event. The first is that the area where it stands was once occupied by brick fields, which specialised in making ornamental bricks thinner than the standard ones, known as 'half bricks'. The second points to the fact that whereas the external walls of the building at ground floor level are of brick, its upper half is pebble-dashed. The third claims that an earlier inn of the same name, which stood further south, right on the beach, was so suddenly overwhelmed by the sea during a great storm in 1869 that only half a brick could be saved – and that this was placed in the foundations of the present pub. The storm is historically true, and it is true that the pub and some cottages were destroyed, but the rescue of the single half brick is pure melodrama.

Hangman's Tree

Another gruesomely named pub was the Hangman's Tree at Rowley Regis in Staffordshire, described by Dunkling and Wright. They describe its signboard as showing a tree with a noose dangling from its branches. The story was that a former landlord had also acted as the local hangman until one day his best friend was condemned to death for some crime; rather than be the executioner, he hanged himself on the tree.

Harvesters, Harvest Home, Harvest Man

See HARVESTERS & WHEATSHEAVES, p. 182

Hawthorn Bush, Hawthorn Tree

There is a Hawthorn Bush pub at West Bromwich and a Hawthorn Tree at Allesley near Coventry; the names may be heraldic in origin, as this plant was shown on the arms of Henry VII. Larwood and Hotten suggest that there could be a folk-loric connection, citing a passage in Reginald Scot's *Discoverie of Witchcraft* (1584) which states that hawthorn gathered on May Day was an antidote to a witch's spells; this parallels an ancient Roman belief that sprays of hawthorn were a magical protection against witchcraft and the Evil Eye. In English tradition, however, the plant usually has a very negative image; there was until recently – and perhaps there still is – a superstition that it is extremely unlucky to bring hawthorn blossom indoors, for this might bring death into the house. Of course, there always remains the possibility that these pubs took their names neither from heraldry, nor from superstition, nor from an awareness of ancient Roman beliefs, but simply from a particularly handsome hawthorn which happened to grow nearby.

See also QUEENS' HEADS & RED LIONS, p. 248

Headless Woman

See QUIET WOMAN

Hercules

One of the most popular legends in ancient Greek mythology told of the hero Herakles, a monster-slayer, famous for his great strength. The Romans changed his name to Hercules, which then passed into English and other European languages. He is generally represented wearing the skin of a lion he had killed with his bare hands; if he has a weapon at all, it is a rough club. There are several pubs named after him in London, including a Pillars of Hercules and a Hercules Pillars, referring to the Rock of Gibraltar and Mount Hacho, which faces it; legend claims they were once a single rock until Hercules tore it apart, making a channel to link the Mediterranean to the Atlantic.

Herne's Oak

Oaks, considered in general, are a popular inspiration for a pub name, carrying patriotic and naval associations ('Hearts of Oak') and making a good subject for a sign-painter. But Herne's Oak at Winkfield in Berkshire refers to a specific tree which once grew in nearby Windsor Park, the focal point of a well-known ghost legend. In Shakespeare's *The Merry Wives of Windsor* (1597) the two heroines of the play decide to make a fool of Sir John Falstaff, who is pestering them with his wooing, by persuading him to disguise himself as a ghost and meet them at midnight under an oak tree in Windsor Park. Describing this ghost, one says:

> There is an old tale goes, that Herne the hunter,
> Sometime a keeper here in Windsor Forest,
> Doth all the winter time, at still midnight,
> Walk round about an oak, with great ragg'd horns;
> And there he blasts the trees, bewitches cattle,
> And makes the cows yield blood, and shakes a chain
> In a most hideous and dreadful manner.

Shakespeare tells us nothing more about Herne, but in 1792 the writer Samuel Ireland said he had heard tell that he had once been employed as a 'hunter' in the sense of a gamekeeper, but had 'committed some great offence for which he feared to lose his situation and fall into disgrace', and so hanged himself on the oak. This fits the traditional belief that suicides haunt the scene of their death.

At different periods, different oaks have been claimed to be *the* tree. One very old pollarded one is marked on a map of 1742 as 'Sir John Falstaff's Oak'; it died and was felled in 1796, so the tradition was transferred to a young tree growing nearby, but this in turn unfortunately blew down in 1863, and another was immediately planted. For some reason this one did not last long either; the tree currently pointed out as Herne's Oak was planted by Edward VII in 1906.

Hob

Discussing the pub of this name at Bamber Bridge in Lancashire, Leslie Dunkling and Gordon Wright state that it refers to 'hobnobbing' with one's friends, i.e. drinking and chatting with them. No doubt that was what they were told at the time (their book was published in 1987, reissued in 1994), but one wonders whether this has always been the favoured interpretation. 'Hob' is a very common term in the northern counties for a type of small (and often mischievous) supernatural being, much the same as a goblin – indeed the two words are often combined – see HOBGOBLIN. Some hobs, it was said, came to live in farms and houses, where they brought good luck; others preferred woods, mounds, or caves.

Apparently they liked bridges too, as there is a Hob Bridge at Gatley (also in Lancashire); perhaps the original hob at Bamber Bridge lived under the bridge. Dunkling and Wright note that at King's Lynn in Norfolk there is a pub named Hob i' the Well, where the 'hob' is definitely thought of as a goblin. One former Hobgoblin pub in Forest Hill (London SE23) has recently changed to the Hob, though this might not necessarily show awareness of the true sense of the word.

Hobbit

Several pubs have taken the name Hobbit or Hobbits, as at Southampton, Weston-super-Mare, Monyash in Derbyshire and Sowerby Bridge in West Yorkshire. They obviously have done so as a tribute to Bilbo Baggins and others of his kin, created by J. R. R. Tolkien in his much-loved fantasy novels – indeed, there is a Bilbo Baggins pub in Eastbourne, East

Sussex. The word 'hobbit' itself, however, goes back before his time and has genuine folkloric roots; it is a very rare variant on the common 'hob' or 'hobgoblin', which was included in a list of some two hundred local types of fairies and bogies compiled by a Victorian folklorist, Michael Aislabie Denham, published in the 1890s. All three derive ultimately from the personal name 'Hob', which in medieval times was the normal colloquial shortening of 'Robin' or 'Robert', now abandoned in favour of 'Rob' and 'Bob'.

Hobby Horse

This pub name, found in Leicester and elsewhere, usually alludes to the general popularity of hobby horse figures in pageants of Tudor and Elizabethan times. These consisted of a man wearing a heavily draped framework slung round him at waist level, which had a horse's head and tail; it hid his legs and feet, so that he appeared to be riding a medieval charger. The term 'hobby horse' is also used of the simple 'cock-horse' toy, a wooden horse-head on a stick which children could 'ride', and of an upright all-concealing disguise, as worn by the 'hooden horses' of Kent.

In Minehead (Somerset), however, the Hobby Horse pub refers specifically to the central figure in a traditional custom observed in that town on the first three days of May. The first description of the Minehead custom dates from 1830; the writer notes that 'it has prevailed for ages, but what gave rise to it is at present unknown'. A number of young men, mostly sailors and fishermen, went round the town with 'grotesque figures' roughly resembling long-tailed horses, which covered and hid those who carried them; they expected people to give them small sums of money, and if anyone refused they would pretend to hit him ten times with a boot. They always visited Dunster Castle, where they got food, beer, and money.

The present Minehead 'horse' is a heavy wooden frame carried on a man's shoulders, draped with a painted cloth and topped with ribbons. Up to the 1880s there was a snapping wooden head fixed to the front of the frame, but this has disappeared; however, it still has a long beribboned tail. The head of the man carrying it pokes out midway, but is hidden by a mask and ribbons. This construction is an eccentric variation on the type of hobby horse used in pageants.

Hobgoblin

There are now a good many pubs of this name – several in London, and others at Aylesbury, Bath, Brighton, Bristol, High Wycombe, Newark and Oxford, for instance. They were formerly owned by the Wychwood brewery and named after that company's Hobgoblin ale, which itself exploits the folkloric associations with hobgoblins of the ancient Oxfordshire woodland that the brewery takes its name from. The word is an old one, well known to writers of the sixteenth and seventeenth centuries, and linked to a series of country names for small elfin creatures (hob, hobthrust, hobman, hobbit), especially in the north of England. These beings are of somewhat mixed character. In some accounts they are said to live in caves or woods, and are regarded as mischievous, though never seriously dangerous; but in many others hobs are said to attach themselves to a house or farm, where they will help with the work, provided nobody annoys them. In Shakespeare's *Midsummer Night's Dream*, for example, a fairy says to Puck:

'Those that Hobgoblin call you, and sweet Puck,
You do their work, and they shall have good luck.'

Presumably the hobgoblin who is now the patron of ale and pubs has particular skill in brewing.

Hooden Horse, Hoodeners' Horse

There used to be a pub at Wickambreaux, near Canterbury, which had the unusual name of Hooden Horse, and there is still one called the Hoodeners' Horse at Great Chart, near Ashford (Kent). These names refer to the old Kentish custom of 'hoodening' on Christmas Eve, when a small group of farm labourers would go from house to house, escorting their 'horse'. This consisted of a wooden head with a hinged clacking jaw, decorated with ribbons and horse brasses, and mounted on a short pole; the man who carried it was bent double, to represent the horse's body, and was hidden by a cloth fixed to the pole. The rest of the group would be ringing hand-bells, or playing a fiddle or melodeon, or singing. There would probably be one man dressed as a woman with a broom (the 'Molly'), and another pretending to be a jockey. When they called at a house, the horse would behave comically, pretending to kick and bite, while the 'jockey' tried to mount it, and the 'Molly' swept the floor. The group would be given beer and cakes, and perhaps money.

The custom was first clearly described in 1809; it was known in about thirty places along the north and east coasts of Kent up to the beginning of the twentieth century, but died out around 1910. After the Second World War it was revived in many places, sometimes with the addition of Morris dancing. 'Hooden' was originally pronounced 'ooden'; it probably means 'hooded', or just possibly 'wooden'. It is very unlikely to refer to the pagan Saxon god Woden, though this romantic idea was put forward in the pamphlet issued when the Wickambreaux pub adopted its name in 1956. Leslie Dunkling and Gordon Wright, in *Pub Names of Britain*, link the custom to the hop harvest; they say that to 'hooden' the hops means to put them in the oast house to dry, and the 'horse' was celebrating this. However, that is done in September, and all records of the Hooden Horse custom place it on Christmas Eve.

There used to be another Hooden Horse in Pembury Road in Tonbridge, but it has been renamed the Somerhill.

See also THE YEAR'S MERRY ROUND, p.310

Hop Inn, Hop'n'Scotch

See PUNS & OLD JOKES, p. 138

Horse

See BLACK HORSE, COCK HORSE, HOBBY HORSE, *or* VALE OF THE WHITE HORSE

Horseshoe

There are a good many pubs called the Horseshoe, or the Three (or Four) Horseshoes. In some cases this may have begun as a reference to farriery, or to a horse fair, but nowadays the horseshoe is always thought of as a lucky charm. This belief has been well known since the late Middle Ages. It is certainly related to the widespread European belief that objects made of iron are powerful against evil supernatural beings; whether the crescent

Puns & Old Jokes

Ideally, an evening's drinking should be a cheerful experience among friends. If the pub's signboard raises a smile, this creates a good atmosphere – and a great many of them do indeed appeal to one's sense of humour. Puns are much favoured. The similarity of 'in' and 'inn' produced the Dew Drop Inn ('Do drop in!') at Oxford; the Hop Inn at Chichester and Winchester (doubly effective because of the association of hops and beer); and the Nobody Inn at Doddiscombesleigh in Devon and elsewhere. There is also the NOG INN at Wincanton, where the pun is on 'noggin', a measure of drink. Dunkling and Wright record with admiration the Hop'n'Scotch at Harrogate, which ingeniously yokes alcoholic references to a playground game. Pubs called the Why Not are generally explained as referring to a famous racehorse of that name in the 1890s, and may well have a horse on the signboard; nevertheless one suspects a lurking pun: 'Let's go and have a drink' – 'Yes, why not?' Others ask, in various spellings, 'Who'd Have Thought It?' Some think this implies that one is surprised at a pub being there at all, or that the landlord was unlikely to get a licence; at Milton Combe the signboard showed astronauts amazed to find beer on the moon. In Plymouth there is one called Nowhere, the idea being that if a man's wife asks him angrily: 'Where have you been?' he can truthfully reply: 'Nowhere, dear, nowhere.' One could also make puns on the name of the innkeeper, or of the town; a Mr Bell, Swan, Hinde, or Bull could name his pub accordingly, while Hatton and Bolton could produce Hat and Tun and Bolt in Tun (a tun being a large barrel). The pub itself might be given an unofficial jocular nickname, e.g. Mucky

Duck for Black Swan, Buzzard and Bastard for EAGLE & CHILD, Goose and Gridiron for Swan and Lyre.

A more elaborate joke, with a satirical edge to it, underlies the frequent pun between heraldic arms and physical arms. Whereas many pubs flatter local 'great families' by taking the name the X Arms and adopting their heraldic device, others in mocking contrast honour the 'arms' of working men – Blacksmith's Arms, Bricklayer's Arms, Butcher's Arms, Forester's Arms, Gardener's Arms, Miner's Arms, and so forth, the craft chosen often being historically linked to that locality. Sometimes the signboard displays the appropriate tools in a heraldic style, but more often it shows a muscular workman with his sleeves rolled up.

A humorous theme dating back to medieval times is to show animals mimicking human activities. The CAT & FIDDLE and the PIG & WHISTLE are two examples that survive, as are also some of the images chosen to illustrate the theme of a WORLD TURNED UPSIDE DOWN. The Hampshire Hog might simply refer to a well-known breed of pig, but not if the sign shows a fat drunken pig, dressed in suit, waistcoat and bow-tie, sitting astride a beer barrel, as in one picture in the modern edition of Larwood and Hotten. These authors mentioned other names of the same type in the nineteenth century: Hog in Armour, Dog in Doublet, Goat in Armour, Ape and Bagpipes, Goat in Boots. The latter they said was a joke against Welshmen, 'the goat having always been considered the emblem of that nation, and the jackboots an indispensable article of Taffy's costume'.

The old style of humour was by no means 'politically correct'. Pubs called the Turk's, Blackamoor's, or SARACEN'S HEAD were common (some still exist); though originating in heraldry, racist mockery was inevitably implied – as it also was in the proverbial LABOUR IN VAIN. Jokes against women were very popular; they include the Quiet/Silent/Headless/Good Woman (see QUIET WOMAN), and the NAG'S HEAD, all of which lampoon women for chattering or nagging, and the even more scathing MAN WITH A LOAD OF MISCHIEF.

See also BELL & MACKEREL, CUCKOO BUSH, CUCKOO OAK, MOON-RAKERS, NOOSE & MONKEY, PIG ON THE WALL *and* TREACLE MINE shape of a horseshoe is also a factor, as some commentators suggest, is more doubtful. Many of the early references specify that horseshoes are a protection against witchcraft, and that they should be nailed to the threshold of a house, to prevent a witch from entering; this was still sometimes being done in the nineteenth century, for in 1813 the antiquary Sir Henry Ellis counted seventeen horseshoes on the thresholds of houses in Monmouth Street (London wc2). Alternatively, the horseshoe could be placed above the doorway – nowadays the usual method – or above the stalls of horses and cattle. In more recent times small ornamental horseshoes have become common as charms.

See also THREE HORSESHOES

House That Jack Built

There used to be pubs of this name at Bristol, Salford, and Wolverhampton, inspired by the well-known nursery rhyme which goes back to the eighteenth century, and begins:

> This is the house that Jack built
> This is the malt that lay in the house that Jack built
> This is the rat that ate the malt that lay in the house
>   that Jack built
> This is the cat that ate the rat that ate the malt …

See also MOTHER GEESE & CATS WITH FIDDLES, p. 46

I

Ilkley Moor

See BAR T'AT

Imp

Dunkling and Wright note that a pub at Southville in Bristol took this name in 1980 in allusion to the nearby *Imp*erial Tobacco factory, but that nevertheless its sign shows a traditional little demon, in the pose of the Lincoln Imp – a small carving in Lincoln Cathedral.

J

Jack & Jill

There are pubs called Jack and Jill in several towns, including Middlesbrough, Stockport and Gainsborough, and also in the village of Clayton in East Sussex. The latter pub takes its name from a conspicuous pair of windmills which used to stand on the crest of the Downs nearby, but the other pubs – and indeed the windmills – allude to an eighteenth-century rhyme, which exists in several versions. It was apparently considered very amusing, for a chapbook of 1820 boasted:

> Read it who will,
> They'll laugh their fill.

Jack & Jill

Its humour, such as it is, depends partly on the slapstick tradition that falling over or getting hit is always funny, and partly on the common nursery rhyme device of deliberate nonsense, for who would go up a hill, rather than down into a valley, to find a well or stream?

The first verse is probably the oldest, and is the only one now well known:

> Jack and Jill went up the hill,
> To fetch a pail of water;
> Jack fell down and broke his crown,
> And Jill came tumbling after.
>
> Then up Jack got, and home did trot,
> As fast as he could caper,
> To old Dame Dob, who patched his nob
> With vinegar and brown paper.
>
> Then Jill came in, and she did grin,
> To see Jack's paper plaster;
> Her mother whipped her across her knee
> For laughing at Jack's disaster.

See also MOTHER GEESE & CATS WITH FIDDLES, p. 46

Jack Horner

See LITTLE JACK HORNER

Jack-in-the-Green

A Jack-in-the-Green is a man covered from head to foot in a mass of leaves fixed to a wooden conical frame seven or eight feet (2.1 – 2.4 metres) in height, so that he looks like a walking column of greenery. It was a tradition of the chimney sweeps in London and other large towns to make such a Jack and escort him through the streets on May Day morning, together with other costumed figures, all dancing to a fiddle and drum. They hoped to be given beer and money for this performance. This urban custom dates from the late eighteenth century; it was quite widespread in Victorian times, but died out in the early twentieth century. In recent decades, however, there has been a strong interest in folk customs, and the Jack-in-the-Green appears once again at May Day celebrations at Hastings, Oxford, Knutsford, Rochester, and elsewhere.

Consequently, there is now a Jack-in-the-Green pub at Rockbeare (Devon), though the sign does not show the wholly leaf-covered mummer of the sweeps' parade. Instead, it shows a young man whose jacket is decorated with tufts of leaves on the shoulders and at the waist, as is his hat; he carries a posy of flowers in one hand and a short pole topped with leaves and flowers in the other; there is a maypole in the background, with a banner saying 'Merry May'. This rendering must be inspired by a passage in William Hone's *Every-Day Book* (1827):

The Jack-o'-the-Greens would sometimes come into the suburbs of London [on May Day], and amuse the residents by rustic dancing. The last of them that I remember were at the Paddington May dance about twenty years ago.... A Jack-o'-the-Green always carried a long walking stick with floral wreaths; he whisked it about in the dance and afterwards walked with it in high estate like a lord mayor's footman.

An almost identical figure is painted on the signboard of the GREEN MAN in Winchester, though without the maypole.

An earlier painting on the Rockbeare sign, mentioned by Leslie Dunkling and Gordon Wright, was of 'a boy garlanded with ivy leaves'. It is a charming idea, but it misled these authors into assuming that it was normal for a sweep's boy to take the central role, 'concealed in a wooden framework covered with leaves and branches' – on the contrary, a full-sized Jack needs a grown man to manipulate it, being far too heavy for a boy's strength.

Jack o' Lantern

This pub name, at Romford in Essex and Loughborough in Leicestershire, refers to the kind of faint, flickering light which was once commonly seen in marshy areas, more usually known as a will-o-the-wisp. According to folk belief, this is caused by a goblin or pixy carrying a little lantern, or a bundle of burning straw (the wisp), with which he hopes to lead travellers astray. The phenomenon was once seriously feared as a danger to people travelling by night. Nowadays little figures representing Jack o' Lantern and his female counterpart, Joan o' the Wad, are sold as lucky charms.

'Jack o' Lantern' can also mean a turnip lantern such as is made at Halloween, offering another possible image for signboard-painters.

Jack o' Lent

In their *Pub Names of Britain* (2nd edn), Leslie Dunkling and Gordon Wright explain this name for a pub in Midsomer Norton (Somerset) as due to 'a local tradition in which the effigy of a knight (who is buried in the local church) was paraded during Lent'. This is rather misleading, for a Jack-a-Lent or Jack o' Lent was not the effigy of a knight, but a crude figure, gaunt and ugly, which was made up of wood, straw, and old clothes. On Ash Wednesday, the first day of Lent, people would parade through the streets with this guy, shouting and jeering; they might end by burning it or shooting it to pieces, or they might hang it up somewhere public and leave it there all through Lent, for boys to throw stones and dirt at. It was ill-treated because it symbolised the six-week season of strict fasting and penance beginning on Ash Wednesday, which was naturally unpopular; alternatively, some said it represented Judas Iscariot. This had once been a widespread custom, often mentioned in the sixteenth and seventeenth centuries, but becoming very rare during the nineteenth.

The 'effigy of a knight', on the other hand, belongs to a customary celebration which is still held on Easter Monday at Ashton-under-Lyne in Lancashire, known as Riding the Black Knight (or the Black Lad). Up to late Victorian times this was a rowdy affair; it is first recorded in 1795. A figure made up of black clothes stuffed with straw or sawdust would be mounted on a horse and paraded through a jeering crowd, and eventually pelted with mud and stones, and shot to pieces. According to legend, it represents a lord of the manor in the fifteenth century, Sir Ralph de Assheton, who is alleged (quite wrongly) to have been exceptionally cruel and to have been shot dead either by one of his tenants or by his wife's relatives. Nowadays, the Riding has become an elaborate pageant.

Several folklorists have noted how like the earlier form of the Riding was to the Jack o' Lent parade, and have suggested that it was originally an Ash Wednesday custom, transferred to a different date. This may be why the explanation offered for the pub name at Midsomer Norton has become confused.

Jack Straw's Castle

This former pub on North End Way, London NW3 (recently turned into flats), took its name from an episode in Wat Tyler's Peasants' Revolt of 1381, when it is said that a group of rebels marched from Clerkenbury to Hampstead and mustered there. Their leader went by the name of Jack Straw, but this was fairly obviously an alias, and probably referred to a traditional figure in seasonal folk revelry. It was, for example, the name conferred on the 'king' of Christmas feasting at Lincoln's Inn in the early sixteenth century. Disguise is an essential element in many folk customs, notably the house-to-house visiting and semi-dramatic performance known as 'mumming', and one simple form of disguise (common in Ireland and Scandinavia) is an all-enveloping straw cloak and a conical straw headdress which also conceals the face. And 'Jack' is, of course, a favourite name for bold young men in English folktales. Historians are divided as to whether it was Wat Tyler himself or one of his lieutenants who was operating under this pseudonym, which is so appropriate to a revolt of countrymen. They also say that there is no evidence to prove that the rebels gathered in Hampstead, and certainly there was no castle there. Some local writers have suggested that the 'castle' may be a joke, meaning simply a hay wagon from which Jack could have addressed his men.

Jacob's Ladder, Jacob's Well

See ANGELS & SAINTS, p. 16

Jacob's Post

This is the name of a post erected on Ditchling Common in East Sussex, and was formerly also the name of the pub adjoining the site. Unlike pubs called Jacob's Ladder or Jacob's Well, it has nothing to do with the biblical patriarch, but refers to a murderer, Jacob Harris, who was hanged on the common in 1734. Some accounts say he was a Jewish pedlar, others that he was a highwayman; he robbed and murdered three people at the inn, and so was executed, as customary, on a gibbet erected as close as possible to the scene of the crime. Tradition says that he was the last man in England to be 'hanged in chains'. It is unclear whether those who said this simply meant that his corpse was tarred, set in an iron framework, strung up again on the gibbet, and left to decay slowly, as was a common practice; or whether they meant that he endured the appalling and archaic penalty of being gibbeted alive (*see* GOLDEN FARMER).

Jacob's Post

Jane Shore

There is a pub called the Jane Shore in Shoreditch in London's East End, for this district traditionally claims to be named after the notorious medieval beauty Jane Shore, who was the mistress of Edward IV (among others). After the king's death she lost her influence at court and fell into poverty; in 1513, Sir Thomas More wrote in his *History of Richard III* that she was 'in beggarly condition, unfriended and worne out of acquaintance'. She died in 1526, and later legend asserted that by then she was completely destitute, and was actually found dead in a ditch – hence Shore-Ditch. This last point is demonstrably untrue, for the place name can be found in documents dating from well before her time; however, her dramatic downfall passed into folklore, as in the ballad entitled 'The Woeful Lamentation of Jane Shore':

> Then those to whom I had done good
> Durst not afford me any food;
> Hereby I begged all the day,
> And still in streets by night I lay.
>
> Thus was I scorned by maid and wife
> For leading such a wicked life;
> Both sucking babes and children small
> Did make their pastime at my fall.
>
> I could not get one bit of bread
> By which my hunger could be fed;
> Nor drink, but such as channel yield,
> Or stinking ditches in the field.

This, weary of my life, at lengthe
I yielded up my vital strength
Within a ditch of loathsome scent
Where carrion dogs did much frequent;

The which now since my dying daye
Is Shoreditch call'd, as writers saye;
Which is a witness to my sinne,
For being concubine to a king.

John Barleycorn

John (or Sir John) Barleycorn is a traditional personification for barley as the basic ingredient in making beer, and hence for the drink itself. A seventeenth-century folksong describes the ordeals 'he' suffers, from sowing, through harvesting, to being ground in a mill, and then being brewed for liquor; it ends by triumphantly pointing out that drink is strong enough to overcome any man. The song is well known in both England and Scotland; Robert Burns wrote a version in 1782. At Bampton in Oxfordshire in the early twentieth century, the song told of three men 'out of the west' who swore to kill John Barleycorn:

They ploughed, they sowed, they harrowed him in,
    Throwed clods upon his head,
And these three men made a solemn vow,
    John Barleycorn was dead.

Then they let him lie for a very long time
    Till the rain from heaven did fall,
Then little Sir John sprung up his head,
    And soon amazed them all.

Then at Midsummer, when 'little Sir John he growed a long beard', men came 'with scythes so sharp / To cut him off at the knee'; others came 'with sharp pitchforks / Who pricked him to the heart', and carted him off to a barn. After that, the threshers came:

> They hired men with crab-tree sticks
>> To cut him skin from bone;
> But the miller served him worse than that,
>> For he ground him between two stones.

But John Barleycorn 'proved the stronger man at last', once he had become liquor:

> And the huntsman he can't hunt the fox
>> Nor so loudly blow his horn,
> Nor the tinker he can't mend kettles or pots,
>> Without a little of Barleycorn.

Drink is powerful indeed; another version vividly describes Barleycorn's revenge on his human persecutors:

> Sir John at last in this respect
>> So paid them all their hire
> That some lay bleeding by the walls.
>> Some tumbling in the mire.

> Some lay groaning by the walls,
>> Some fell i' th' street down right;
> The wisest of them scarcely knew
>> What he had done o'er night.

Another ends with a warning against drink:

> It will make a boy into a man,
>   A man into an ass;
> To silver it will change your gold,
>   Your silver into brass.

There are pubs called (Sir) John Barleycorn in Nottingham, Cambridge, and Hitchin.

See also HARVESTERS & WHEATSHEAVES, p. 182

John Bull

There are pubs named after John Bull, the conventional stereotype of an Englishman, in Exeter and elsewhere. This figure was invented in 1712 by a Scottish writer, Dr John Arbuthnot, who wrote a political satire contrasting 'honest, bold, plain-dealing John Bull' with his deceitful enemies the Dutch Nick Frog and the French Louis Baboon. He became far better known in cartoons from the late eighteenth century onwards, sometimes drawn as a bull, sometimes as a bulldog, but most often as a heavy-built man, gruff-looking, and gorging on beef, beer, and plum-pudding.

Jolly Farmer

See HARVESTERS & WHEATSHEAVES, p. 182

King & Miller

See SIR JOHN COCKLE

King & Tinker

In Whitewebbs Lane, in Enfield on the northern outskirts of London (formerly Middlesex), there is a very old pub which has been known since the beginning of the eighteenth century, if not earlier, as the King and Tinker. It takes its name from a ballad which tells how James I became separated from his companions while out hunting deer, and went into an alehouse, where he sat at the same table as a tinker. They talked merrily together, and the tinker happened to say that he would dearly like to see the king, for he had heard he was in the neighbourhood. That would not be difficult, answered James, for if the tinker would mount behind him he guaranteed that they would soon find the king. So they rode off together, and in due course came to where the nobles and courtiers were gathered. Astonished at seeing so many fine men, the tinker asked how he could know which one was the king. 'He will be the only one with his hat on,' James replied. The tinker looked puzzled, for all the nobles had doffed their hats – and then he realised that the man he was riding with had not. In horror at his own disrespectful behaviour, he fell to his knees and begged forgiveness, but the king merely laughed, and knighted him there and then.

Various places have claimed to be the setting for this adventure, one of them being Enfield Chase; hence the name of the pub.

King Arthur

Stories about King Arthur, originating in Wales and other Celtic-speaking areas, had reached England (via French romances) by the twelfth century, and most people of that period believed he had really existed. Considering his great importance in the legendary history of Britain and in literature, it is surprising that he is not more widely celebrated when pubs are being named. However, his supposed birthplace at Tintagel in Cornwall does have both a King Arthur's Arms and a King Arthur's Castle, and there is a King Arthur at Gower in Glamorgan, not far from a crag long known as Arthur's Seat. Another town which has named a pub for him is Glastonbury in Somerset, which has had strong Arthurian associations for over eight hundred years, since it claims a link with Avalon itself.

The legends of Arthur all agree that he had been mortally wounded in battle, but what happened next was a mystery; it was generally said that he had been taken to the enchanted Isle of Avalon, a place not to be found on any earthly map. Maybe he had been buried there, or maybe he had been healed and would one day return – no one knew.

Then in 1191 the monks of Glastonbury Abbey announced a sensational discovery, vividly described by the chronicler

Gerald of Wales, who visited the abbey the following year. He says the monks were excavating their graveyard on instructions from King Henry II, because he had been told by 'an ancient Welsh bard, a singer of the past, that they would find [Arthur's] body at least sixteen feet (4.8 metres) below the earth, not in a tomb of stone, but in a hollow oak'. And so they did

King Arthur

– two skeletons in an oak, one that of a very tall man and one that of a fair-haired woman, together with a lead cross bearing the inscription: 'Here lies buried the renowned King Arthur with Guinevere his second wife, in the Isle of Avalon'. The skeletons were transferred to a marble tomb within the abbey itself (the site of which is now marked by an inscribed stone slab).

It is a good story, rather too good to be true. The monks may well have accidentally unearthed prehistoric skeletons in a tree-trunk coffin, but the cross allegedly proving their identity as Arthur and Guinevere is a medieval forgery, not genuine work of Iron Age Britons. One can guess at the motives for this dramatic deception. The abbey, needing funds to rebuild after a recent fire, would profit well from visitors coming to a hero's tomb; Henry II had political reasons for wishing to convince the Welsh that Arthur was truly dead and would never return to lead an uprising against the English.

But the story has never died, and to this day visitors to Glastonbury dream that this is indeed Avalon, the last resting place of King Arthur.

King Coel

The town of Colchester traditionally claims that it was founded by a certain King Coel or Cole, who is said to have lived in the third century AD, and honours his memory in the name of a pub. According to the very unreliable medieval historian Geoffrey of Monmouth, Coel was at first merely Duke of Colchester, but rebelled against the then king of Britain (an even more shadowy figure with the unlikely name of Asclepiodotus), and reigned himself for a few months before dying of natural causes. All this is sheer fiction; however, Geoffrey also says that Cole had a learned and musically gifted daughter Helena who married a Roman senator and became the mother of the future Emperor Constantine – and she at least really did exist, whoever her father may have been.

It is not this dubious history which has made King Cole famous, but a nursery rhyme dating from around 1700:

> Old King Cole was a merry old soul,
> And a merry old soul was he;
> He called for his pipe and he called for his bowl,
> And he called for his fiddlers three.

He is a very suitable patron for a pub, and is also commemorated at the FIDDLERS THREE.

See also MOTHER GEESE & CATS WITH FIDDLES, p. 46

King Lud

Up to the end of the twentieth century there were two notable pubs of this name in London, the Old King Lud at 78 Ludgate

Hill, EC4, and the New King Lud at 3–4 Seacole Lane. The building which housed the former (now a restaurant) still displays carved bearded heads on its façade, representing its ancient patron. There is also a King Lud pub at Wishaw in Scotland, which is rather more surprising, since the legendary figure from Britain's pseudo-historical past whom they commemorate is always associated with London.

According to Geoffrey of Monmouth's *Histories of the Kings of Britain* (c.1136) – a highly unreliable work, which was nevertheless accepted as a good authority even in Elizabethan times – Lud was king of Britain at the time of Julius Caesar, and in 66 BC he became the first to fortify the town of London with a wall, one particular gate in which was therefore known as Ludgate. Geoffrey was not too far out in his dating of the fortifications (though Lud himself is a fiction), for while the city wall and gates of his time were medieval structures they were built on the foundations of older Roman ones, parts of which would still have been visible. The original Roman gate he referred to was built *c.* AD 200. Its medieval successor was demolished in 1760, and statues of Lud and his two sons which had stood there were transferred to the church of St Dunstan-in-the-West in Fleet Street, where they can still be seen. Nowadays, some people say that Lud's bones still lie in a secret vault, deep underground on the site where his gate once stood.

King Mark

The King Mark pub at Newquay is named after a legendary king of Cornwall who figures in a tragic love story in medieval romance. Though no longer young, King Mark decided to marry a beautiful Irish princess named Iseult (or Isolde), and sent his nephew Tristan to fetch her to Cornwall. Iseult's wait-ing-woman had prepared a magic potion which would make Iseult and Mark fall deeply in love, thus ensuring the success of the marriage, but by ill luck it was Tristan and Iseult who drank it together. Despite their instant love, Tristan was bound by loyalty to his uncle to bring Iseult to be his bride, and the mar-riage took place as planned. The rest of the romance tells of the various tricks by which the young lovers contrived to meet and, for a while, avoid discovery; of Mark's fury when he did learn their secret; how they were forced to part, but eventually were reunited in death. None of the versions of the story shows much sympathy for Mark, and Sir Thomas Malory's *Morte D'Arthur* gives a particularly unfavourable view of him.

L

Labour in Vain

It is thought that this rather curious name, known in London from the seventeenth century to the nineteenth, was originally meant to imply that the pub bearing it served such excellent beer that anybody trying to equal it would be wasting their time. The name itself is now rare, and few if any of the pubs using it still display the sign which traditionally illustrated it, for this is regarded as offensive – one side showed a woman scrubbing a black child in a tub, while on the other side she was scratching her head to see that he was as black as ever. There used to be examples of this sign at Horsehay (near Telford, Shropshire), Westergate (West Sussex), Eaton Bray (Bedfordshire), Yarnfield (Staffordshire), and Old Swinford (Worcestershire). It was sometimes accompanied by the rhyme:

> Washing here can now be seen,
> She scrubs both left and right.
> Although she'll get him middling clean,
> She'll never get him white.

The underlying idea is a proverbial one, that any attempt to change someone's basic nature is futile. Various classical Greek and Roman authors wrote of 'washing an Ethiopian white' to mean that it is foolish to labour at an impossible task, while the Bible asks: 'Can the Ethiopian change his skin, or the leopard his spots?' (Jer. 13:23).

Some people preferred to think their pub sign commemorated a local scandal. At Albury in Hertfordshire and at Westergate in Sussex they said it was about a woman who had an affair with a West Indian and bore his child while her husband was away; now she was desperately trying to get it white, before he came home from his travels. The Albury pub was closed in the 1950s. The Westergate one was still going strong in 2003, though there was a plan afoot to remove the original sign, as being racist; local people defended it, arguing that it showed a real episode of history dating from the eighteenth century. Local opinion prevailed at first, but two years later the pub was sold, and the new owners changed the name and turned it into a restaurant.

At Yarnfield the original signboard was taken down in 1993 after complaints that it was racist. It was replaced by one showing a farmer sowing corn, with a flock of birds following and gobbling it up, but in 2009 this in turn was removed and the original sign rehung.

Lady Godiva

The city of Coventry has, naturally enough, named one of its pubs after the famous local heroine, Lady Godiva, who died in 1057. She was a devout lady, the wife of Earl Leofric of Mercia, and a generous donor to Christian causes. But what has made her famous is the legend of her naked ride through the streets of the city, told many years after her death by the chroniclers Roger of Wendover in the twelfth century and Matthew Paris in the thirteenth; they saw it as a noble act, undertaken in response to an unreasonable demand by a tyrannical husband. The people of Coventry, they explain, were burdened by a heavy tax which Earl Leofric could remit if he so wished. So, as Roger of Wendover puts it:

The saintly countess . . . often besought the earl, her husband, with earnest prayers, to free the town, by the guidance of the Holy Trinity and of the Holy Mother of God, from this slavery. The earl upbraided her for vainly seeking something so injurious to him and repeatedly forbade her to approach him again on the subject. Nevertheless in her female pertinacity she exasperated her husband with her unceasing request, and extorted from him the following reply: 'Mount your horse naked,' he said, 'and ride through the market place of the town from one side right to the other while people are gathered there, and when you return you shall claim what you desire.' And the countess answered: 'And if I wish to do this, will you give me your permission?' And the earl said: 'I will.'

Then the countess Godiva, beloved of God, on a certain day, as it is said, mounting her horse naked, loosed her hair from its bands, and her whole body was veiled, except for her fair white legs. Her journey done, unseen by a soul, she returned rejoicing to her husband, who accounted it a miracle. Then Earl Leofric granted a charter freeing the city of Coventry from its servitude and confirmed it with his seal.

It is impossible to guess now whether there is any grain of historical fact behind the story; probably not, since it has echoes of legends about female saints robed in their own hair, and of fairytales about clever girls solving apparently impossible tasks. Later versions of the Godiva story switch the emphasis from her holiness to her cleverness; it was now said that she arranged that everyone should stay indoors with closed windows as she rode by. People could hear the horse's hoof-beats, but they did not see her. And so she returned home, wrote an Elizabethan chronicler, 'with her honour saved, her purpose obtained, her wisdom much commended, and her husband's imagination utterly disappointed'.

By 1659, a new character had been added to the legend: PEEPING TOM, who opened a window to see the naked Godiva riding by, and was struck blind. He too is now commemorated by a pub.

Lady of Shalott

This name, found at Louth in Lincolnshire, is derived from a tale in Arthurian tradition as mediated through nineteenth-century literature; it is the title of an attractive and popular poem by Tennyson (who was born at Somersby, only a few miles from Louth). This tells of a lady who, because of a spell laid upon her, lives in seclusion in Shalott, an island in a river that flows past Camelot. She is under a taboo never to look out of her castle window, and spends her days weaving a tapestry based upon the reflections of the outside world which she sees in a great mirror. Seeing Sir Lancelot ride past one day, she forgets the spell and runs to the window to see him better; at this, her mirror cracks and she feels death coming to her. So she takes a boat:

Lying, robed in snowy white
That loosely flowed to left and right –
The leaves upon her falling light –
Through the noises of the night
    She floated down to Camelot:
And as the boat-head wound along
The willowy hills and fields among,
They heard her singing her last song,
    The Lady of Shalott.

Heard a carol, mournful, holy,
Chanted loudly, chanted lowly,
Till her blood was frozen slowly,
And her eyes were darkened wholly,
    Turned to towered Camelot;
For ere she reached upon the tide
The first house by the river side,
Singing in her song she died,
    The Lady of Shalott.

Tennyson is here reworking the poignant story of Elaine of Astolat from Book 18 of Malory's *Morte D'Arthur*, but altering the name of her home to something closer to that in a thirteenth-century Italian version, *La Donna di Scalotta*, for the sake of the convenient rhyme of 'Shalott' and 'Camelot'. In Malory, there is no mirror, and no spell. Elaine is the daughter of Sir Bernard of Escalot, in whose castle Sir Lancelot is staying in order to take part anonymously in a tournament. When he is seriously wounded she helps nurse him, and falls so deeply in love that when he is well enough to leave she pleads openly:

Fair knight and courteous knight, have mercy upon me, and suffer me not to die for thy love. What would ye that I did? said Lancelot. I would have you to my husband, said Elaine. Fair damosel, I thank you, said Sir Lancelot, but truly, said he, I cast me never to be a wedded man. Then, fair knight, said she, will ye be my paramour? Jesu defend me, said Sir Lancelot, for then I would reward your father and brother full ill for their great goodness. Alas, said she, then must I die for thy love.

Once Lancelot is gone, Elaine can neither eat, nor drink, nor sleep. She dictates a letter of farewell to him, saying that she dies 'a clean maiden' and urging him to pray for her soul. Then she tells her father what to do when she dies:

And while my body is hot let this letter be put in my right hand, and my hand bound fast with the letter until that I be cold, and let me be put in a fair bed with all the richest clothes that I have about me, and so let my bed and all my richest clothes be laid with me in a chariot unto the place where Thames is; and there let me be put within a barget, and but one man with me, such as ye trust to steer me thither, and that my barget be covered with black samite over and over; thus father I beseech you let it be done.

When the black barge reaches Westminster, Arthur, Guinevere, and the knights go to view this 'fairest corpse' clad in cloth of gold, 'and she lay as though she had smiled', and they weep to read her letter. Lancelot grieves, saying 'she was both fair and good, and much was I beholden unto her, but she loved me out of measure'.

Lady of the Lake

The Lady of the Lake, who has given her name to a pub in Lowestoft, on the coast of Suffolk, is one of the recurrent characters in romances about King Arthur and his knights. She is not usually given a personal name, and is probably a literary development of the many nameless fairies known as 'White Ladies' in British and European folklore who were traditionally believed to haunt pools and rivers. In Arthurian tales the Lady of the Lake is usually a force for good. She is said, in French romances, to have rescued the infant Lancelot from enemies who meant to kill him, and to have reared him in her underwater palace until he was old enough to go to Arthur's court. In Thomas Malory's *Morte D'Arthur* she intervenes several times to warn Arthur of various dangers and to assist his knights, but her most important deed is to give Arthur his sword, Excalibur:

> So [Arthur and Merlin] rode till they came to a lake, the which was a fair water and broad, and in the midst of the lake Arthur was 'ware of an arm clothed in white samite, that held a fair sword in that hand. Lo! said Merlin, yonder is that sword that I spake of. With that they saw a damosel going upon the lake. What damosel is that? said Arthur. That is the Lady of the Lake, said Merlin; and within that lake is a rock, and therein is as fair a place as any upon earth, and richly beseen; and this damosel will come to you anon, and then speak ye fair to her that she will give you that sword.

The Lady tells Arthur that the sword is indeed hers, and that she will gladly give him both sword and scabbard if he will give her a gift when she asks it of him. He agrees: 'And so they went into the barge, and when they came to the sword which the hand held, Arthur took it up by the handles and took it with him, and the arm and the hand went under the water.'

Lamb & Flag

There are pubs simply called the Lamb in many towns and villages throughout the country, and in most cases the reference is merely to the local importance of sheep-rearing and the wool trade. Others are named after a person called Lamb. But the Lamb and Flag at Oxford and elsewhere, which appears at first glance to be one of the arbitrary 'combination names', is in fact a religious symbol which goes back to the early centuries of Christianity and has been passed on from church art to heraldry, and then on to the modern world. A lamb is the symbol of Jesus Christ in his role as sacrificial victim, an interpretation based on several Bible texts, most notably John the Baptist's words about him: 'Behold the lamb of God, that takes away the sins of the world' (John 1:29). In medieval art this *Agnus Dei*, 'Lamb of God', is shown with one of its forelegs hooked round the staff of a banner which bears a red cross; this is to express the idea that Christ's death became a triumphant victory. It is this banner which in modern terms has become the 'flag'.

From about the fourth century onwards, tablets of white wax stamped with the *Agnus Dei* were highly prized among Catholics as protective religious amulets; they were made by melting down the unused stumps of church candles, especially the large Pascal Candle. The Lamb of God was also adopted as a heraldic device by various organisations, both secular ones such as the Guild of Merchant Tailors, and religious ones such as the Knights of St John of Jerusalem and the Knights Templar.

Since the latter two had a particular concern for the well-being and safety of travellers, it is easy to see why their emblem was appropriate for inns.

See also ANGELS & SAINTS, p. 16

Lambton Worm

The pub of this name in Chester-le-Street (Durham) commemorates one of the best-known tales of dragon-slaying in English folklore – for 'Worm' here is used in its medieval sense of 'serpent, dragon' – which was first put into print by Robert Surtees in 1820 in his *History of Durham*. The story goes that at some unspecified date in the Middle Ages a young knight of the Lambton family (whose castle lies a little over a mile from the village) committed the sin of going fishing on a Sunday, in the river Wear. To make matters worse, he cursed freely because for a long time he caught nothing, and when at last he did, it was only an ugly little thing, rather like a newt or worm. He angrily tossed it into a nearby well, thought no more about it, and went off to the Crusades. While he was away the worm grew bigger and bigger, till it was so long that it could coil nine times round a nearby hill, and became the terror of the countryside.

The Lambton Worm

When Young Lambton returned home, he was horrified, and swore he would destroy the monster. The problem was, as he soon discovered, that this worm had the power to join itself up again whenever it was cut in half, so nothing he could do would kill it. Then, on the advice of a witch, he had his armour studded with razor blades, and took up a position on a rock in the middle of the river. The worm wrapped itself round him, hoping to crush him, and was cut to pieces by the razors; what is more, the pieces fell into the river and were swept away by its rapid flow, so the creature could no longer rejoin its severed parts.

The witch's price for her good advice had been that Young Lambton should kill the first living creature which came to him after the battle, and he had agreed. He left orders that his dog should be released as soon as he blew his bugle, thinking that it would rush to meet him and that an animal's life would be enough to please the witch. Unfortunately, the orders were forgotten, and instead of the dog it was Lord Lambton himself who came out to welcome his son. Young Lambton could not kill his own father, so he broke his word to the witch. She cursed him and his family, saying that for nine generations no one who held the title would die in his bed.

The legend has been often retold, and a simple version of it, ignoring the witch and her curse, is the subject of a lively folk-song, beginning:

> One Sunday morning Lambton went
> A-fishing in the Wear,
> And catched a fish upon his hook
> He thought looked very queer,
> But whatten a kind of fish it were
> Young Lambton couldn't tell;
> He wouldn't fash to carry it home,

So he hoyed it in a well.

Chorus: Whisht, lads, and hold yer gobs,

    I'll tell you all an awful story;

    Whisht, lads, and hold yer gobs,

    I'll tell you about the Worm.

Lammastide

It is unusual for a pub to be named after a date or season, but such was the case with the Lammastide at Hinton in Gloucestershire. 'Lammas' comes from the Anglo-Saxon word for 'loaf-mass', and was originally a religious festival at which loaves made from freshly harvested grain were brought to church and blessed – in other words, an equivalent to the modern Harvest Thanksgiving services. It took place on 1 August. Although the religious importance of Lammas faded, this day and those immediately following (comprising 'Lammastide') remained popular in many districts as a time for fairs and local festivals.

See also THE YEAR'S MERRY ROUND, p. 310

Lancelot

The name of Sir Lancelot, most famous of the Knights of the Round Table, is occasionally found attached to pubs. The most interesting instance is one in Liverpool, because it may reflect the romantic speculations of some Lancashire historians in the nineteenth century. They claimed that Lancelot had been brought to Lancashire as a baby when his royal parents were forced to flee from their kingdom of Brittany; that it was in Lancashire that a Lady of the Lake fostered him in her underwater realm after they died; and in Lancashire that he slew the murderous and gigantic Sir Tarquin. There is no support for these localisations in Malory or in earlier medieval texts.

Leprechaun

Since there has long been a flourishing Irish community in Liverpool, it is understandable that the city should also have a pub called the Leprechaun, for this is a well-known creature from Irish folklore. A leprechaun is a type of small goblin or fairy-man, who is always seen on his own; sometimes he is busy mending shoes, for he is said to be the fairies' cobbler. Above all, he is the owner and guardian of great wealth, either in the form of a crock of gold or of a magic purse which is never empty. There was once a man who crept up on a leprechaun and grabbed him, and swore he would squeeze him to death if the little fellow did not show him where the gold was hidden. So they set off, the man still holding the leprechaun very tightly, and never taking his eye off him for a second, until – well, some say the leprechaun suddenly squealed, 'Look out for that horrible big dog!', or 'There's a house on fire over there!', or maybe he just threw a pinch of snuff in the man's face, making him sneeze. But whatever it was, the man looked away for a moment, and by the time he looked back the leprechaun had vanished.

Lincoln Imp

There is naturally a pub named after the Lincoln Imp in Lincoln itself, and another in Scunthorpe. The Imp is the figure of a little grinning demon, horned, furry, and about twelve inches tall, sitting with one foot crossed over his knee; he can be seen carved high up on one of the pillars of the Angel Choir in Lincoln Cathedral. It is on the north side, which is appropriate, since in medieval symbolism the north is associated with the Devil, and with Hell. The carving dates from the thirteenth century.

There are several versions of the story, differing slightly about how the imp got into the cathedral but agreeing that once he was inside he began causing as much disturbance and damage as he could. The angels ordered him to stop, but he simply laughed at them, so they turned him to stone.

Lion, Golden Lion, Red Lion

See QUEENS' HEADS & RED LIONS, p. 248

Little Jack Horner

This pub name, found at Stockport (and the shorter version 'Jack Horner', found in Worthing, Sussex), is another that is taken from a nursery rhyme:

> Little Jack Horner
> Sat in the corner
> Eating his Christmas pie;
> He put in his thumb
> And pulled out a plum,
> And said, 'What a good boy am I!'

It is often said that this is a political joke dating from the time of the Reformation, and means that a certain Thomas Horner acquired the Manor of Mells in Somerset, a piece of property belonging to Glastonbury Abbey. The last abbot had hoped that by giving this manor to Henry VIII he could persuade him to spare the abbey, so he sent his steward Horner to London with the deeds, hidden in a pie – but the disloyal steward kept them for himself. In their *Oxford Dictionary of Nursery Rhymes* (1951), Iona and Peter Opie showed that this 'explanation' only dates from the nineteenth century; it is true that Thomas Horner did exist, and did obtain that property, but there is no reason to think that he stole the deeds – in fact, a Tudor chronicler refers to him having 'bought the lordship of Mells' from the king. Whatever the truth of the matter, the story is the origin for the colloquial phrase 'a plum job'.

See also MOTHER GEESE & CATS WITH FIDDLES, p. 46

Little John

One of the most popular stories about Robin Hood tells how Little John – so called because he was unusually tall and burly – arrived in Sherwood Forest to challenge him to a quarterstaff fight (or to a wrestling match), and after a hard tussle knocked him into a river. Robin took it all as a joke, and invited Little John to join the outlaw band, after which they had many adventures together.

It is appropriate that one of the pubs named after Little John should be in the village of Hathersage (Derbyshire), since a tradition going back at least to the early seventeenth century claims that he was both born and buried there. There are two stones in the churchyard, more than three yards apart, which are said to mark the head and foot of his grave; this is much farther apart than is normal, and would imply that he was almost eight feet (2.4 metres) tall. The grave was opened in 1784 by one of the local gentry, who removed a thighbone which is said to have measured 2 feet 5 inches (74 centimetres); however, he then suffered a series of accidents and misfortunes which convinced him to have the bone reburied.

Load of Mischief

See MAN WITH A LOAD OF MISCHIEF

London Stone

In London's Cannon Street, EC4, there is a plain stone, some two feet high (60 centimetres), set in a recess of the wall of an empty building and protected by an iron grille. This is the London Stone, which allegedly once marked the very centre of the city, and not far off is the pub which takes its name from it. A plaque beside the stone records what little is known of its history:

> This is a fragment of the original piece of limestone once securely fixed in the ground now fronting Cannon Street Station. Removed in 1742 to the south side of the street, in 1798 it was built into the south wall of the church of St Swithun London Stone which stood here until demolished in 1962. Its origin and purpose are unknown, but in 1188 there was a reference to Henry, son of Elwyn de Londonstane, subsequently Lord Mayor of London.

It is unclear just how old the stone is; there are occasional mentions of it in various documents from the late eleventh century onwards, none of which explain just why it was considered important. One historical episode seems to confirm its symbolic importance; Elizabethan chroniclers tell how when the rebel Jack Cade entered London in 1450 he 'struck his sword on London Stone' as he proclaimed himself 'lord of this city'; Shakespeare used this episode in *Henry VI Part II*.

A more elaborate account was contributed to the journal *Notes and Queries* in January 1862 by 'Mon Merrion' – a misprint for Môr Meirion, the bardic name of the Rev. Richard Williams Morgan. According to Morgan, it should rightly be called the Brutus Stone, for Brutus, grandson of Aeneas and allegedly the founder of Britain, brought it with him from Troy, because it enshrined his luck, and set it up as an altar to Diana, the goddess who had guided him to his new land. It therefore became the 'luck' or 'soul' of London; if it were destroyed, disaster would befall the city. Others say (but cannot prove) that it first stood in the forum of Roman London, as the central 'milestone' from which all distances in the country were measured. Modern occultists claim that it must have been a Druidic megalith, and/or a 'marker' on a ley line, and/or the stone from which Arthur pulled the sword. In his novel *The House of Dr Dee* (1993), Peter Ackroyd represented this Elizabethan magician as searching for a lost antediluvian city below the streets of London, of which this stone alone remained above ground as a source of magic. Needless to say, there is no supporting evidence for any of these enticingly dramatic speculations.

Long Man of Wilmington

This pub at Patcham, north of Brighton in East Sussex, takes its name from a famous landmark, the figure of a giant carved into the north face of Windover Hill at Wilmington, about fifteen miles further east. See the GIANT'S REST (Wilmington) for the associated stories.

Lover's Leap

This pub at Stoney Middleton in the Peak District of Derbyshire stands at the foot of a high, perpendicular rock which has been known as Lover's Leap since the beginning of the nineteenth century. According to Ebenezer Rhodes in his *Peak Scenery* (1824):

> From the summit of this fearful precipice, about the year 1760, a love-stricken damsel of the name of Baddeley threw herself into the chasm below, and, incredible as it may appear, she sustained but little injury from the desperate attempt. Her face was a little disfigured, and her body bruised, by the brambles and the rocky projections that interrupted her fall, but she was enabled to walk to her home with very little assistance.

Rhodes adds that the experience cured her of her passion, so that she remained unmarried and 'ever afterwards lived an exemplary life in the neighbourhood of the place that had been the scene of her folly'. Later Victorians, apparently unwilling that an attempted suicide should go unpunished, declared that she 'remained sadly crippled for the rest of her life'. Nowadays interest usually centres on the curious and mildly amusing factor which is generally said to have saved her life: her skirts billowed out and acted as a parachute.

Luck Penny

One might assume that the luck penny which provided the name of a pub in Stafford was yet another lucky charm or talisman, like a four-leafed clover or a horseshoe. This is not so. The term refers to an old custom at fairs and markets that someone selling horses, cattle or other livestock should hand back some small fraction of the purchase price as a goodwill gesture to the buyer.

~M~

Mad Hatter

There are or were pubs called the Mad Hatter (or Hatters) in Manchester, Warrington, and Edinburgh, certainly alluding to the character in Lewis Carroll's *Alice in Wonderland*. However, this figure, like his companion the MARCH HARE, is not purely Carroll's invention. 'Mad as a hatter' was already a proverbial expression before he wrote, but the explanation is uncertain; some commentators think it refers to the ill effects of mercury compounds used by hatters in their trade, which caused twitching.

Magog

London once had a pub called the Magog in Russia Row, EC3, which has been demolished. It used to have two figures of giants at the door, in allusion to the legend of GOG & MAGOG.

Magpie

Pubs named the Magpie are fairly common; there are also variations such as the Pie, the Magpie and Crown, or the Magpie

The Magpie

and Stump – the latter showing the bird perched on a tree stump, which some authorities believe was a misunderstanding of the heraldic crest of Anne Boleyn, which consisted of a white falcon on the root of a tree. Though the magpie is unpopular with gamekeepers and other countrymen, it is of course immediately recognisable and easily painted, which is an advantage as a visual emblem.

In folklore, it is most famous as an omen, usually of ill, and has been so since Shakespeare's time, if not before. Seeing a single magpie invariably means bad luck (some even said, death), but two or more portend a variety of coming events, some good and some bad, depending upon the number seen at once. These are described in verses first recorded in the eighteenth century which are found in many different versions. As usual with superstitions, the older ones are grimmer than the modern. The verse usually counts up to seven, which forms a climax, but there are occasional elaborate versions going up to twelve. Variants include:

> One for sorrow, two for mirth,
> Three for a wedding, four for a birth
> [or 'death', or 'dearth']

> Five for heaven, six for hell,
> Seven you'll see the devil himsel'.

Or, more common nowadays:

> Five for silver, six for gold,
> Seven for a secret never to be told.

The longest recorded comes from Lancashire in the late nineteenth century:

> One for anger, two for mirth,
> Three for a wedding, four for a birth,
> Five for rich, six for poor,
> Seven for a witch, eight for a whore,
> Nine for a burying, ten for a dance,
> Eleven for England, twelve for France.

In *English Inn Signs*, the 1951 updating of Jacob Larwood and J. C. Hotten's *History of Signboards*, it is said that a carved wooden sign of the Magpie and Horseshoe was still to be seen in Fetter Lane in London at that date. Perhaps the original landlord prudently reckoned that the good luck of the horseshoe would cancel the bad luck of the single magpie.

Maid Marian

There are pubs dedicated to Marian (or Marion), heroine of the Robin Hood legend, at Norwich and at Arnold (near Nottingham). She was not originally an important character in the story – indeed, the medieval ballads which are its earliest sources never mention her at all. However, when Robin Hood's exploits became a topic for the professional stage (as opposed to folksongs, rural entertainments, and local anecdotes) Marian was introduced, no doubt to provide dramatic variety and a romantic plot. She appeared first in a play by Anthony Munday (1598), and has remained a popular figure ever since. According to Munday's version, Robin was no mere yeoman but the rightful Earl of Huntingdon in the reign of Richard I, betrothed to the beautiful and equally aristocratic Matilda (whom the king's brother, Prince John, also loved). When Robin was outlawed through his wicked uncle's plot, Matilda followed him to the forest, where she took the name of Marian and soon became a skilful archer.

Man & Scythe

See HARVESTERS & WHEATSHEAVES, p. 182

Man in the Moon

Several pubs of this name (e.g. in Cambridge, Ipswich, Norwich, and West Heath in Birmingham) deliberately changed it to Man *on* the Moon in 1969 to celebrate Neil Armstrong's landing, and repainted their sign to show the astronauts, their rocket, or their landing module. But others, such as the one in Chalk Farm Road, London NW1, kept to the older, folkloric interpretation. From medieval times onwards, it has been said, usually as a joke, that the dark blotches on the moon's face show a man carrying a bundle of thorny sticks and a lantern, and followed by a dog. It was said he was put there as a punishment for gathering sticks on a Sunday (an idea suggested by the Bible, Num. 15:32–6, where a man is stoned to death for this sin), or for having stolen the sticks, or for strewing branches of thorn bush on a church path to stop people going to the services. The legendary figure is still well remembered, partly because Shakespeare uses him to comic effect in

The Man in the Moon

A Midsummer Night's Dream, and partly because of a nineteenth-century nursery rhyme:

> The man in the moon
> Came down too soon
> And asked his way to Norwich;
> The man in the south,
> He burnt his mouth
> By eating cold plum porridge.

Another folk rhyme, recorded in 1913, better reflects the legend:

> The Man in the Moon was caught in a trap
> For stealing the thorns from another man's gap.
> If he had gone by, and let the thorns lie,
> He'd never been Man in the Moon so high.

See also MOTHER GEESE & CATS WITH FIDDLES, p. 46

Harvesters & Wheatsheaves

Writing in 1608, the poet Thomas Heywood produced a song of five verses on the names and clientele of London pubs, of which the first verse runs:

> The Gentry to the *King's Head*,
> The Nobles to the *Crown*,
> The Knights unto the *Golden Fleece*,
> And to the *Plough*, the Clowne.

Since 'clown' was a contemptuous term for a peasant or yokel, it is clear that Heywood regarded the Plough as a low-class name. Nevertheless, the vital importance of farming to past generations ensured that names referring to it soon became popular, while its rather idealised and nostalgic appeal in our own times probably means they will remain popular for the foreseeable future. The Jolly Farmer and the Farmer's Boy used to be common, and since cereal crops are the basis for making beer, ale and whisky, it is natural for pubs to celebrate their cultivation, from initial ploughing to eventual harvesting. The names PLOUGH, Plough and Horses, and Plough and Harrow are widespread; there is also a Ploughboy at Lincoln, a Ploughshare at Beeston in Norfolk, and a more up-to-date Plough and Tractor at Great Knightley in Essex. The pubs called Speed the Plough at Hitchin, at Barton-in-the-Clay in Bedfordshire, and elsewhere are quoting a phrase which is actually an old-fashioned prayer or blessing, meaning 'May God grant success to the plough'.

The popular song 'JOHN BARLEYCORN' describes the whole process of sowing, harrowing, reaping, threshing, and grinding the barley in terms of a series of tortures which its hero triumphantly endures, and which transform him either into beer or into strong malt liquor – the Barley Bree which gives its name to an Edinburgh pub. In either form, John Barleycorn can defeat any man.

There are pubs celebrating the reapers themselves by the name of Harvest Man or Harvester(s); Dunkling and Wright described the sign-board of the Harvesters at Stockwood near Bristol as one 'that says it all', since on one side it shows a band of traditional reapers wielding scythes, and on the other a modern combine harvester. Incidentally, the Crossed Scythes and the Man and Scythes at Sheffield do not refer to agriculture but to Sheffield's steel industry, which produced the best scythes. Once the corn was cut it would be bundled up into sheaves which were set upright in the field and left there for two or three weeks for the grain to dry out and ripen; it was said that the Sunday church bells should ring 'twice over wheat and three times over oats'. This stage is recalled in the names Barley Sheaf and Wheatsheaf, the latter being particularly wide-spread because a sheaf featured on the coat of arms of both the Brewers' and the Bakers' Companies. When the sheaves were ready, they were brought to the farm itself; the last cartload was brought in ceremonially, the cart being decorated and the reapers singing and cheering as they accompanied it in procession. The farmer would then treat them to a good meal. This celebration was known as the Harvest Home, and there are several pubs of that name. Finally the sheaves were built up into a stack; the BARLEY MOW at Oswestry and the Barley Stack at Brampton in Cumbria refer to this. Eventually the grain would be threshed and taken to the mill; the name Plough and Sail originally meant the sail of a windmill, though some sign-painters mistakenly show a sailing ship.

A fairly new addition to the repertoire of pub names is CORN DOLLY. This too refers to a harvest custom which was first recorded in the late sixteenth century. When the corn was almost entirely reaped, the last tuft was left uncut in the centre of the field, and plaited into an orna-mental shape; the reapers would then try to cut it down by throwing their sickles at it from a distance. This ornamental tuft was known as the corn dolly (or baby, maiden, old woman, hag, or mare); it would be kept at the farm for luck, usually for a year, sometimes until it fell to bits. These customs naturally became impossible once harvesting was done by machine. In the 1960s and '70s, however, making corn dollies became popular as a craft; some of the patterns were traditional, others too complicated ever to have been made in the field.

Man with a Load of Mischief

It is said that William Hogarth painted the original sign for a pub of this name in Oxford Street in London, now demolished, as a way of paying for his drink; it was much copied. The joke is a sexist one. The man carries on his shoulders his wife, who is drinking from a bottle, and is linked to him by the chains of matrimony; she in turn is holding a monkey and a magpie, symbols of mischief and incessant chatter. Below, a caption ran:

> A monkey, a magpie and a wife
> Is the true emblem of strife.

Nowadays, the message can be milder. Dunkling and Wright describe the signboard of one pub called the Load of Mischief, at Churchill near Axbridge in Somerset, as showing 'an attractive girl pushing a barrow-load of monkeys'.

March Hare

There are March Hare pubs in Nottingham, Biggleswade, Winchester, Worcester, and elsewhere, in allusion to the character in *Alice in Wonderland*, who was himself named from the proverbial comparison 'as mad as a March hare'. Hares do indeed behave wildly in March, their breeding season, when they chase one another round the fields and have 'boxing matches'. It used to be thought that this was the behaviour of males competing for females, but naturalists have now found that what is happening is that males are chasing females who fight them off, because they are not yet willing to mate.

The March Hare

Marrowbone & Cleaver

At Kirmington in Humberside the pub called the Marrowbone and Cleaver takes its name from a kind of crude musical instrument which butchers used to make for their own amusement. Hollow marrowbones of beef can be cut to different sizes so as to produce sounds of different pitch when struck with a cleaver, in a kind of parody of hand-bell ringing. Butchers used to 'play the bones' as a celebration at weddings, especially for one of their own number.

May Garland

This pub name (found in the village of Heathfield in East Sussex) refers to a widespread and long-lasting way of celebrating May Day. There were various types of 'garland', but all involved a display of spring flowers. One type was a wreath hung above one's door or in a church. Another was a portable display – sometimes a simple wreath fixed to a pole, sometimes a construction of greenery and flowers shaped like a bell, a pyramid, or a globe – which was carried from house to house by children, usually little girls, who would sing at people's doors in the hope of being given pennies. Originally, village children had done this in their own way, without adult involvement, but in the later part of the Victorian era teachers started organising more formal events for schoolchildren, giving prizes for the best garland, teaching maypole dancing, choosing a May queen, and so forth.

See also THE YEAR'S MERRY ROUND, p. 310

Maypole

Pubs called the Maypole or the Old Maypole can be found in Cambridge and Derby, at Wilford in Nottinghamshire, at North Mimms in Hertfordshire, at Sittingbourne in Kent, and elsewhere, for this is a universally understood symbol of traditional merrymaking. In Tudor and Elizabethan England it was the custom to cut down a tall, slender tree in preparation for May Day, lop off its branches, paint it in bright colours, decorate it with flower garlands, greenery, flags, and ribbons, and erect it somewhere where it could be the focal point of the celebrations. Some places kept their maypole all year round, but it would need replacing from time to time, as the base rotted in the wet earth. People would dance round it on May Day and other occasions too – but they did not plait ribbons as they went, for that particular form of dancing, now so well known, was only invented in the 1830s. Originating in stage performances, ribbon-dancing was soon adopted by enthusiastic schoolteachers and organisers of fêtes, and by now can be regarded as a tradition in its own right.

See also THE YEAR'S MERRY ROUND, p. 310

Merlin's Cave

The famous wizard of Arthurian legend has a Merlin Hotel named after him at Pontypridd in Glamorgan, and pubs in Leeds, at Swindon in Wiltshire, and at Andover in Hampshire, plus a Merlin's Cave at Chalfont St Giles (Buckinghamshire). This last has the fullest story, for it presumably alludes to the sad tale of Merlin's doom, as told in various medieval romances up to and including Thomas Malory's *Morte D'Arthur*. Despite his age and great wisdom, Malory tells us, he 'fell in dotage upon one of the damsels of the Lady of the Lake, that hight [was called] Nyneve' (or, in other sources, Nimue or Vivien). He was so besotted with her that he would never let her out of his sight, but she made him swear that he would never use any enchantment on her, to get her to sleep with him. Then she took advantage of his infatuation to persuade him to teach her his most secret spells. At last, having learnt all she could and being very weary of him, she found a way to be rid of him:

> And so on a time Merlin did show her a rock whereat was a great wonder and wrought by enchantment that went under a great stone. So by her subtle working she made Merlin to go under that stone to let her know of the marvels there, but she wrought so there for him that he came never out, for all the craft he could do. And so she departed and left Merlin.

Malory sets this story somewhere in Cornwall, but does not link it to any precise locality. However, the Elizabethan poet Edmund Spenser in Book III of his *Faerie Queene* draws upon a Welsh local legend which talked of a Merlin's Cave under Merlin's Hill, about 2½ miles north of Carmarthen in Wales, describing it as a 'dreadful place', a 'hideous hollow cave':

> There the wise Merlin whylome wont (they say)
> To make his home low underneath the ground,
> In a deepe delve, far from the view of day,
> That of no living wight he mote be found,
> When so he counsel'd with his sprites encompast round.

Spenser warns his readers not to go inside:

> But dare thou not, I charge, in any case
> To enter into that same balefull Bower,
> For fear the cruell Feendes should thee unwares devowre.

Instead, anyone who puts his ear to the ground will hear the 'ghastly noise' of iron chains and brazen cauldrons rumbling far below, and horrible groans, because a gang of demons is still at work down there, trying to build a wall of brass to surround Carmarthen; Merlin set them this task shortly before he was made captive by the spells of the Lady of the Lake, and never returned to release them. Modern local lore says that Merlin himself lies in the cave (which is completely hidden from human view), imprisoned there by the lady, and that it is his groans which can be heard.

There is another Merlin's Cave at Tintagel in Cornwall, a long tunnel piercing the rocky cliffs of the headland, which can only be seen or entered at low tide, for at high tide the sea fills it. Like other Arthurian place names in this area, it was probably inspired by the popularity of Arthurian tales in the late Victorian period, and the implication appears to be that it was there that Merlin lived and performed his magic, rather than that he was buried or imprisoned in it by enchantment.

In his *London Signs* (1972), Bryant Lillywhite suggests another explanation: that the pub name may have been inspired by a picturesque grotto adorned with magical and astrological symbols and containing a waxwork figure of Merlin, which had been constructed in 1735 in the royal gardens at Richmond, at the queen's request. Antony Clayton's *The Folklore of London* (2008) tells of a New Merlin's Cave in Margery Street, London WC1 (demolished in 1996) which had existed since about 1730 alongside pleasure gardens and a skittle ground. Both these examples suggest that the eighteenth century took a relaxed and light-hearted view of Merlin's 'magic'.

Mermaid

This is one of the oldest secular pub names on record, generally found in seaports such as Portland in Dorset and Rye in East Sussex. There was an alehouse called the Mermaid at Rye in 1300, which may have begun as early as 1156, and is certainly the direct forerunner of the Tudor inn built on the same site and still extant. There is no story to explain the name, but it must be related to Rye's status as a major port in the Middle Ages. London too is a port, and there was a famous Mermaid Tavern in Cheapside, supposedly a favourite haunt of Shakespeare and other Elizabethan poets; it was burnt down in the Great Fire of 1666.

Mermaids are ambiguous figures in seamen's lore. On the one hand, they were believed to bring storms and cause shipwrecks, and so were feared. On the other hand, they were regarded as sexy; they were often shown carrying a comb and a mirror, which were standard attributes of the Whore of Babylon in

religious art; twin-tailed mermaids would be represented holding an up-turned tail in each hand in a pose of sexual display.
Probably the explanation is that medieval moralists took the
mermaid, like her Classical Greek forerunner the siren, as a
symbol for sensual pleasures which lure men to sin and damna-
tion, such as drink and sex. In fact, some religious writers said
bluntly that 'mermaid' was a symbol for 'prostitute'. In view of
this, one may wonder whether some Mermaid pubs offered a
service which would be much appreciated by seamen.

The Mermaid Inn on Blackshaw Moor near Leek in
Staffordshire takes its name from a small pool about a mile
away, the Mermaid Pool, which had an eerie reputation in the
eighteenth and nineteenth centuries. It was reputed to be bot-
tomless, and to be the home of an evil mermaid who would rise
to the surface at midnight and seize any passer-by and drown
him. A Victorian landowner had once planned to drain the
pool; he hired workmen to dig a drainage ditch, but the mermaid appeared and threatened that she would send the water to
flood Leek and all the countryside around, so they immediately
abandoned the work. Some people said this mermaid had once
been a human girl; a man named Joshua Linnet had courted
her, and when she rejected him he took his revenge by accusing
her of witchcraft, whereupon she drowned herself in the pool. A
few days later, as he was passing the pool, she reached out and
dragged him in; his drowned corpse was later recovered, with
deep scratches on the face.

Dunkling and Wright note in their *Pub Names of Britain* (rev.
edn) that a pub named the Tinners Arms at Zennor in Cornwall
has a mermaid on its signboard; an earlier sign showing a tin
miner had been stolen. A mermaid was chosen because of a
romantic local legend. This tells of a handsome young tinner

named Matthew Trewhella, who had a very fine voice and sang in Zennor church choir. From time to time, people noticed a beautiful woman who would appear in the church and listen intently to the music, though nobody knew who she was; nor could they see where she

The Mermaid

went after the service ended. She often seemed to be watching Matthew, and he was watching her. And one Sunday he followed her when she left; he was seen heading for the shore, but after that he was never seen again, and neither was the mysterious woman. However, some time later a ship's captain reported seeing a mermaid out in the cove, so the people of Zennor reckoned that she was the one who had lured Matthew away.

Finally, Dunkling and Wright list the Mytton and Mermaid at Atcham near Shrewsbury. Sir John Mytton, they explain, was a local squire who died in 1834, famous as a huntsman and also for frequently 'hunting' the 'mere maids' of the village. On one side, the signboard shows him mounted and holding a tankard of ale, 'and a miniature mermaid is seen emerging from the froth'; on the other, a mermaid sits combing her hair, but her mirror shows the reflection of Sir John 'wearing hunting rig and a lecherous grin'.

Midas Touch

One must admire the wit of whoever decided to name a pub in London's Golden Square the Midas Touch. According to

Classical Greek legend, Midas was a fabulously rich king, and a worshipper of the wine-god Dionysus. One day Silenus, oldest and most drunken of the satyrs who followed Dionysus, was found fast asleep in the rose gardens of the king's palace. The gardeners brought him as a captive to Midas, who, far from being angry with the intruder, feasted him for five days. When Dionysus heard of this, he sent a message to King Midas offering him whatever reward he might wish, in return for his kindness. 'Then grant that whatever I touch will turn to gold,' said Midas. And so it was. The furniture, the walls and pillars, the flowers in the garden, all turned to gold as soon as Midas touched them. Unfortunately for him, so did any piece of food or drop of liquid which touched his lips. Within a few hours the king was desperate with hunger and thirst, and had to beg the god to withdraw his gift. Dionysus laughed, and told him to go and wash it off in the river Pactolus. And from that day to this, the sands of that river shine like gold.

Nowadays, when we say someone 'has the Midas touch' we mean that he makes money easily out of any enterprise, and that this is a fine thing. But the Greeks told the story of Midas as a warning.

Miller of Mansfield

See SIR JOHN COCKLE

Minerva

The Minerva pub in Plymouth is a good instance of the use of mythology at second hand. Its first owner was a retired sea captain who named it after the last ship he had commanded, but the ship itself was obviously named after the Roman goddess of wisdom and of the women's crafts of spinning and weaving. The mythology was not in fact forgotten when the pub was designed; Dunkling and Wright record that 'There is a stained-glass window showing this goddess at the front of the pub, and a statuette of her behind the bar.'

Molly Malone

This name, given to pubs in Glasgow and in Hitchin in Hertfordshire, is taken from a traditional Irish song about a pretty Dublin girl who sold shellfish from a barrow, as her father and mother had done before her. She came to a sad end:

> She died of a fever,
> And nothing could save her,
> And that was the end of sweet Molly Malone;
> But her ghost wheels a barrow
> Through streets broad and narrow,
> Crying 'Cockles and mussels! Alive, alive-o!'
>   'Alive, alive-o-o! Alive, alive-o-o!'
>   Crying 'Cockles and mussels! Alive, alive-o!'

Moonrakers

This name refers to a traditional anecdote mocking an allegedly stupid act by men from a particular village – most famously, those of Bishop's Cannings in Wiltshire, but also of Gotham in Nottinghamshire and Piddinghoe in Sussex. It is found not only at Swindon and Pewsey in Wiltshire, where its local relevance is obvious, but also in places far from any of the villages concerned; in the latter, it is sometimes given a modern reinterpretation as an allusion to the James Bond film.

The original Moonraker joke belongs to a widespread type, and in its simplest form may well go back to medieval times. It was briefly mentioned by the lexicographer Francis Grose in 1787: 'Some Wiltshire rusticks, as the story goes, seeing the figure of the moon in a pond, attempted to rake it out.' Later versions recorded by various Wiltshire writers give more detail. They say some men riding past at night noticed the country-men poking about in the pond with long-handled hay rakes, and asked what they were doing. One replied, pointing at the reflection of the full moon, 'Why, we be a-raking for thicky gurt big cheese wot be fallen in our pond.' The riders burst out laughing at such a pack of fools, and went on their way. Little did they know that the men from Bishop's Cannings had made fools of them, since what they had really been doing was raking up some barrels of smuggled brandy which they had earlier hidden from the revenue men by sinking them underwater. This of course reverses the whole meaning of the joke; it now goes to show that Wiltshire men, far from being fools, are unusually cunning.

See also HIGHWAYMEN & SMUGGLERS, p. 208

Morris Dancers

Pubs of this name can be found at Castleton in Derbyshire, and at Scarisbrick, Ormskirk, and Bolton (all three in Lancashire). There is also a Morris Clown at Bampton near Oxford, so called because in that village the team of dancers always includes one taking the role of Fool. Indeed, considering the

popularity of Morris dancing in the twentieth cen-
tury, and the fact that the
dancers so often choose the
courtyards of pubs as the
venue for their perform-
ances, it is surprising that
similar names are not more
common.

The Morris Dancers

Morris dancing is the
major form of folk dancing in England. Its history can be traced
back to the later fifteenth century, and there are many references to it in the sixteenth and seventeenth. It nearly died out
in the nineteenth century, but was rediscovered by Cecil Sharp
in 1899; thanks to his enthusiasm in recording and publicising
it, a vigorous revival began shortly before the First World War,
and still continues. There are several regional styles. The best
known is the Cotswold Morris, where six-man teams dance
in one spot, facing each other in two lines of three, clashing
sticks in time to the music, or waving large handkerchiefs. In
Lancashire, however, the teams are larger and their dances are
designed to be used in processions, e.g. when escorting a rushcart.

See also THE YEAR'S MERRY ROUND, p. 310

Mother Blackcap

In the eighteenth century there was an inn of this name in the
rural area to the north of London which later became Camden
Town, very near the better known MOTHER REDCAP. It is mentioned in evidence at the trial of a man called Edward Phipps

for theft, at the Old Bailey in 1774; the victim said in evidence: 'I have lodgings in the country, between Mother-Red-Cap's and Mother-Black-Cap's.' It is not clear whether the latter is the same establishment as the Mother Black Cap inn in the Hampstead Road referred to in *The Times* in 1793, and/or the Mother Black Cap in Camden High Street where an inquest was held in 1844, in a building still extant. At some time during the nineteenth century the name was simplified to the Black Cap, which it still bears, and which some people believe to be a reference to the black cap formerly put on by judges when pronouncing a sentence of death.

There is no evidence as to what the original story behind the name Mother Blackcap may have been; perhaps it was nothing more than a reference to some landlady's normal way of dressing. However, inside the present-day Black Cap there is a decorative ceramic tile, in a late-nineteenth-century style, which does imply that a tale of some sort was current at that period. It shows an angry witch, wearing the conventional pointed black hat, cursing a group of three drunken men inside the inn; through a window can be seen a distant gallows, bearing a hanged man. Maybe the story was that they laughed at her for her hat, and that she retorted that before long they would see a judge put on his black cap and send them to the gallows.

In 1987, a successful film entitled *Withnail and I* included several scenes shot at a pub in Notting Hill which, for the purposes of the film, was given the name Mother Black Cap and was supposedly sited in Camden Town. It is not known whether the script writers knew about the old name of the inn, or whether they accidentally re-created it by blending its modern name with that of the Mother Redcap. But as a result of the film's popularity, the Notting Hill pub has discarded its own name and has become the Mother Black Cap.

Mother Hubbard

At Loughton in Essex and at Doncaster in Yorkshire there are pubs called Mother Hubbard. The name is taken from a fourteen-verse poem by Sarah Catherine Martin published in 1805, 'The Comic Adventures of Old Mother Hubbard and her Dog', probably modelled on an older anonymous version which had only three verses. It immediately became extremely popular, and was constantly reprinted; the opening lines are still familiar as a nursery rhyme:

> Old Mother Hubbard
> Went to the cupboard
> To fetch her poor dog a bone;
> But when she got there
> The cupboard was bare
> And so the poor dog had none.
>
> She went to the baker's
> To buy him some bread
> But when she came back
> The poor dog was dead.

Fortunately, as later verses show, the dog is not dead at all, but merrily engaged in various nonsensical activities – smoking a pipe, standing on his head, and so forth. Finally:

The dame made a curtsey,
The dog made a bow
The dame said, 'Your servant',
The dog said, 'Bow-wow'.

See also MOTHER GEESE & CATS WITH FIDDLES, p. 46

Mother Huff Cap

There is a pub of this name at Great Alne in Warwickshire. Dictionaries give 'huffcap' as an old name for strong ale, dating from Elizabethan times, but do not commit themselves as to what exactly it implies. One possibility could be that it made drinkers quarrelsome (cf. 'huffing and puffing', being 'in a huff'). Another is that the ale had a particularly frothy head, that this was called its 'cap', and that blowing this off was called 'huffing' it. Neither theory has been actually proved, but one scrap of evidence in favour of the first one is that in the Vale of Evesham (Worcestershire) 'huffcap' was the name of a type of perry, a drink made from pears which though often strong does not produce a head of froth. However, the pub sign at Great Alne has opted for the second; it shows a buxom barmaid holding out a foaming tankard.

Mother Redcap

Currently, there are several pubs of this name, including one at Sheffield and an Old Mother Redcap at Blackburn. It was also the older name of a famous coaching inn in Camden High Street, London, which was renamed the World's End in 1985, though the old sign is still on display in the bar. There is another

Mother Redcap in London's Holloway Road; according to some editors of Samuel Pepys's *Diary*, this is the unnamed hostelry to which he refers in his entry for 24 September 1661: 'So we rode easily through and only drinking at Halloway [Holloway] at the sign of a woman with cakes in one hand and a pot of ale in the other, which did give good occasion of mirth, resembling her to the maid that served us.'

As a nickname for a living person, 'Mother Redcap' has been known since the sixteenth century, with various implications, none of them respectable. There was, for example, a jestbook entered in the Stationers' Register in 1595 entitled *Mother Redcap her Last Will and Testament, containing sundry Conceited and Pleasant Tales Furnished with Much Variety to Move Delight*. If, as is likely, these were dirty jokes, 'mother' may imply 'bawd'. There is also evidence from the seventeenth century that 'Mother Redcap' was a general nickname for an 'ale-wife', i.e. a woman running an inn, which would match Pepys's description of the sign. By the middle of the nineteenth century it had become a popular humorous name for a witch. At Sadler's Wells in 1857, in the pantomime *Harlequin and Beauty & the Beast*, the first scene showed Mother Bunch, Mother Goose, Mother Redcap and Mother Hubbard, with brooms, stirring a huge cauldron. The same nickname is given in local folklore to a witch who is supposed to have lived on Wallsea Island in Essex.

Local tradition in Camden Town maintains that the inn was so called because it was built on the site of a cottage where a witch called 'Mother Damnable' (aka 'The Shrew of Kentish Town') had lived in the seventeenth century, and that 'Mother Redcap' was an alternative name for the same woman. However, it is likely that these were originally two different people (both probably fictional). To add to the difficulties, there is a record of a Mother Damnable inn in Camden in 1704, which apparently refers to the same building. According to an old pamphlet quoted in Samuel Palmer's *History of St Pancras* (1870), the woman's real name was Jennie Bingham, and she had a bad reputation. Her parents had been accused of witchcraft, and she herself was believed to have murdered two out of the four men she lived with at various times in her life. She was strikingly ugly, kept a huge black cat, and always wore her red bonnet and a grey shawl 'with black patches which looked at a distance like flying bats'. The pamphlet says that many people went to her to have their fortune told and their diseases healed, which would imply that she was regarded as a Wise Woman rather than a witch. On the other hand, it also says that she got the blame when any misfortune occurred, and mobs would hoot at her. When she was dying crowds gathered at her cottage, expecting to see the Devil come to fetch her.

According to some guidebooks, there was a second Mother Red Cap at a later date, who was simply the hostess of the inn and brewed remarkably good ale. In the nineteenth century the inn had a placard which boasted:

> Old Mother Redcap, according to her tale,
> Lived twenty and a hundred years by drinking this good ale!
> It was her meat, it was her drink, and medicine beside,
> And if she still had drunk this ale, she never would have died.

This rhyme was used elsewhere too, e.g. at Luton.

In the aftermath of the French Revolution, when red caps took on a whole new meaning, the name was sometimes given a political twist. There is a cartoon by George Cruikshank, dated 1821, entitled 'The Mother Red Cap Public House in opposition to the King's Head'. Both establishments display placards. The King's Head declares itself to be 'the original house of call for loyalists', and is serving a few quiet respectable people; there is a church nearby. But the Mother Red Cap, which calls itself a 'radical house of call', is besieged by a rowdy drunken mob. The sign shows a fat raddled woman wearing a ruff and a pointy hat, not, as one might expect, the Republican Cap of Liberty. Cruikshank must have wanted to include an allusion to the alleged witch in his political satire.

Mother Shipton

There are, or have been, pubs of this name in many parts of England, for the prophecies of Mother Shipton were at one time as well known in popular culture as those of Nostradamus. Regrettably, a fine London example, on the corner of Prince of Wales Road and Malden Road, NW5, had its name altered in the 1980s. The most famous, however, still exists; it is the one at Knaresborough in Yorkshire, where the original sign (painted on copper, and said to date from the eighteenth century) showed her as a round-shouldered old peasant woman, leaning on a broom, and accompanied by a cat; it bore a couplet:

> Near this Petrifying Well
> I first drew breath as records Tell.

The well mentioned here is Knaresborough's other great attraction, a spring of water with such high mineral content that articles left in it will eventually turn to stone. The village has long claimed that Mother Shipton was born there in 1488; this claim is based on Richard Head's pamphlet *The Life and Death of Mother Shipton* (1667). However, there is no trace of her in the parish records, and the first text to mention her (*The Prophesie of Mother Shipton*, 1641) implies that she lived in York, in the reign of Henry VIII. It is in any case very doubtful whether she ever really existed.

In the early accounts, her most famous prophecy concerned Cardinal Wolsey. Hearing that he meant to visit York, she remarked that he would never reach the city; furious, he sent disguised noblemen to question her, but she knew at once who they were, and repeated that although the cardinal might indeed see York, he would never enter it. 'He will,' replied one of the nobles, 'and when he does you will be burnt as a witch.' Not long afterwards Wolsey, on his way to York, halted for the night at a mansion in Cawood, some eight miles away; that very night he was arrested and taken away on the orders of Henry VIII, without ever setting foot in York itself.

Her fame was so great that later generations believed she had foretold the calamities of their own times, such as the Civil War and the Great Fire of London. Indeed, an eyewitness to the latter disaster reported that many superstitious Londoners refused to join in fire-fighting efforts, declaring that the total destruction of the city was certain, since Mother Shipton had foreseen it. Instead, they 'folded their arms and looked on', or took to looting.

Then in 1862 a hack writer named Charles Hindley produced a daring hoax: a booklet entitled *The Life, Prophecies and Death of the Famous Mother Shipton*, which reprinted material from the old pamphlets, but added ninety-four lines of rhyming 'prophecies' which are simply his own invention. They contain clear allusions to such Victorian discoveries and events as steam power, telegraphy, railways, ballooning, the Crystal Palace, the

Crimean War, the Gold Rush, and 'horseless carriages', by which Hindley meant trains, though modern interpreters claim they are cars. Finally, Doomsday was dramatically announced:

> The world then to an end shall come
> In eighteen hundred and eighty-one.

This date may have been chosen because its figures remain the same whether it is read forwards or backwards or upside down, like numbers in a magic square. In 1872 Hindley, challenged by a contributor to *Notes and Queries*, confessed that the lines were his own invention. Even so, when the fatal year of 1881 arrived there was panic in some rural areas, with people leaving their houses and spending nights on end in churches or in the open fields, praying. There was even one London child who died of a fit which, her parents told the inquest, had been brought on by her hysterical terror that the world was about to end.

Mother Shipton is still a tourist attraction at Knaresborough, where pamphlets about her are available, and include Hindley's verses as if they were genuine. During most of the twentieth century the Doomsday prediction appeared, but altered to read 'In nineteen hundred and ninety-one' – a date which can at least be read back to front, though not upside down. It has now been dropped.

✺ N ✺

Nag's Head

There are many pubs of this name. If the sign simply shows a horse's head, this is of no significance for folklore, and may have originally been meant to indicate that the innkeeper also kept horses for hire. There was a time, however, when it would have been seen as an opportunity for a sexist joke against women who nag their husbands, and a few instances of this interpretation remain. At Martock in Somerset the sign shows an ugly, bad-tempered woman, while at St Leonard's in East Sussex it bears

The Nag's Head

the image of a woman who is silenced by wearing a 'scold's bridle', a kind of metal gag pressing painfully on the lips and tongue, which was a traditional punishment for quarrelsome women, especially those who turned their bad temper against their husbands. Paul Corballis in his *Pub Signs* (1988) shows an example of this image from one of a set of miniature signs issued by the Whitbread brewery as advertisements in the 1930s.

Nell Gwynne

Nell Gwynne, the best remembered and most popular of Charles II's mistresses, who died in 1687, is commemorated in the names of pubs in Hereford, at Arnold (near Nottingham) and elsewhere; she is often represented on the signboard with a basket of oranges, since she worked as an orange-seller in Drury Lane Theatre as a teenage girl, before becoming an actress and a noted beauty. There is one traditional anecdote about her which is more legend than truth, namely that it was at her suggestion that the king founded the Royal Hospital in Chelsea for old soldiers. It is said that one day a crippled and destitute ex-soldier came up to her carriage begging for alms, and she was so grieved to see a man who had fought for his country in such a plight that she persuaded the king to make permanent provision for all such men. The story was current some hundred years or so after her death, for it is mentioned in David Lysons's *Environs of London* (1795), with the additional detail that there was a pub called the Nell Gwynne in the Pimlico Road (not far from the Royal Hospital), with her portrait on the sign and an inscription giving the story. Currently two London pubs are named after her: the Nell Gwynne Tavern in Bull Inn Court, WC2, and Nell of Old Drury in Catherine Street, just opposite the theatre where she once worked.

Nevison's Leap

The Nevison's Leap pub at Pontefract in Yorkshire commemorates a certain John (or possibly William) Nevison, who was born in that town in 1640, moved to London in his twenties, became a highwayman, ran protection rackets, and was eventually hanged at York in 1684. His claim to fame rests on a story told by Daniel Defoe in his *Tour through the Whole Island of Great Britain* (1724–6), but since this was written fifty years after the event the tale may have grown considerably in the telling. In 1676 he robbed a man on the open road at Gad's Hill in Kent, at four in the morning, and immediately rode his mare to Gravesend and took the ferry over to the Essex shore. He then rode across country to Chelmsford, where he stopped half an hour to refresh his horse; then on through Cambridge to Huntingdon, where he took an hour's sleep.

> Then holding on to the North Road and keeping a full larger gallop most of the way, he came to York the same afternoon, put off his boots and riding clothes, and went dressed as if he had been an inhabitant of the place, not a traveller, to the bowling green, where among other gentlemen was the Lord Mayor of the city. He singling out his lordship studied to do something particular that the Mayor would remember him by, and accordingly lays some odd bet ... and then takes occasion to ask his lordship what o'clock it was; who, pulling out his watch, told him the hour, which was a quarter before, or a quarter after, eight at night.

The result was that when he was charged with the robbery he could produce the Lord Mayor himself and other respectable witnesses to swear he was playing bowls in York on the very day of the crime, and since the jury accepted that it was impossible to be in two places so far apart in one day, he was acquitted. After which, knowing he could not be tried twice for the same crime, he boasted freely of his alibi; Charles II sent for him to hear his tale, and when Nevison said he had ridden so fast that even Old Nick (the Devil) could do no better, the king called him 'Swift Nick', and the name stuck.

It was obviously this anecdote which inspired the novelist Harrison Ainsworth in 1834 to invent Dick Turpin's amazing ride to York, and the feat is now invariably credited to Turpin. A curious result of the confusion can be seen on p. 59 of the 1951 *English Inn Signs*, the revised version of Larwood and Hotten's classic *A History of Signboards*. This shows a double-sided signboard at Gad's Hill, undated, but clearly modern; on one side, a highwayman is robbing travellers, while on the other he is playing bowls – but, alas, the pub in question is called the Dick Turpin. It is good that Nevison is at least remembered correctly in his own Yorkshire birthplace.

See also HIGHWAYMEN & SMUGGLERS, p. 208

Nine Maidens

The Nine Maidens pub in Dundee commemorates a local legend of death, heroism and dragon-slaying which purports to explain the names of various smaller places a few miles from the city, and which goes back to the eighteenth century, if not earlier. The starting point was a well at Pittempton (no longer extant), called the Nine Maidens' Well. It was said that there was a man at Pittempton who had nine daughters, and one Sunday evening he told the eldest to go and draw water. She did not return, so he sent the next, then the next, and the next,

Highwaymen & Smugglers

Crime becomes thrillingly romantic once it is safely distanced in the historic past – the further back, the better. Robin Hood is now universally seen as a merry hero who 'robbed the rich to give to the poor', even though only one among the thirty or so old ballads celebrating him says that he 'did poor men much good'. He and his companions have many pubs named in their honour, and nobody now recalls the hostile attitude of some older references (see THREE NUNS).

Similarly, in their own time highwaymen must have been feared and loathed by many of their potential victims, even if they were also admired by some for their reckless courage when facing death. This ambiguity was already humorously exploited in John Gay's *The Beggar's Opera* (1728), but the major turning point was Harrison Ainsworth's novel *Rookwood* (1834); ever since then, they have been represented as glamorous, witty, brave, gallant towards ladies, loyal to their comrades, and so forth. There are several pubs named after DICK TURPIN, by far the most famous of them, and even more pubs that claim that he used to drink there, or hid there, or stabled his horse there. Swift Nick Nevison, original hero of the amazing ride to York, is also commemorated in a pub (see NEVISON'S LEAP), as are SIXTEEN-STRING JACK, and the WICKED LADY, Kathleen Ferrers, a highway*woman*.

Smugglers, like highwaymen, are usually seen in folklore as lovable rogues rather than the violent men they often were; unlike highwaymen, however, they are not generally remembered as individuals but as anonymous groups, or members of a named gang. As such they feature in the stories of many pubs (both in coastal areas and along the routes to London) where it is said that they would meet to plan their work, and would hide their contraband (or themselves) in cellars and secret rooms, behind huge fireplaces, or in underground tunnels leading to the sea or to some other building. Such traditions may very well have a good deal of truth in them. It is more doubtful whether certain villages were ever as thoroughly honeycombed with smugglers' tunnels, many of them linked to pubs, as their local lore asserts. There are also a few more elaborate smuggling legends, e.g. the humorous explanation for the MOONRAKERS, and one version of the gruesome BUCKET OF BLOOD. Related names include Smugglers' Barn, Smugglers' Den, Smugglers' Haunt, Smugglers' Roost, and (at Anstruther in Fife) just plain Smugglers.

The evil innkeeper is a recurrent figure in folklore, reflecting the understandable fears of travellers in past centuries. It was said, for instance, that highwaymen would gather at the isolated Windwhistle Inn in Somerset, tethering their horses to rings which can still be seen attached to an outer wall. Worse still, the landlord was a murderer; any traveller who arrived there alone would be lured into the cellar, robbed, and have his throat cut. The corpse would then be secretly buried or thrown down a well; according to rumour, one might see the landlord riding off by night, with a sinister bundle slung across his horse. One explanation for the QUIET WOMAN pub name involves a wicked landlady who used to murder solitary travellers, and was beheaded for her crimes; even more wicked was the landlord of the OSTRICH at Colnbrook. In his *Byways in Berkshire and the Cotswolds* (1920), P. H. Ditchfield tells how in the 1880s two skeletons were found under the roots of blown-down trees behind an inn at Blewbury, and local folk remembered it had once been kept by 'a surly ruffian [who] was suspected of robbing and killing his guests', though no bodies were ever found; he was curiously fond of planting trees in his paddock. In these two cases the names of the pubs do not draw upon the legend, but elsewhere they do, stressing by their choice of name and/or signboard that the criminal paid the just price for his deed (see CANNARD'S GRAVE, TUCKER'S GRAVE, and JACOB'S POST).

Bloodthirsty tales are now often exploited as semi-humorous attractions. Consequently, there are now pubs celebrating such notorious figures as the London barber Sweeney Todd (see SWEENEY & TODD)and the Scottish cannibal Sawney Bean (see SAWNEY BEAN'S HOWFF), both of whom are almost certainly fictional, however much the tourist industry may deny it; there is even one named after the all too real serial killer Jack the Ripper, in Whitechapel in London's East End.

till all nine had gone to fetch water, and not one had returned. A dragon had killed and eaten them all. A youth named Martin, who had loved one of the sisters, went to Pit*tempt*on and at*tempt*ed to kill the monster with his club, but only wounded it, and it *drag*ged itself to Bal*dragon*. Martin pursued, and struck it again at *Strikemartin* (now called Strathmartin); he finally killed it at *Martinstane*. These puns are enshrined in a jingle supposedly spoken by the dying dragon:

> I was tempit at Pittenpton,
> Draglit at Baldragon,
> Stricken at Strikemartin.
> And killed at Martinstane.

Nobody Inn

See PUNS & OLD JOKES, p. 138

Nog Inn

There is a Nog Inn at Wincanton and another at Honiton in Devon. Whoever first named them was no doubt intending a pun either upon 'nog', a type of strong beer, or 'noggin', a small measure of liquor. At Wincanton, however, the current sign-board has Irish lettering, and the image of an elf or leprechaun. This suggests that a more recent landlord has linked the name to the Irish myth of Tir na nÓg, 'The Land of the Ever-Young'. This is a blissful and beautiful Otherworld, which is said in some tales to be an island out in the western ocean, and in others to be an underground kingdom in Ireland itself, whose secret entrance is through one or other of its prehistoric burial mounds. It is the home of elves and ancient gods, where there is an unending supply of delicious food and drink. It is occasionally visited by favoured humans.

See also PUNS & OLD JOKES, p. 138

Noose & Monkey

It is only in recent years that a pub in Aberdeen has acquired this striking name, replacing the equally curious My Father's Moustache. It is the choice of a new landlord, who hails from Hartlepool in County Durham. He obviously was struck by the coincidence that the same anecdote is told as a joke about the men of Boddam, a coastal village near Aberdeen, and about those of Hartlepool. It is impossible to decide to which place it 'really' belongs. The Boddam version belongs to local oral tradition, which in some families is said to go back to the latter part of the nineteenth century. It tells how a ship called the *Anna* was wrecked just off Boddam in 1772 (though there is no evidence to confirm this); the crew were drowned, or abandoned ship, but a monkey remained on board. In Scottish law, an abandoned ship with livestock still on board is not deemed to be a wreck, and so cannot be claimed as salvage. Therefore, to make sure of their booty, the boarding party of local men hanged the monkey. Some versions add that they ate it. There is now a folksong, first printed in 1965, beginning:

> A ship went out along the coast
> And all the men on board were lost,
> Except the monkey, who climbed the mast,
> So the Boddamers hanged the monkey-O!

The Hartlepool version appears to have originated in the 1850s as a song by a professional comedian named Ned Corvan, with the refrain, 'The fishermen hanged the monkey-o'. Here, the motive is different. It is said that the wreck was that of a French ship during the Napoleonic wars, the only survivor being a pet monkey dressed in sailor's clothes. The men of Hartlepool, thinking all Frenchmen were small and skinny, decided that this was a French spy, and hanged it.

Nowhere

See PUNS & OLD JOKES, p. 138

Nutshell

This tiny one-room pub in Bury St Edmunds (Suffolk) holds the record as the smallest in Britain. From a folklore point of view, it is interesting to note the dried-out bodies of three or four cats fixed to the ceiling. It is not unusual to find 'mummified' cats hidden away in hollow walls or among roofing timbers of old houses, of any period from medieval times to the eighteenth century, when these are being repaired or demolished. They were put there deliberately, and a few had been arranged in hunting postures and accompanied by a dead rat or bird. In such cases the purpose is obvious – the dead cat would protect its home from vermin – and it is sometimes said that those found in the roof or near a chimney would be a protection against fire. More commonly, it was simply felt that they were 'lucky', and that if one was discovered it would bring bad luck to remove it. The cats displayed at the Nutshell may have been found in that building itself, or brought from other old houses of the town; there are others in the Moyses Hall Museum.

Oak

See GOSPEL OAK, HERNE'S OAK, *or* ROYAL OAK

Old Father Thames

Overlooking the river Thames at a site in London SE11 stands a pub aptly named the Old Father Thames. The idea of a male god as the personification of a major river was common in Classical Rome and Greece; he would be conventionally represented in art as a mature, bearded figure, reclining, and holding a jar from which the waters of his river unceasingly flowed. There is a statue representing the Thames in this way at St John's Lock, near Lechlade in Gloucestershire, where the rivers Leach and Thames meet. Englishmen would be quite familiar with such river-gods from their reading of classical authors; in the eighteenth century the poet Thomas Gray referred to 'Father Thames', and Alexander Pope to 'Old Father Thames'.

Old Harry

The Old Harry pub at Poole in Dorset was named after one of a pair of tall rocks which once stood in the sea near the entrance to the harbour and were known as Old Harry and His Wife. Such names imply a legend claiming that they had once been living beings – almost certainly giants – who had been turned to stone.

Old Man & Scythe

As far back as Ancient Greece, a thin old man carrying a scythe and an hour-glass was the conventional way to represent Old Father Time; the image probably arose from a confusion between Greek *chronos*, meaning 'time', and Cronus, the name of the god of agriculture, whose emblem was a scythe or a sickle. It was, and still is, familiar in art.

At Bolton in Lancashire, however, the fine old inn called the Old Man and Scythe, which once had this picture on its sign,

The Old Man & Scythe

later changed it to that of a fool swinging a scythe. Perhaps the original associations with time, old age, and eventual death were felt to be too grim. The more recent sign refers to an anecdote about Sir William Trafford, a rich local landowner who supported the Royalists in the Civil War of the seventeenth century. Hearing that Cromwell's victorious troops were coming to search his house for treasure, he hid as much of it as he could under a huge pile of straw, disguised himself as a labourer, and capered about, slashing at the empty air with a scythe. Cromwell's men assumed that he was the village idiot, and left him in peace while they searched the house, where of course they found nothing.

Stories of seemingly half-witted actions which are in fact part of a cunning plan are more commonly told of village communities than of an individual.

Old Nick

It may seem odd to name a pub after the Devil, but this was what happened at Wootton Bassett in Wiltshire, for 'Old Nick' has been a humorous term for Satan since the seventeenth century. Why this should be so is unknown. It may simply be the common human nickname for anybody called Nicholas, but there is also a possibility that it is related to a word found in several Germanic languages for supernatural beings of various types – the Scandinavian *Neck* or *Nökk*, for example, who was believed to be a male water-demon inhabiting rivers and waterfalls, who might sometimes drown people; the *Nykur*, an Icelandic water-horse which was definitely malevolent; or the German *Nickel*, a mischievous goblin found in mines.

Old Nun's Head

The pub of this name is at Nunhead Green, London SE15. The story told to explain it is a fine example of the way tales are invented to 'explain' a name, and the name is then cited as 'proof' of the tale. It is claimed that the pub was built on the site of a convent which was suppressed at the Reformation, with the Mother Superior allegedly being beheaded. It is hardly necessary to say that there is no historical record of any such execution.

Old Tup

For the explanation of this pub name at Gamesley in Derbyshire, see DERBY TUP.

Ostrich

This pub at Colnbrook in Buckinghamshire dates from around 1500, and is on the site of a medieval hospice. Its unusual name is sometimes said to be a corruption of 'hospice', but might be a humorous allusion to the bird's traditional reputation of being able to swallow anything; it might also have a heraldic origin, since ostrich feathers are found on some coats of arms. Be that as it may, the inn became famous as the scene of a crime. According to *The Pleasant Historie of Thomas of Reading* by Thomas Deloney (*c.*1600) there was once a landlord named Jarman who, with the help of his wife, used to murder rich travellers who stayed the night there, by a method worthy of Sweeney Todd. A trapdoor in the floor under the guest's bed would open at dead of night, hurtling him down into a vat of boiling ale in the kitchen. The corpse would then be thrown into the local river and swept away downstream. Fifty-nine people died this way, undiscovered. The sixtieth was a man named Thomas Cole. After his horse was seen wandering loose, enquiries were made, Jarman fled, and the truth was revealed. Delaney says that is why the river is called the Cole; modern tellers go further, saying the corpse was actually found floating, at which the finders exclaimed: 'Cole-in-brook!' and so the whole village got its name.

See also HIGHWAYMEN & SMUGGLERS, p. 208, QUEENS' HEADS & RED LIONS, p. 248

Owl & Pussy Cat

The nonsense rhyme written by Edward Lear (1812–88) is now so well known to children that it practically counts as folklore; it begins:

> The Owl and the Pussy Cat went to sea
> In a beautiful pea-green boat.
> They took some honey and plenty of money,
> Wrapped up in a five-pound note.

The signs of the Owl and Pussy Cat at Redchurch Street, London E2, at Kingston-upon-Thames (Surrey), in Leicester, and at Laindon (Essex) show the scene.

P

Pack of Cards

This pub, at Coombe Martin in Devon, was originally the home of a man named George Ley who had made his fortune as a gambler, and became an inn after his death in 1716. The design of the building is said to be based on the mathematics of a pack of cards: four storeys, one for each suit, thirteen doors on each floor for the thirteen cards in a suit, and (it is said) originally fifty-two windows for the total number of cards in a pack, though some have been blocked up. If this is all literally true, the house would have been a fine example of a 'folly', i.e. a building designed according to one man's whim rather than architectural convention or practical advantage. If not, the account is an instance of folklore based on the fascination of numbers, similar to the claim that a cathedral has 365 pillars, or a large house 365 windows, 'one for each day of the year'.

Pearly King

During the later nineteenth century, London's costermongers (i.e. street traders and barrow boys) began decorating their working clothes with rows of mother-of-pearl buttons. It is said that the first to do so was a teenage orphan named Henry

Croft, born in 1862. Before long the fashion evolved into an elaborately patterned and expensive costume, after which the costers were nicknamed 'pearlies'. Their descendants still make and wear these costumes, as a jealously guarded privilege, and the head of the leading family in a particular borough is its king or queen. Leslie Dunkling and Gordon Wright mention a Pearly King pub in the East End of London at the time they wrote, and a former Pearly Queen pub, also in the East End. Neither is listed in current telephone directories, which is sad, since there are still pearly kings and queens keeping up the old tradition, and they would make appropriate and picturesque emblems for a pub.

Peeping Tom

At Burton Green, on the south-western outskirts of Coventry and close to the University of Warwick, is the Peeping Tom, honouring the notorious character in the legend of Lady Godiva. Early written accounts (from 1235 onwards) never mention him, but he certainly featured in tradition by the seventeenth century, for in 1659 a visitor to Coventry was shown a statue which, he was told, represented a man who had been miraculously struck blind because he tried to spy on Godiva as she rode naked through the town; this 'statue' may well be the same life-size wooden figure of a man in Tudor armour, with damaged eyes, now standing in the Cathedral Lane Shopping Centre. It is said to date from about 1500; there is no record of what its original context and purpose may have been. There is also a painting of Godiva's ride in Coventry Museum, dated 1586, in which a small figure can be seen looking from the window of a building in the background. He may be meant to be

Tom; if this is the case, he must have become part of the story in Elizabethan times.

From 1765 onwards, Tom often had a place in the city's Godiva pageants. Sometimes the wooden figure was paraded, sometimes displayed in the window of an inn overlooking the processional route. In the early part of the nineteenth century he was represented by a human actor inside a little 'house' mounted on a wagon, who poked his head out of the window and amused the crowd by his comments.

Pegasus

Two Greek myths mention a wondrous winged horse named Pegasus; according to one tale it was ridden by the hero Perseus, and according to the other by the hero Bellerophon, each of whom was on a quest to destroy a monster. A winged horse makes an instantly recognisable image. There are pubs named Pegasus, the Flying Horse, or the Winged Horse at Bristol, Banbury, Vange, and elsewhere, but these are not necessarily inspired directly by mythology, since in the Second World War a flying horse was adopted as the insignia of British airborne troops. Moreover, as Dunkling and Wright point out, 'Flying Horse' was a name used by rapid stagecoaches. As so often, one would need to know whether the pub has a pictorial signboard, and if so whether this has been altered over the years, in order to know how the name is locally understood.

Pelican

The most likely reason why a pub would be named the Pelican, as is the case at Chew Magna in Somerset, is in allusion to the heraldic arms of some local family. But behind the heraldry lurks a piece of medieval folklore and religious symbolism, for in heraldry and in church art the bird was shown standing above a nest containing its chicks, and stabbing its own breast with its beak, so that the dripping blood fed them – an image technically known as 'The Pelican in her Piety'. It is the name given to a pub at Bridgend in Wales.

This belief about pelicans, which was widespread among medieval writers, probably arose from mistaken observation, since they do indeed feed their chicks by regurgitating half digested fish from the large pouch below their beaks. But St Jerome and other Christian writers saw in this a theological lesson about the Fall of Man, the Wrath of God, and the redemptive power of Christ's sacrificial blood. Pelicans, they wrote, love their chicks dearly, but the chicks rebel and beat with their wings against their parents' faces. In punishment, the male pelican strikes the chicks dead. But the female, pitying them, opens her side and lets the blood gush over the dead chicks; they revive sufficiently to feed on it, and thus are restored to life. Because of this allegory, a pelican stabbing its breast became the recognised symbol in art for charity in general, and more particularly for Christ's self-sacrificing love of humanity.

See also QUEENS' HEADS & RED LIONS, p. 248

Pendle Witch

Nowadays, stories of the 'Lancashire Witches' or 'Pendle Witches' are well publicised as tourist attractions – hence the pubs called the Pendle Witch in Clitheroe, Lancaster, and Sabden, and at Atherton in Greater Manchester. The reality behind the stories is a grim example of the darker side of folk belief. On two occasions in the early seventeenth century, in 1612 and again in 1633, villagers from the area of Pendle Forest in Lancashire were charged with killing or maiming people and livestock by witchcraft and put on trial at Lancaster Assizes. In 1612, fourteen of the twenty accused were hanged, one died in jail before the trial, two were pilloried and jailed, and three were acquitted. In 1633, thirty people were accused; seventeen were convicted but later acquitted, the chief witness (a young teenage boy) having admitted that he lied. The first case was reported in dramatic detail in a pamphlet by Thomas Potts, clerk of the court, and both have been thoroughly studied by historians.

No single figure stands out from the reports as being *the* Pendle witch. Those most central to the affair of 1612 were two women in their eighties known as Old Demdike and Old Chattox, their respective married daughters Elizabeth Device and Ann Redfearne, Elizabeth's daughter Alison, and an unrelated and much wealthier woman, Mrs Alice Nutter, whose husband and son had supposedly been killed by the spells of Old Chattox and her daughter. She protested her innocence to the last. At first Elizabeth Device also denied the charges, until her nine-year-

The Pendle Witch

old daughter Jannet gave evidence against her, saying she had 'a spirit in likeness of a brown dog' which killed people. The two other Device children, Alison and James, also denounced their mother and grandmother for various magical acts, including making wax images and plotting to steal a Communion host; so Elizabeth confessed. She later withdrew her confession, but it was still used as evidence against her. Alison herself (who was eleven) was accused of bewitching a pedlar, producing symptoms which must surely be those of a stroke:

> By this devilish art of witchcraft his head is drawn awry, his eyes and face deformed, his speech not well to be understood, his thighs and legs stark lame; his arms lame, especially on the left side, his hands lamed and turned out of their course; his body able to endure no travail.

Alison confessed to this charge. Old Demdike confessed to having made a pact with the Devil twenty years previously; he met her in Pendle Forest in the form of a boy called Tibb, and gave her a dog to be her familiar, which she fed with her blood. However, she died in prison before sentence was passed. Old Chattox confessed to killing Robert and Christopher Nutter, and was hanged, as were all the Device family apart from Jannet, though Elizabeth now protested her innocence. Most of the others also denied any guilt, 'crying out in very violent and outrageous manner, even to the gallows, where they died impenitent'.

In 1633, the accusations depended almost entirely on a boy called Edmund Robinson and his father. Edmund swore that he had been turned into a horse by a woman who then rode him to a gathering of about sixty witches who were holding a magical feast in a barn. He claimed that when he saw them pulling on ropes that went up into the roof, and roast meat, milk, and butter coming down the ropes, he got scared and ran home. The magistrates authorised Edmund to go around the villages to markets and churches, and pick out any women he could recognise as having been at the feast; he was paid a fee for each one he denounced. One was Jannet Device; she and sixteen others were condemned to death after 'devil's marks' (i.e. warts or moles) were found on their bodies. Fortunately some of the judges, dissatisfied, referred the cases first to the Bishop of Chester and then to the King's Council. Edmund admitted that his stories had been devised by his father 'for envy, revenge, and hope of gain'.

Pendragon

Pendragon, literally meaning 'Dragon's Head', was a title given to British chieftains and war leaders when they took command in times of particular danger, probably implying that they had authority over warriors of several different tribes. In Arthurian legend, however, it is applied to one man only – King Uther, the father of Arthur. According to Geoffrey of Monmouth, Uther adopted the name Pendragon and took a golden dragon as his personal emblem and battle-standard because of a vision in which a star's rays turned into a dragon, from the mouth of which two more rays shot out, indicating the extent of the realm his son Arthur would rule. There is a Pendragon Inn in Cardiff which has a double Arthurian relevance, since it is in a road called Excalibur Drive.

Phantom Coach

This pub, at Canley near Coventry, is on an old coaching route running from that city to Cheltenham, so the name is appropriate. In English legends, tales of phantom coaches are quite common; they are allegedly to be seen galloping along this or that particular road, possibly drawn by headless or fiery horses, and usually carrying the ghostly form of some wicked land-owner doomed to wander the earth on account of his sins. Here, however, the story as given by Leslie Dunkling and Gordon Wright does not fit the pattern; they say the pub got its name because there was once a coach which set out from there one night, and was never seen again.

See also GHOSTLY BARMAIDS & HAUNTED CELLARS, p. 278

Phoenix

As a pub name (found in York, Bristol, Manchester, and else-where), the Phoenix might have been chosen because it is a frequent emblem in heraldry, or it might directly refer to the mythical bird which symbolises rebirth after disaster. According to tradition, there is never more than one phoenix on earth at any one time, but it lives to be five hundred years old; when it feels its death approaching it builds a nest, in which it lays a single egg. Then it bursts into flame and burns itself up, so that the warmth will hatch a new phoenix from the ashes. The myth originated in Ancient Egypt, where the creature was named the Benu Bird, and was usually described as a heron, or as a huge golden hawk with a heron's beak. The name 'phoenix' was given to it by the Greek writer Herodotus in the fifth century BC, meaning that its

The Phoenix

plumage was as brilliant as Phoenecian purple dye. Medieval writers associated the bird with Arabia, not Egypt.

See also QUEENS' HEADS & RED LIONS, p. 248

Picketty Witch

Originally, the name of this pub at Yeovil (Somerset) simply referred to a tree – a wych-elm grown in such a way as to form a 'pike' or point. Not surprisingly, people felt that a witch is more colourful and exciting than an elm, so the sign now shows a typical witch in her trademark pointy hat. 'Picketty' is now taken to mean 'irritable, hard to please'.

Pied Piper

The story of the Pied Piper has become familiar to English children through the influence (direct or indirect) of a lively poem written by Robert Browning in 1842. But, as Leslie Dunkling and Gordon Wright shrewdly observe, the likely reason it has given a name to pubs at Scunthorpe, Stevenage, Middlesbrough, and elsewhere is that it provides an opportunity for a punning joke on people being 'pie-eyed', i.e. drunk.

The tale is of course a German one, set in the town of Hamelin (Hameln in German), and recounting an event which, it is claimed, occurred there in 1284. There are various versions from the fourteenth and fifteenth centuries, differing slightly in their details, but the central point is that a stranger came into the town on 26 June 1284 and took 130 of its children away with him to a hill outside the town, and they were never seen again. It seems reasonably certain that something did happen on this date. However, these first sources say nothing about rats or curiously coloured clothes, and though one does mention a silver pipe it does not make clear that it was magical. By the sixteenth century, the story had developed more dramatic features. It was now said that the stranger was a piper (dressed in a multicoloured coat) who undertook to clear the town of a plague of rats. He did so, luring them into the river Weser, where they drowned. But then the citizens regretted having promised him a large fee, so they made excuses not to pay, and he went off in a rage. On 26 June he returned, dressed as a hunter. Again he played his fife, but this time it was children who ran after him; he led them out of the town and into a cave in a mountain. They were never seen again – though some accounts said that they came out alive, hundreds of miles away, in Transylvania.

This last detail, which at first sight seems wholly fantastic, may hold the clue to a plausible historical explanation for the legend. It is a fact that in the thirteenth century a German bishop in Bohemia sent emissaries to recruit young families in Lower Saxony, including the Hamelin area, in order to establish a German population in his diocese; similarity of surnames in the two regions proves that his plan was successful. The tale of the Pied Piper could therefore express the grief of the people of Hamelin at the emigration of a generation of young folk.

The story reached Britain via Richard Verstegan's *A Restitution of Decayed Intelligence in Antiquities* (1605), but remained little known until Robert Browning took Verstegan's account as the basis for his poem, which proved immensely popular.

Pig & Whistle

This name, which is found at Scunthorpe (Lincolnshire), in Manchester, and elsewhere, is one of those which give rise to all sorts of implausible theories based on the assumption that something which looks like a joke cannot *really* be a joke, but must be due to somebody somewhere misunderstanding something perfectly rational and not in the least funny. In this case, 'whistle' is claimed to be a corruption of 'wassail', itself derived from Old English *wæs hæl*, 'Be healthy!', a phrase used in drinking a toast and as a greeting. As for the pig, some link it to *piggen*, 'milking pail', assuming beer was served in pails; others to a type of mug called a 'pig'; others think it a corruption of 'peg' in the sense of a measure of liquor. One very farfetched theory, mentioned in Eric Delderfield's *British Inn Signs*, proposes that the 'wassail' greeting is being combined with Danish *pige*, 'girl, maiden', producing 'Hail, Virgin' as a variation on 'Hail, Mary'. Others accept that 'whistle' means what it appears to mean, but say 'pig' means 'peg'; they explain that when a potboy was sent to get cider or beer he was ordered to whistle while drawing the peg from the barrel, to prove he was not having a drink himself. No actual evidence is offered to back up any of these ideas.

There is also disagreement on the age of this name. Delderfield thinks it 'a very old sign', but Larwood and Hotten point out that there is not a single example of it in Bryant Lillywhite's *London Signs*, a large collection of nineteenth-century material, and that it is still far from common (currently, examples can be found in Manchester, Chelmsford, and Scunthorpe). On the other hand, they quote the *Oxford English Dictionary* as recording several instances of a seventeenth-century phrase 'going to pigs and whistles', meaning 'going to rack and ruin'.

But one should never underestimate the appeal of sheer surreal nonsense to the English sense of humour. And there certainly are precedents in the Middle Ages for the joke of imagining a pig as a musician. One of the carved wooden misericords in Winchester Cathedral, dating from around 1300, shows a sow playing a double pipe while suckling her piglets; other misericords in Ripon Cathedral, Manchester Cathedral, and Beverley Minster show a pig playing the bagpipes to dancing piglets. In the latter cases we probably have an additional cruel joke (similar to that of the cat playing upon the cat-gut fiddle), for medieval bagpipes were made from pigs' bladders or stomachs.

See also PUNS & OLD JOKES, p. 138

Pig on the Wall

It is a long-standing Shropshire joke to claim that the men of the small village of Gornal were so stupid that they heaved a pig up onto a wall so that it could enjoy watching a band go past on its way to nearby Dawley. This was on the occasion of a procession honouring Captain Webb, a citizen of Dawley, who had become the first man to swim the English Channel, in 1875. As so often, what was once a sneer has turned into a source of pride for the people concerned; in recent years a pub in Upper Gornal previously known as the Bricklayer's Arms has been renamed the Pig on the Wall.

The name is also found at Droylsden (Greater Manchester), though there the explanation given to Leslie Dunkling and Gordon Wright was more humdrum; they were told that the pub had been built on the site of a former pig farm, some of its beams and bricks being reused in the new building. The traditional joke itself, like others about the silly behaviour of fools, was formerly told in many communities.

Pillar of Salt

This very unusual pub name occurs at Droitwich in Worcestershire and at Northwich in Cheshire, and is appropriate to the historical importance of salt production in the economy of both towns. The allusion is to the biblical story of Lot's wife. She and her husband were fleeing from the doomed cities of Sodom and Gomorrah, which God was about to destroy with fire from heaven, but (despite strict instructions from an angel) she could not resist stopping to look back at the city for a moment. So God punished her by turning her into a pillar of salt.

Until well into the twentieth century a pub was primarily a meeting place for men only, so sexist humour is common in pub names (see NAG'S HEAD and QUIET WOMAN). It may well be that the tale of Lot's wife was seen as an amusing example of a woman getting what she deserved for her curiosity and disobedience.

See also ANGELS & SAINTS, p. 16

Pindar of Wakefield

This name, for a pub in London WC1, refers to a character in one of the later Robin Hood ballads, popular from the middle of the seventeenth century onwards. A 'pindar' or 'pinder' was a man officially employed to catch stray horses or farm animals, especially any that wandered into fields and damaged the crops, and to take them to the village pound. Their owners would have to pay to get them back. The ballad tells how Robin Hood and two of his comrades were walking through a cornfield near Wakefield in Yorkshire when a pindar angrily ordered them to get back on the path. Robin refused, and the two of them fought. They were equally matched, and after a while agreed to call it a draw. Robin invited the pindar to join his band, and he agreed.

Plough

The Plough, or the Plough and Horses, is a very common name for a pub, obviously appropriate in country districts, and usually there is no folklore attached to it. But sometimes even the simplest of names can become linked to a story. At Beddington (in what was formerly Surrey, now part of Greater London) there is a Plough Inn in Plough Lane, near the entrance to the Beddington Caves, and these caves, according to rumour, were merely the beginning of an amazingly long secret tunnel. A certain 'Shudderus' wrote in the *Croydon Review and Timetable* of January 1880:

> Rumour goes so far as to say that the cave originally extended right away to Brighton, and that by its means smuggled goods

The Plough

were introduced to Surrey and thence to London. The cave was discovered, I was told, by some person who was ploughing above it, and who suddenly found himself in the robbers' den. In confirmation of this assertion, my informant pointed to the figure of a man and a plough on the signboard at host Watkinson's hostelry as being the picture of the identical man and of the plough he was directing at the time.

Secret tunnels are among the most popular themes of local folklore throughout England, and are regularly linked to memories of the smuggling era. However, few (if any) can rival this one for the sheer impossibility of its length, or can boast of a signboard as 'proof'.

Plough & Harrow, Plough & Horses, Plough & Sail, Plough & Tractor, Ploughboy, Ploughshare

See HARVESTERS & WHEATSHEAVES, p. 182

Printer's Devil

There are pubs called the Printer's Devil in Bristol and in Fetter Lane, London. The latter has on its signboard the picture of an apprentice pulling a demon by the nose, in much the same way as St Dunstan did (see DEVIL & DUNSTAN).

On one level, the term printer's devil simply refers to an apprentice who does menial jobs of fetching and carrying, mixing tubs of ink, and so forth for the men in the printing works (similarly, a junior legal counsel can be called his principal's 'devil'). But it invites colourful 'explanations', of which there are several, ranging from the fairly plausible – printers' apprentices tend to get blackened by the ink, or that William Caxton, the first English printer, had an assistant named Deville – to the fanciful and folkloric. It has been said, for instance, that the famous Renaissance printer Aldus Manutius of Venice was suspected of black magic, and that a black African boy who worked for him was dubbed 'the printer's devil'. Best of all is the rumour that every printing office has a resident imp or demon who delights in surreptitiously messing up the type so as to create misprints, causing sheets of paper to stick together, abstracting whole pages from the centre of books, and so forth. A devil of this species is, obviously, a gremlin in disguise.

Punch & Judy

It is clear why a pub in London's Covent Garden Piazza bears this name, for it was in Covent Garden that in May 1662 Samuel Pepys came to see the performance of 'an Italian puppet play which is very pretty, the best I ever saw'. This is the first record of a 'Punch' show in England; it was probably a novelty at the time. Unfortunately Pepys does not describe the plot of the play he saw, but later in the seventeenth century there are references to the fights between Punch and his wife and to 'a senseless dialogue between Punchinello and the Devil … through a tin squeaker'. The basic plot was not actually printed until 1828, but must have gradually developed through many decades of oral tradition. Its publication in print did not fossilise it, for later generations of showmen have added characters and episodes, and modified and updated the dialogue to keep the humour topical. There is an annual gathering of Punch showmen in the grounds of St Paul's Church, Covent Garden, in May.

There is also a Punch Tavern near Ludgate Circus in London EC4 which took its name from street puppet shows given nearby, and in turn inspired the name of the magazine *Punch*, which was first thought of in that pub, in 1841. The Punch and Judy at Margate in Kent and the one at Bournemouth in Hampshire were probably so named because the puppet show has been a very popular open-air entertainment at seaside towns throughout the twentieth century.

Punchbowl

Normally, this name simply refers to the large bowl in which the hot drink 'punch' is mixed and served, but at Hindhead in Surrey it refers to a landscape feature – a large, deep, steep-sided hollow in the hillside known as the Devil's Punchbowl. Rather surprisingly, there is no full-scale legend to account for its existence, merely a vague notion that the Devil mixes his drink there, and that when mists gather in the hollow they are a sign that his hot punch is steaming.

Puss in Boots

The story of Puss in Boots as we know it originally came from Charles Perrault's collection of French fairytales (1697), but was soon translated, and is now one of the stories most familiar to English children. It is also a favourite subject for pantomimes.

There was once a miller who had three sons, but was so poor that when he died and the two eldest had inherited the mill and its donkey, all that was left for the third was a cat. But the cat said: 'Don't worry, I'll make your fortune, if you give me a bag and a good pair of boots.' Then the cat went hunting. Whenever he caught tender young hares, or tasty partridges, he would stuff them in his bag and march off to the king's palace, saying: 'I bring you a gift from my master, the Marquis of Carabas.' Then one day when the king was due to drive past a certain river, the cat told his mas-

Puss in Boots

ter to strip naked and bathe in the river, and when the king's carriage appeared the cat started screaming: 'Help! My master is drowning! And his clothes were stolen by robbers while he was swimming!' Of course the 'drowning man' was rescued at once, and when the king heard that this was the marquis who had sent him so many presents, he gave him fine clothes and invited him to ride in the carriage. The cat marched on ahead, and whenever he passed men working in the fields, he ordered them to tell the king that this land belonged to the Marquis of Carabas. Finally he killed an ogre, and pretended that his castle and treasure belonged to the marquis – who was thus able to marry the king's daughter.

Some pubs named after this tale display on their sign a magnificently booted cat striding along with a bag on his shoulder, presumably containing the gifts for the king. This can be seen at Macclesfield (Cheshire) and Hazelwood (Derbyshire); sometimes a milestone is shown, which may indicate some influence from the story of Dick Whittington and his cat. The Puss 'n' Boots at Acomb (Yorkshire) has a variation in which the cat is waving his hat and holding a large bag. The Puss in Boots at Stockton (Greater Manchester) used also to show the striding cat, but the sign was repainted in 1994 and now shows the scene on the river bank.

At Hazelwood there are verses on the reverse of the sign which may refer to the fact that Puss's owner was a miller's son – unless perhaps the pub itself once belonged to a miller – and promising the customer a 'cheering bate', i.e. a pleasant pause for refreshment:

> The water kindly turns the mill,
> While I grind corn for many.
> Ale, I hope, may farther still
> Assist to turn the penny.
>
> Then try, my lads, how soon or late,
> How ale your strength recruits.
> You'll always find a cheering bate
> At honest Puss in Boots.

Occasionally, the fairytale is set aside in favour of some joke. The sign on the Macclesfield pub at one time represented a drunken cat (in boots, of course), leaning happily against a lamp-post.

Quiet (Silent, Headless, Good) Woman

Pubs with these names have as their sign a headless woman in period costume, in some cases holding her head under her arm. This is a sexist joke. Men have for generations criticised women for talking far too much, and especially for nagging, arguing and answering back to their husbands. In short, the only way to silence a wife is to cut her head off. In several places the message is reinforced by a verse:

> Here is a woman who's lost her head.
> She's quiet now – you see, she's dead.

Or there may be a suitable proverb, as at Earl Sterndale (Derbyshire), where the sign says: 'A soft answer turneth away wrath', a biblical quotation (Prov. 15:1). Local tradition adds that a former landlord cut off his wife's head because her chattering irritated him so much.

The underlying idea goes back to medieval Christian morality, which followed the teaching of St Paul that 'man is the head of woman', and that a woman should 'learn in silence and subjection' (1 Cor. 11:3; 1 Tim. 2:11). This was so generally accepted that it was even a Dutch proverb that 'A good woman goes without a head'.

The eighteenth-century artist William Hogarth wittily exploited these associations in one detail of his picture *Times of the Day: Noon*. In a bustling street stands an inn with the headless woman as its sign (no actual name given, for in Hogarth's time inns relied on pictures, not words, to identify them); a furious woman is leaning out of its upstairs window, shouting and throwing a joint of meat into the street, while her milder-looking husband tries to restrain her.

However, many places have adopted different explanations for the sign, either because the older one had been forgotten, or because it seemed inadequate or offensive. There used to be a Quiet Woman pub on Matlock Moor in Derbyshire (later the site of a sporting club) which was said to be haunted by a headless woman – the ghost of a wicked landlady who used to murder solitary travellers who spent a night there, and was eventually hanged and beheaded for her crimes. The Silent Woman Inn in Wareham Forest (Dorset) has two stories, one serious and one flippant. Either the decapitated victim was a saintly girl martyr killed by Viking raiders, or she was a former landlady who loved gossiping so much that smugglers took this drastic step to make sure she would never give them away. Up to the 1990s, there was a Quiet Woman pub at Halstock in Dorset; there the explanation is that it refers to a local saint, Juthwara, whose head was cut off by her stepbrother after she was falsely accused of staining the family honour by becoming pregnant; she calmly picked her head up and carried it into Halstock church, where she laid it on the altar before falling dead. The pub is now a house offering bed-and-breakfast, which displays an attractive medieval-style signboard showing Juthwara carrying her head.

In the modern world, minor female saints are irrelevant, and sexist jokes are frowned upon. Consequently, these names are sometimes reinterpreted in the light of history. Jacob Larwood and John Hotten described a double-sided pub sign at Widford in Essex, showing Henry VIII on one side and a headless woman on the other, implying a reference to the decapitation of Anne Boleyn. They suggested that this could have arisen from the amalgamation of two pubs, a King's Head and a Headless Woman. Be that as it may, the idea certainly has popular appeal. At Leek (near Stoke-on-Trent in Staffordshire), the sign of the Quiet Woman is quite unambiguous – a female ghost carrying her head, with Henry VIII in the background.

One legend, about the Headless Woman at Duddon in Cheshire, draws upon local history, interpreting her silence as an act of heroism during the Civil War. In the 1860s the pub displayed a notice telling the tale; it is quoted by Jacob Larwood:

A party of Cromwell's soldiers, engaged in hunting down the Royalists in the Chester district, visited Hockenhall Hall, but found that the family being warned of their coming had buried all the silver and other valuables and then fled for safety, leaving only a faithful old housekeeper in charge of the Hall, thinking it unlikely that the soldiers would do her any harm.

The soldiers, being incensed at finding nothing of value, locked up the housekeeper in the top room and proceeded to torture her to tell them where the valuables were hidden. She remained faithful, and was finally murdered by the soldiers cutting off her head. Tradition says that afterwards on numerous occasions she was seen carrying her head under her arm, walking along the old bridle path between Hockenhall Hall and the spot where it comes out on the Tarporley Road near to the public house.

The story still features in local guidebooks, some of which say the faithful servant was a cook, not a housekeeper, called Grace Trigg. They add that the Roundheads carried her body and head from the Hall to a cottage to hide them, and that this cottage later became the pub. Some say her ghost occasionally appears in the pub, or on the road leading to it.

~ R ~

Rainbow & Dove

This name is still to be found at Harlow and Leicester, and in the reversed order of Dove and Rainbow at Hartshead near Sheffield. The reference is of course to the story telling how Noah learnt that the Flood was at an end when the dove he sent out from the ark returned with an olive branch in its beak (proving that living trees were beginning to emerge from the retreating waters), and how God created the rainbow as a pledge of His promise never to send such a flood again (Genesis 9). It is also probable that the former popularity of this sign in London was partly due to its use as the heraldic emblem of the Dyers' Company, chosen in allusion to the rainbow-like brilliance of their work. More generally, doves are widely seen as symbols of peace, and rainbows of hope. 'Rainbow' alone is also found as a pub name in various places.

See also ANGELS & SAINTS, p. 16

Rainbow's End

There is a pub of this name at Steeple Langford in Wiltshire. Like Crock of Gold, it refers to the proverbial saying that there is wealth and happiness to be found at the foot of the rainbow, provided one can reach the actual spot before the rainbow fades – an impossible task.

Ram

A ram was the emblem of the Worshipful Company of Clothworkers, and is a common pub name in areas which depended on sheep-rearing and the wool trade. The symbol became particularly important to the people of Derbyshire, and inspired a humorous folksong, for which see DERBY TUP.

See also QUEENS' HEADS & RED LIONS, p. 248

Ram Jam

At Stretton, near Oakham in Rutland, is the oddly named Ram Jam Inn. Some say it is so called after a particularly potent drink which one of its landlords used to serve, the recipe for which was lost when he died; others give as explanation an anecdote about a trick played on a landlord's wife. There was once a traveller – some say a highwayman – who had been staying at the inn and realised he would be unable to pay the heavy bill he

The Ram

had run up. So he convinced the landlady that he knew a magic spell which enabled him to draw both mild ale and bitter out of the same barrel, and that he would teach it to her. Curious, she agreed to take him into the cellar. There he produced an augur and drilled a hole in one side of the barrel, and as the beer began to gush out he told her to plug the hole with her thumb, so as not to waste any. Then he did the same on the other side, telling her to plug that hole too, with the thumb of the other hand. Then he ran off, took his horse, and galloped away, leaving his bill unpaid and the furious landlady still embracing the barrel, her thumbs both ram-jammed tight in it. It was quite a while before anyone heard her shouts.

See also HIGHWAYMEN & SMUGGLERS, p. 208

Rattlebone Inn

This fine sixteenth-century inn in the village of Sherston takes its name from a highly dramatic local tale, and has an equally dramatic sign to go with it. In the year 1016 there was a battle between the English army of King Edmund Ironside and Danes led by Canute at a place named Sceorstan, which can be confidently identified as the village of Sherston in Wiltshire. No details are given, but over the centuries a story grew up that a warrior called Rattlebone had done great deeds for England. The name sounds implausible, and no such person has been historically identified. The antiquarian John Aubrey was the first to mention the legend, in the seventeenth century, in his collection of notes on Wiltshire history; he connects it to a statue in the church and to a popular rhyme which seems to have been devised in order to account for the ownership of certain estates:

In the wall of the Church Porch on the outside, in a niche … is a little figure about 2 foote and a half high, ill done, which they call *Rattle Bone*, who, the tradition is, did much service against the Danes, when they infested this part of the countrey …

Mem. The old women and children have these verses by tradition, *viz*:

> 'Fight well Rattlebone.
> Thou shalt have Sherstone.'
> 'What shall I with Sherstone doe,
> Without I have all that belongs thereto?'
> 'Thou shalt have Wyck & Willesly,
> Easton towne and Pinkeney.'

These are hamlets belonging to this parish. Their tradition is that the fight was in the ground called the Gaston. *Quaere*, what it signifies?

The battered little statue in the church porch is late medieval, and though Aubrey was told it represented a warrior with his shield, it is more likely to be a saint holding a book. But it happens that the object looks rather like a roof-tile, and the figure seems to be clutching it tightly to his stomach – and so by the eighteenth century the tale had grown to its fullest version, involving an act of courage and endurance reminiscent of legendary heroes such as the Irish Cú Chulainn. The brave warrior John Rattlebone, it was said, had fought valiantly until a savage sword thrust ripped his belly open, and his guts began to spill out. Undaunted, he crammed them back in, picked up a fallen tile, and held it firmly against the wound to keep it closed. And then he went on fighting. Once the battle was won, he fell dead – some say upon the very spot where the inn now stands.

The inn sign displays Rattlebone's heroism, as he flourishes his sword in one mailed fist and clutches the tile in the other. Besides the current version, the one that existed in the 1960s can be seen in Eric Delderfield's *British Inn Signs and their Stories*.

Raven in the Tower

The semi-tame ravens of the Tower of London have been famous for many years, so it is no surprise to find a pub of this name nearby, in Tower Bridge Road, London SE1. It is often said – especially by tourist guides – that if these ravens were to die out, or fly away, the White Tower itself, together with the kingdom of Britain, would fall. They are carefully tended by the Yeomen of the Guard, and their wings are clipped to make sure that they never do abandon their home. The rule is that there should always be at least six of them; those that die are buried in the Raven Cemetery (located in a dried moat near the Watergate), and their names inscribed on the Raven Memorial Headstone. In 2007, the current six were named Hugin and Munin (Odin's ravens in Norse myth), Bran and Branwen (semi-divine characters in the *Mabinogion*), Gwylum, and Cedric.

How old the story is, and indeed how long the ravens have been around, is problematic. The popular tradition is that they were already there in the time of Charles II. He had at first wanted them destroyed because the Astronomer Royal complained that their droppings were obscuring the telescope of his observatory in the White Tower; however, he was warned that this would cause the White Tower to collapse and would threaten Charles's throne and kingdom, so he spared the ravens and moved the observatory to Greenwich instead. A good story, but pretty implausible as history. Moreover, recent research by Dr Geoffrey Parnell (Keeper of Tower History at the Royal Armouries) found no evidence for their presence in the Tower before the 1890s, when there were two pet ravens; in 1903, there were five, and a visitor noted that if one died it was replaced at once.

As for the belief that to lose them would bring disaster on the whole country, it may have developed during the Second World War, for the first known published mention of it is in the *Evening Standard* of 15 October 1949. Dr Parnell says that Winston Churchill knew it, and took it sufficiently seriously to ensure that when the birds were killed in an air raid the news was kept secret, and that they had been replaced by the time the Tower was reopened to the public in 1946. A related belief was recalled by Sir Iain Moncrieffe (in a talk given to the Folklore Society in 1980): while stationed with the Scots Guards at the Tower during the 1940 London Blitz, he was told that if a raven died someone in the Tower would also die. One day a raven did die, and next day one of the Yeoman Warders died.

There is also a belief, amusingly described in Peter Bushell's *London's Secret History* (1983), that the birds are capable of taking their revenge on anyone who harms or insults them. He was told that some time in the 1930s a guardsman stationed at the Tower kicked a raven, and shortly afterwards broke both legs by falling into the moat while sleepwalking. At about the same period, a visiting Nazi officer sneered at one of the ravens, remarking that 'We Nazis prefer the eagle', whereupon the bird promptly bit him on the ankle.

Red Dragon

A Red Dragon has been the national emblem of Wales for many centuries, possibly even from the seventh century, when it is said to have been the standard of King Cadwallader (d.689), though it is more likely that the symbolism was popularised – perhaps even created – by a famous episode in Geoffrey of Monmouth's *History of the Kings of England*, which dates from around 1136. He tells how the prophet Merlin, while still a boy, revealed that there were two dragons fighting each other in a cavern under a mountain in Wales. One was white, and represented the Anglo-Saxon invaders of Britain; the other, which was red, stood for the Celtic Britons, and would, he foretold, eventually drive out the white one. Since the Welsh are direct descendants of the Britons, the Red Dragon has become their patriotic symbol and appears on the national flag. This is its meaning at any Red Dragon pub in Wales (e.g. those at Port Talbot and Wrexham), but when the same name appears in England the reference may be to the armorial bearings of some local family.

Red Lion

See QUEENS' HEADS & RED LIONS, p. 248

Ring o' Roses

This pub name, at Holcombe in Somerset, is a prime example of the way an unproven and speculative theory takes on a life of its own and lodges immovably in the public imagination. It comes, of course, from the nursery rhyme and singing game 'Ring-a-ring o' roses', which has been known in Britain

Queens' Heads & Red Lions

Heraldry in itself is not folklore but a learned code of symbols governed by strict rules, and applied to the requirements of a social elite. Its symbols, however, are quite often based on old beliefs about mythical creatures such as the PHOENIX, the dragon (see GREEN DRAGON or RED DRAGON), the UNICORN, the WYVERN, or the WILD/GREEN MAN, which are thus passed down to more modern times. It can also itself become a source of legend, when stories are devised to account for its dramatic but puzzling images, e.g. the BEAR & RAGGED STAFF, the SARACEN'S HEAD, and the EAGLE & CHILD. It must be borne in mind that heraldic devices would be well known to the whole local community, not simply to the family that bore them; they could be seen carved on houses, painted on carriages, and (most importantly) carved on tombstones and memorial plaques in the village church.

Heraldry has been a major influence on the development of pub signs and names. Many refer explicitly to the coats of arms of aristocratic and landowning families, calling themselves the Norfolk Arms, Salisbury Arms, and so forth; the signboard will usually reproduce the full arms. This choice generally indicates that the inn stands on, or near, an estate of the family in question, as when one finds a Marlborough Arms at Woodstock, a mere stone's throw from Blenheim Palace, seat of the dukes of Marlborough. On the other hand, when a London pub is called the Marlborough Arms, it is more likely to be a tribute to the duke as a military hero rather than a signal that he or his descendants had a town house in the area – local historical records would have to be checked in order to get to the bottom of the matter.

Instead of reproducing a whole coat of arms, it is simpler to select a single clear image from it – the crest, perhaps, or one of the two 'supporters', or one motif from the shield. Many 'animal' signs are believed to have originated in this way, though they have since been frequently repeated without any awareness of their older meanings, and in places where it would be irrelevant anyway. Originally, the WHITE HART was the badge of Richard II, the White Boar of Richard III, the Blue Boar of the earls of Oxford, the Red Lion of John of Gaunt, the White Horse of the Hanoverian kings – examples could be multiplied. The Tudor Rose has a particularly significant history; it has both red and white petals, and was invented by Henry VII to symbolise his role in bringing the Wars of the Roses to an end by combining the claims of the Yorkists and Lancastrians (whose badges were a white and a red rose respectively). The Feathers (or the Three Feathers, or the Prince of Wales' Feathers) refers to the triple ostrich plumes forming the crest of every Prince of Wales since the Black Prince in the fourteenth century. Heraldry quite often involves jokes; the earls of Derby, whose family surname was Ferrers, chose three horseshoes for their arms, as a pun on 'farriers', and this is one possible source for THREE HORSESHOES as a pub name.

Heraldry is not of course exclusive to the aristocracy and gentry. It was very much used by medieval guilds and by their successors, the various livery companies and trade associations, not to mention colleges, banks, sports clubs, counties, and towns. Crests from trade coats of arms have often been adopted as pub signs: the RAM from the Worshipful Company of Clothworkers, the Dolphin from fishmongers, the Wheatsheaf from bakers, Three Tuns from brewers, and so forth. In some cases, instead of using some version of the old guild emblem, the sign-painter has chosen to create suitable 'arms' from scratch. Eric Delderfield's book includes some fine examples (the Plaisterer's Arms at Winchcombe in Somerset, the Baker's Arms at Broad Camden and the Butcher's Arms at Sheepscombe, both in Gloucestershire) which are based on realistic renderings of the appropriate tools, laid out in the manner of a conventional coat of arms. Trade heraldry can also be the immediate source – though not the ultimate explanation – for apparently nonsensical pub names such as the ELEPHANT & CASTLE (the Cutlers' Company), the Goat and Compasses (Cordwainers; see PUZZLING PAIRS, p.112), not to mention the Green Man and Still (Distillers).

since the 1880s, and in America since the 1790s. For many decades nobody thought it particularly mysterious or sinister. But someone in the latter half of the twentieth century (it is not known who) launched the idea that the rhyme commemorates either the medieval Black Death or the seventeenth-century Great Plague. It is claimed that 'roses' refers to a rash, 'posies' to flowers which people carried in the belief that sweet scents warded off the disease, and that 'Atishoo, atishoo, we all fall down' mimes the death of the victims. It is true that people did carry posies for this reason, and that there is a superstition that sneezing can be an omen of death unless a bystander says 'Bless you!' The rest of the argument, however, makes no sense medically – neither rosy rashes nor sneezing are plague symptoms. Moreover, variations of the game both in Britain and abroad show that it often ended with the children curtseying and bowing rather than falling over. It is also unlikely that the rhyme dates back to the seventeenth century, let alone the fourteenth. None of these considerations, however, are likely to kill off the dramatic 'explanation'.

According to a journalist writing in *The Times* on 29 May 2000, the Holcombe pub claims to have acquired its name in the fourteenth century, when it was relocated 'after the Black Death apocryphally wiped out all but one resident from its original settlement one mile away'. A fine melodramatic legend, but the journalist was wise to add the crucial word 'apocryphally'.

See also MOTHER GEESE & CATS WITH FIDDLES, p. 46

Ring o' Stanes

The name of the Ring o' Stanes at Glenrothes refers to a prehistoric stone circle at nearby Bilbirnie. This stands in what is now a built-up area, but was once open country. It was traditionally known as the Druids' Circle, in accordance with the persistent theory that all such monuments had been erected by Druids as places of worship, possibly involving human sacrifice. This idea was quite plausible when it was first proposed by seventeenth-century antiquarians, and was accepted as orthodox history for several generations; even nowadays, when archaeology has proved that the stone circles were built many centuries before Druids existed, it still has some power in popular imagination.

Roaring Meg

From the late seventeenth century to the early nineteenth, Roaring Meg was the name of an inn in Hereford, and it is now that of a pub at Biddulph, near Stoke-on-Trent (Staffordshire). Both were so named in honour of Roaring Meg, a mighty seventeenth-century cannon which was used by the Parliamentary army during the Civil War when it was besieging Biddulph Hall in 1643, and again at the siege of Goodrich Castle in Herefordshire. It was said to be at that time the largest piece of ordnance ever cast in England. When the latter siege ended, the Parliamentary commander, Colonel Birch, who was Governor of Hereford, had the cannon taken to that city and displayed in a street there; it gave its name to a nearby inn until it was removed to Castle Green in 1839. It can currently be seen in the ruins of Goodrich Castle.

In earlier generations, Meg seems to have been a particularly popular name for very large guns; there is a fifteenth-century one called Mons Meg in Edinburgh Castle, a Long Meg of Westminster at the Tower of London, and another seventeenth-century Roaring Meg at Derry in Northern Ireland. The custom of giving such weapons female nicknames continued into modern times; a German long-range cannon which was used to shell Paris during the First World War was known as Big Bertha.

An intriguing new development is that Roaring Meg is now sometimes thought of not as an actual weapon but as a mythic personification of recklessness and ferocity associated with it, a kind of modern valkyrie. A current rock band has adopted the name Roaring Meg; on their website they describe their heroine as 'a mythical six-foot-six emerald-eyed, beer-swigging, tattooed, leather-clad fiery red-head, who roams the Underworld astride a flaming cannon'. This idea may have been inspired by the legend of the human Long Meg of Westminster after whom the Tower gun is named, which was known from the 1580s onwards; she is said to have been a remarkably tall and strong woman who used to batter thieves, bullies, and other male wrong-doers with her cudgel, and often dressed as a man. It is probably also relevant that in eighteenth-century slang a 'roaring girl' was a female pickpocket, and a 'roaring boy' a street hooligan.

Robin Hood

There are pubs named for Robin Hood not only in Nottingham, the scene of so many of his alleged exploits, but in many towns and villages all over the country. He has been a popular hero for some six hundred years, yet the early songs and plays give very few factual details about him, and those they do give are so inconsistent that historians have never been able to pin down just when and where he lived – was it in the reign of Richard I, or in that of Edward II? Was he an outlaw in Sherwood Forest, or in Inglewood (a royal forest near Carlisle), or in Barnsdale,

Robin Hood

some thirty miles from York? Was he simply a yeoman archer, or a man of noble birth, cheated of his inheritance? Perhaps there never was a single 'Robin', and it is just a nickname for any secretive, hooded, clever outlaw?

Whatever the historical reality may or may not have been, by Tudor times he was seen as a cheerful rogue, not a serious criminal, even though he lived by poaching deer in the king's forests; he was famed for archery, wrestling, and quarterstaff fighting. Games and pageants featuring him and his companions were regular entertainments for May Day and Midsummer festivities. A few versions of the legend claimed that he would only steal from the rich in order to give to the poor, and this is the trait now best remembered. Some Victorian writers saw him as a patriot fighting on behalf of the native English against oppressive Norman barons and the wicked King John. Gradually he came to typify cheerful courage, cheeky resistance against petty tyrants, and the freedom of an idyllic life in the forests.

A good many pubs are named Robin Hood and LITTLE

JOHN, referring to the most famous of Robin's 'Merry Men'. These often display a rhyme, which may have begun as a joke about a pub where the landlord's name was John. The version at Castleton runs:

> Kind gentlemen and yeomen good,
> Come in and sup with Robin Hood.
> If Robin Hood he be agone,
> Come in and sup with Little John.

Another version, cited by Bryant Lillywhite, is:

> Come here, my boy, if you be dry,
> The fault's in you, and not in I.
> If Robin Hood from home is gone,
> Come in and drink with Little John.

One detail often mentioned in stories about Robin is that he and his men were always dressed in green – useful camouflage, obviously, for anyone lurking in a forest. As a result, from the middle of the nineteenth century onwards pubs called the GREEN MAN often chose to put him on their signboards. This is less common now, other interpretations of the name having become more popular, but the Green Man at Turnstall (Suffolk) still shows Robin Hood drawing his bow.

Rose & Crown

See PUZZLING PAIRS, p. 112

Round Table

There is a Round Table pub in London WC2, between Covent Garden and Leicester Square, though there seems to be no particular reason why this legendary institution of King Arthur's knights should be commemorated there. A more appropriate setting would be Winchester in Hampshire, since the town's Great Hall displays a masterpiece of medieval carpentry – a huge table-top, eighteen feet (5.4 metres) in diameter and weighing a ton. It is thought to have been made on the orders of Edward I, who was an enthusiastic admirer of Arthurian legends, for the feasting at a tournament in Winchester in 1290. Later, the legs were removed and the table-top was hung against the wall of the hall, as the chronicler John Hardyinge noted in the middle of the fifteenth century:

> The round table at Wynchester began,
> And there it ended, and there it hangeth yet.

The striking painting which now adorns the table (making it look very like a gigantic dartboard) is a piece of Tudor propaganda, reinforcing the claim often made by this dynasty that they were descended from Arthur, and thus his rightful successors both in England and in Wales. The centre of the board is a Tudor rose, and the picture of Arthur enthroned at the top is in fact a portrait of Henry VIII when he was still a young man. This decoration probably dates from 1516, when Henry was hoping to be elected Emperor of the Holy Roman Empire; medieval historians believed that Arthur had not only been king of Britain but had been victorious in wars in Europe, so an Arthurian connection would have added to Henry's European prestige. In 1522, when the man who did become Emperor, Charles V, visited England, Henry showed him the Winchester table as an authentic relic of Arthur's reign.

Roundstone

A pub of this name stands at a crossroads on the bypass to the north of East Preston (West Sussex), just below Highdown Hill; up to the 1970s its sign showed a skeleton pinned under a millstone with a stake driven through its central hole, but struggling energetically to get out. A painting of the same scene used to hang in the bar, till it was stolen in 1976. The story was that a suicide, or a criminal, had been buried at the crossroads, but would emerge and roam around at night, terrifying the neighbourhood. There was a mill on Highdown, owned by a certain John Oliver (a famously eccentric local character, who died in 1793), so the villagers asked for a millstone to lay on the grave. The miller agreed. The heavy stone was placed on top of the corpse and a stake driven through, so the revenant could never get out again, however hard he tried.

Presumably at some stage this black humour was thought too gruesome, for there is now a milder version of the story which simply says that the grindstone of Oliver's mill accidentally fell, rolled down the hill and crushed a man walking along the lane; it was so heavy it could not be removed, so the victim was left beneath it. The current pub sign shows a millstone only.

Rowan Tree

The Rowan Tree pub in Aberdeen takes its name from a species of tree (*Sorbus aucuparia*, also called mountain ash or witan) which was used in many parts of the British Isles as a charm against fairies, witchcraft, and the Evil Eye until late in the nineteenth century. Its twigs, preferably those bearing its red berries, would be hung up over the door of the house, the cowshed, or the dairy as a general protection from evil forces, or over one's bed to prevent nightmares. These specific uses have died out, but some people still regard it as a lucky tree to have in one's garden.

Royal Oak

Royal Oak is one of the most popular pub names, found far and wide throughout the country, and refers primarily to an actual historical event – the celebrated escape of Charles II after his army was defeated at Worcester in 1651, when he climbed into an oak tree at Boscobel to hide from Parliamentary soldiers. Secondarily, in some places it refers to one or other of various Royal Navy warships bearing the name. Nevertheless, there is a link to folklore too, since 29 May was celebrated as Royal Oak Day from 1661 till late in the nineteenth century by the people in general, and till the middle of the twentieth century by children. This date was both Charles II's birthday and the anniversary of his triumphal entry to London at his Restoration in 1660. It was instituted as an offi-

The Royal Oak

cial holiday, with church services of thanksgiving, and many places soon added various popular celebrations copied from May Day, such as Morris dancing and setting up a maypole. Above all, it was a day when everybody wore sprays of oak leaves (often gilded or beribboned) pinned to their clothes or hats; children went on doing this as late as the 1950s, and usually also carried a bunch of nettles with which to sting the arms or legs of any child not wearing leaves. At one time houses too were decorated with leafy oak twigs at their doors; it would be pleasant if some Royal Oak pubs were to revive the custom.
See also THE YEAR'S MERRY ROUND, p. 310

Rumples

Dunkling and Wright, in their *Pub Names of Britain*, record 'Rumples' as the rather strange name of a pub in Rye (East Sussex) which turned out, on examination of the signboard, to refer to the goblin in one of Grimms' fairytales which is well known in Britain. This tells of a girl whom a king married because he thought she could spin flax into gold, as her mother had foolishly boasted. To her great dismay, he locked her up with a vast heap of flax, ordering her to make gold of it, on pain of death. Then a goblin appeared and did the task for her, but his price was that he would carry off her firstborn child, unless she could guess his name within a year. She tried many times, in vain, until one day when the year was almost up the king happened to tell her that he'd seen a goblin in the woods, dancing with glee and shouting: 'My name is Rumplestiltskin, but she'll never guess it!' So when the goblin next appeared, the girl told him his true name, and he was so furious that he split in two.
See also MOTHER GEESE & CATS WITH FIDDLES, p. 46

Rushcart

It is mildly surprising to find this pub name in the Yorkshire town of Sowerby Bridge, since it was in Lancashire and Cheshire that the custom of rush-bearing evolved into a celebratory procession involving a highly decorated cart. The practice of strewing rushes on the floors of buildings for warmth and comfort is an old one, well known in medieval and Elizabethan times; it persisted longer in churches than in houses because their flooring often consisted of beaten earth (rather than flagstones) in the eighteenth or even well into the nineteenth century. Rushes needed to be regularly replaced once a year, in July or early August; this was a communal activity, culminating in a procession bringing the fresh supply to the newly cleaned church. In earlier times this would have been a sedate, religious affair, but by the middle of the eighteenth century many villages had turned it into an elaborate festival. The rushes would be piled high on a cart, with a strong sheet thrown over them, to which were stitched all manner of silver objects borrowed for the occasion from the wealthier local households – silver spoons, snuffboxes, watches, mugs and trinkets – plus ribbons and garlands of flowers. The cart was escorted by drummers, fiddlers, and Morris dancers; it would parade all round the village (stopping at various pubs) before eventually reaching the church.

See also THE YEAR'S MERRY ROUND, p. 310

S

St George

See GEORGE & DRAGON

Salamander

There is a pub in Bath called the Salamander. In modern zoology, this is the name of one family of newt-like amphibians, but in Ancient Greece it referred to a mythical reptile, rather like a lizard, which was supposed to be so intensely cold that it could live in the midst of fire, putting the flames out by mere contact with its body. Later, in Renaissance Europe, the occultist Paracelsus appropriated the name for one of the four elemental spirits which he believed inhabited each of the four elements (earth, air, fire, water); naturally, it was the spirit of fire. Pub owners, however, were probably unaware of Paracelsus, and more inclined to celebrate a famous racehorse called Salamander which won the Grand National in 1866.

Salutation

This, one of the oldest recorded names for an inn, originally referred to the Gospel episode more commonly known as the Annunciation, which recounts how the archangel Gabriel appeared to the Virgin Mary and greeted her with the words: 'Hail, full of grace, the Lord is with thee, blessed art thou among women' (Luke 1:26–8). In medieval times both Mary and Gabriel would be represented on the sign, the latter bearing a scroll on which these words were written, but after the Reformation this scene was felt to be too Popish. A few examples survived into the seventeenth century, but Puritanism put an end to them. Either Mary was no longer shown, and the inn became known simply as the Angel; or the name and image became that of the Soldier and Citizen; or the old name was kept but the sign altered to show two men shaking hands or bowing to each other. Dunkling and Wright report that in the 1970s the Salutation at Gibb in Wiltshire showed 'a Victorian gallant kneeling before his lady-love'.

See also ANGELS & SAINTS, p. 16

Samson & the Lion

See ANGELS & SAINTS, p. 16

Saracen's Head (or Turk's Head)

A Saracen's (or Turk's) head, glaring fiercely and wearing a turban, is a fairly common device in heraldry; it implies that the family in question claimed that one of its ancestors had been a Crusader, for 'Saracen' was a general medieval term for an Arab or Muslim. It is likely that most of the older pubs adopting this name were alluding to the coat of arms of a local family, though Eric Delderfield suggests that the choice may also reflect hostility towards the Barbary pirates of later centuries. One pub which certainly claimed a link to the Crusades was the Saracen's Head at Ettington in Warwickshire, now a private house. According to the legend, a knight and squire were returning from the Crusades, carrying a severed head as a battle trophy. They stopped to drink from a spring in the village, and accidentally dropped the head into the water, where it eventually became fossilised. This was said to be the reason why the local branch of the Shirley family had a turbaned head carved as a heraldic crest on their monuments in Ettington church, and on their mansion, Ettington Park. However, when dealing with local legends associated with concrete objects, it is generally safer to think that the object does not commemorate the story but, on the contrary, gave rise to it.

See also QUEENS' HEADS & RED LIONS, p. 248

Sawney Bean's Howff

The pub of this name at Saltcoats, Clyde, is drawing upon one of the most horrific of Scotland's legends – and one well exploited by the tourist industry. In Scottish, a howff is a haunt or regular meeting place – often a favourite tavern – and Sawney Bean was (allegedly) the head of a family of cannibal brigands living in a cave somewhere in Galloway in the late sixteenth century. They would ambush, rob, and kill travellers, especially by night, and regularly ate the bodies. Despite their many murders, and despite the occasional discovery of severed limbs on the shore, they escaped discovery because their cave appeared to be inaccessible. Sawney's evil career lasted for twenty-five years, during which time the size of his family increased through incest, until in the end there were forty-eight of them. Eventually they were hunted down on the orders of James VI (later James I of England), and taken to Edinburgh to be executed. According to one account, Sawney and the other men had their hands, feet and genitalia cut off, and were left to bleed to death in the presence of the women and children, who were then burned alive. According to another, the burning took place first; the men were forced to watch it, after which they were hanged, drawn, and quartered.

Historians reject this gruesome tale as baseless. They point out that there are no contemporary records of the allegedly numerous disappearances of travellers in Galloway, nor of the executions in Edinburgh. The whole story rests on an English source printed in 1734, *The Lives and Actions of the Most Famous Highwaymen* by 'Captain Charles Johnson' (a pseudonym), together with five English chapbooks of the late eighteenth and early nineteenth centuries – long after the period when Sawney is supposed to have lived. It is strongly suspected of being propaganda designed to show Scotland as a barbarous land where horrific crimes can flourish until suppressed by royal authority – which, by the eighteenth century, would mean English authority.

Scholar Gipsy

The Scholar Gipsy pub at Kennington, near Oxford, should really be classed as one named after a literary work, in this case a poem by Matthew Arnold which was published in 1853. However, there is some folklore in its background, since Arnold's inspiration was a local legend recorded by Joseph Glanvil in the seventeenth century:

> And near me on the grass lies Glanvil's book,
> The story of an Oxford scholar poor,
>   Of pregnant parts and quick inventive brain,
> Who, tired of knocking at preferment's door,
>   One summer morn forsook
> His friends, and went to learn the gipsy lore,
>   And roamed the world with that wild brotherhood,
>   And came, as most men deemed, to little good,
> But came to Oxford and his friends no more.

It was said that the student's ghost still haunted the area, and Arnold tells how he was sometimes to be seen sitting by some river, or gazing out over the fields, or wandering the autumn woods, forever young, and forever deep in poetic meditation.
See also GHOSTLY BARMAIDS & HAUNTED CELLARS, p. 278

Sea Witch

Nowadays it is likely that the first thing that comes to mind on hearing the name of the Sea Witch Hotel in Poole (Dorset) is the cartoon character of the villainous Ursula in Walt Disney's film *The Little Mermaid* (1989), which is based on a story by Hans Andersen. But there is an older traditional meaning, exemplified by the Sea Witch pub which stood on the banks of the Thames at Greenwich from the 1830s until it was destroyed in the bombing of London in 1940. A sea witch was one who could use her magic powers to control the winds at sea and raise storms and tempests. According to Cornish legend, there was a witch named Madgy Figgy at St Leven who was often to be seen sitting on a roughly chair-shaped rock when storms were raging, luring ships to their doom. The parish register of Wells-next-the-Sea, a small port in Norfolk, records in December 1583 the deaths of some men in a shipwreck attributed to magic, and explains the spell used:

> Perished upon the West coast, coming from Spain, Richard Waller [and thirteen others, listed] whose deaths were brought to pass by the detestable working of an execrable witche of Kings Lynn, whose name was Mother Gabley, by the boiling or rather labouring [beating] of certayn Eggs in a payle full of colde water, afterward proved sufficiently at the arraignment of ye said Witche.

It is sometimes claimed nowadays that some sea witches raised the storm which scattered the Spanish Armada, thus helping Drake and saving England from invasion. It is a good story, but not an old one.

There was a persistent legend in the days of sailing ships that some witches could 'sell the wind' to sailors. What they sold was a piece of string with three knots in it; if the ship was becalmed, untying one knot would bring a mild but favourable wind; the second knot brought a stronger one; but if the impatient sailor untied all three, there would come a gale strong enough to wreck his ship. This spell was generally credited to the far-off witches of Lapland, but occasionally to those closer home; Ranulf Higden, a fourteenth-century writer, says there were witches on the Isle of Man who used it.

The sea witch in Hans Andersen's story is a wholly supernatural being, living on the seabed. Her house stood in a weird forest of polyps, half animal and half plant, with tentacles like long wriggling worms; it was built from the bones of the drowned. The mermaid visits her to obtain a magic potion which will split her tail into two legs, even though this will cause her pain at every step she takes, and even though she has to pay for the potion by having her tongue cut out. As Andersen wrote the tale, all her courage is in vain; the human prince she loves marries another, and she dies of grief. Disney, and other modern retellers, naturally preferred to punish the witch and give the mermaid a happy ending.

Seven Sisters

The Seven Sisters Road which links the London districts of Tottenham and Holloway commemorates a group of seven large elm trees which formerly stood outside a tavern there, the tavern itself being also named the Seven Sisters. According to a legend recorded in the late nineteenth century, a father told his seven daughters to plant one tree each before they all parted; one of them grew up crooked, but that was because the girl who planted it was a cripple.

Seven Wives

Appropriately, this pub name is to be found at Green End in the town of St Ives – but the one in Huntingdonshire, not the one in Cornwall. As its sign proves, it refers to the 'catch' rhyme (known since around 1730):

> As I was going to St Ives,
> I met a man with seven wives,

Each wife had seven sacks,
Each sack held seven cats,
Each cat had seven kits.
Kits, cats, sacks, wives –
How many were there going to St Ives?

See also MOTHER GEESE & CATS WITH FIDDLES, p. 46

Shamrock

Since the shamrock has been famous as the national emblem of Ireland since the end of the seventeenth century, it could well be the case that pubs called the Shamrock, such as the ones at Cheltenham in Gloucestershire and Standish in Lancashire, either have an Irish landlord or serve numerous Irish customers. The traditional explanation given for the plant's symbolic importance is that when St Patrick was trying to teach the newly converted Irish the Christian dogma of the Trinity he showed them a shamrock leaf, saying, 'Is it not as easy for Father, Son, and Holy Ghost to be one God, as for three leaflets to make up one leaf?'

However, there might also be an allusion to good luck, since a four-leafed shamrock (like a FOUR-LEAFED CLOVER) will make anyone who picks and keeps it lucky in gambling and racing, provided he always carries it with him and never lets anybody else see it.

Shoe

At Exton near Southampton (Hampshire), Leslie Dunkling and Gordon Wright reported that there was a pub named the Shoe, with a signboard illustrating the nursery rhyme:

> There was an old woman who lived in a shoe,
> She had so many children she didn't know what to do;
> She gave them some broth without any bread,
> She whipped them all soundly and put them to bed.

Modern editors find this embarrassing, and soften the ending, so it is worth also quoting an earlier and fuller version (1797) found by Iona and Peter Opie, where the humour is even blacker:

> There was a little old woman, and she liv'd in a shoe,
> She had so many children she didn't know what to do.
> She crumm'd 'em some porridge without any bread,
> And she borrow'd a beetle [= a mallet], and she knocked 'em
>   all o' the head,
> Then out went th'old woman to bespeak 'em a coffin,
> And when she came back, she found 'em all a-loffin'.

See also MOTHER GEESE & CATS WITH FIDDLES, p. 46

Shovel & Boot

See PUZZLING PAIRS, p. 112

Silent Woman

See QUIET WOMAN

Silver Ball

The Silver Ball pub in the Cornish town of St Columb owes its name to a custom which can be proved to have existed there in the 1590s, and may well be older – its annual hurling match on Shrove Tuesday afternoon. It is played with a wooden or cork ball about the size of an orange, coated with silver, which is thrown or carried, but rarely kicked. The game begins on the market square, and the goals are about two miles apart. There is no limit on the number of players, so there may well be a hundred or more taking part; the aim of each team is to carry the ball to its own goal, or to get it across the parish boundary in any direction. It is a very lively affair, during which shopkeepers find it advisable to board up their windows.

See also THE YEAR'S MERRY ROUND, p. 310

Silver Tassie

A tassie is, in Scottish, a large cup or goblet, and 'The Silver Tassie' is a song by Robert Burns which has given its name to pubs in Lochgellie, Johnstone, and Hamilton. It is the song of a soldier about to leave for some war overseas:

> Go fetch to me a pint of wine
>   And fill it in a silver tassie,
> That I may drink, before I go,
>   A service to my bonny lassie. ...

> The trumpets sound, the banners fly,
>   The glittering spears are ranked and ready
> The shouts o' war are heard afar,
>   The battle closes deep and deadly.

> It's not the roar of sea or shore
>   Wad make me longer wish to tarry,

> Nor shouts o' war that's heard afar –
> It's leavin' thee, my bonny Mary!

Simple Simon

The reason that a pub at Emscote in Warwickshire took this name was that there was a large pie factory on the other side of the road, and a well-known nursery rhyme about the misadventures of a fool, beginning:

> Simple Simon met a pieman
> Going to the fair;
> Said Simple Simon to the pieman,
> Let me taste your ware.

See also MOTHER GEESE & CATS WITH FIDDLES, p. 46

Sir John Barleycorn

See JOHN BARLEYCORN

Sir John Cockle

The pub of this name at Mansfield in Nottinghamshire takes its name from the hero of a humorous ballad, 'The King and the Miller of Mansfield'. There are also pubs called the Miller of Mansfield and the King and the Miller in various towns.

Various versions of the ballad are known from the late seventeenth century, and one is printed in Thomas Percy's *Reliques of English Poetry* (1765). It exploits an old and always popular theme – that of a king who, being accidentally separated from his courtiers, encounters a peasant who fails to recognise him and speaks roughly to him, or casually admits to lawbreaking. In Percy's version it is Henry II, in others Henry VIII.

The ballad opens by telling how one summer day:

> Henry, our royall king, would ride a-hunting
> To the greenwood so pleasant and faire;
> To see the harts skipping, and dainty does tripping,
> Unto merry Sherwood his nobles repaire.

As dark fell, Henry lost his way in the wood and found himself wandering alone. At length he met a 'rude miller' and asked him the way to Nottingham, but the miller retorted that he looked like 'a gentleman thief', and would get a crack over the head with a cudgel if he came any closer. The king persuaded him, with some difficulty, that he was an honest man in need of a night's lodging, and could pay for it, so they set off for the miller's house in Mansfield. There the miller said he would be well lodged; he could share his son Richard's bed for the night, with fresh straw and good brown hempen sheets. But Richard has some doubts about this:

> 'Art thou not lousy, nor scabby?' quoth he;
> 'If thou beest, then surely thou lyest not with mee.'

The king assures the lad that he is quite clean, and they all sit down to a hearty supper, including a fine venison pasty. The king says he has never eaten anything so good as this dainty dish. Richard, the miller's son, says they eat such meat every day, and never pay a penny for it:

> 'From merry Sherwood we fetch it home here;
> Now and then we make bold with our king's deer.'

He explains that they always keep two or three fat deer hidden in the roof, but that the king must never hear about it, and Henry promised to keep their secret. Next morning, inevitably, the courtiers who have been searching for their missing lord arrive at the miller's house, where the family realise who their guest must be, and are terrified to think they will be hanged for poaching. The king draws his sword – not to behead the miller, but simply to dub him a knight, as Sir John Cockle. The name is presumably meant as a bawdy pun.

Judging by parallel tales elsewhere, this is probably where the original legend ended. Percy's version, however, has a second section telling how the king later summoned the miller to court for a feast on St George's Day. Here the humour is mere coarseness. When the king asks Richard if he remembers how they shared a bed, he replies that he certainly does, because 'Thou with thy farting didst make the bed hot.' Horrified, the miller tells his son to watch his language, only to fall into similar coarseness himself:

> 'Thou whoreson unhappy knave,' then quoth the knight,
> 'Speak cleanly to our king, or else go shite!'

But Henry finds it all highly amusing, and after a feast he makes Sir John Cockle overseer of Sherwood, with £300 a year, though warning him: 'Take heed now you steal no more of my deer.'

Sixteen-String Jack

This was the nickname of John (or Jack) Rann, an eighteenth-century highwayman famous for his love of gaudy dress; he wore bright ribbons on his riding breeches, eight on each leg. There are pubs named after him at Theydon Bois near Epping and Stratford St Mary near Colchester. Historically he was not a particularly significant criminal, and would have been forgotten long ago if he had not been taken up by the Victorian hack-writers who produced 'penny dreadfuls', cheap sensational fiction serials printed in weekly instalments for schoolboys and young working-class readers. Highwaymen were a popular subject. Sixteen-String Jack was the hero of a serial of his own, but more significantly was given a major role as one of Dick Turpin's comrades in *Black Bess, or The Knight of the Road* by Edward Viles, which ran for 254 weekly parts and was eventually published in book form in 1868.

See also HIGHWAYMEN & SMUGGLERS, p. 208

Skimmington Castle

The Skimmington Castle pub on Reigate Heath, which already existed as a beerhouse in the 1890s, perpetuates the local place name Skimmington Hill. Around 1900, it was the home of a James Bonny, who, besides running the pub, advertised 'J. Bonny & Son's Pure Mineral Waters, Skimmington Castle, Reigate, manufactured from the Celebrated Skimmington Castle Spring Water (sterilized), guaranteed absolutely pure by analysis.'

What remains mysterious is how the name Skimmington came to be attached to the hill at all, for it refers to a custom, not a locality. 'Skimmington riding' or 'skimmety riding' was the term generally used in the south and south-west of England for a traditional way in which a community would express its disapproval of someone who had offended against social norms, more generally known as 'rough music'. Many instances have been recorded from the sixteenth century to the nineteenth, and even a few in the first part of the twentieth. Typically, it would be aimed at adulterers, sexual deviants, people whose marriage or cohabitation was considered scandalous, women who beat or bullied their husbands (or vice versa), couples who were cruel to their children. People would gather after dark and march round the village in procession till they reached the offender's home, making as much din as they could by banging on pots and pans, blowing whistles and horns, and shouting insults. They would parade an effigy of the guilty party, setting it to 'ride' on a pole, on a donkey, or in a cart, and often ending by hanging or burning it. The process was repeated for three nights. The aim was to humiliate the offender, and if possible to drive him or her out of the village. As George Roberts, author of a *History and Antiquities of Lyme Regis and Charmouth,* wrote in 1834, 'A skimmington riding makes many laugh, but the parties for whom they ride never lose the ridicule and disgrace which it attaches.'

One can only hazard a guess that perhaps in this area skimmington processions used to assemble on one particular hill, thus giving it its name.

Smugglers, Smugglers' Barn, Smugglers' Haunt, Smugglers' Roost, Smugglers' Den

See HIGHWAYMEN & SMUGGLERS, p. 208

Spaniards Inn

The Spaniards Inn, in Spaniards Road, Hampstead Heath, London NW3, was built in the early eighteenth century and is supposed to be named after two brothers, Francesco and Juan Porero, who are said to have been the original owners. The story goes that they fought a duel over a woman whom they both loved, and that one or both died as a result, and may have been buried in the garden. An alternative explanation assumes that the name goes back to the seventeenth century; this theory claims that the Spanish ambassador to the court of James I had a house on this site which he left to his valet, and that the latter turned it into an inn. However, the pub devotes far more attention to its alleged links to the highwayman Dick Turpin, many of whose robberies took place on nearby Hampstead Heath.

See also HIGHWAYMEN & SMUGGLERS, p. 208

Spectre

The pub at Pluckley in Kent, formerly known as the Black Horse, rechristened itself as the Spectre, a name which is probably unique, and obviously chosen to reflect the proud boast that this is 'the most haunted village in England'. Its reputation as such goes back at least thirty years, and the number of alleged ghosts is considerable – though Alan Bignell wrote, in his *Kent Lore* of 1983, that it was becoming hard to find anyone who had actually seen one. The ghosts include a highwayman, a monk, a miller, an old gypsy, a soldier, a suicidal farmer, a suicidal schoolmaster (said to have hanged himself in the pub), a woman with a dog, and a Red Lady and a White Lady, both supposed to have belonged to past generations of the local landowning family.

See also GHOSTLY BARMAIDS & HAUNTED CELLARS, p. 278

Speed the Plough

See HARVESTERS AND WHEATSHEAVES, p. 182

Spotted Cow

This is a fairly common name for a pub, two examples being found in Manchester, and others at Angmering (Sussex), Hartlepool (County Durham), Aylesford (Kent), in Leeds, and elsewhere. It is true that some breeds of cow do indeed have blotches of a different colour, so the name may simply be descriptive. However, there could be a reference to a lively folksong which was widespread in the nineteenth century, and is still popular with folk singers. It begins:

> One morning in the month of May
> As from my cot I strayed,
> Just at the dawning of the day
> I met a charming maid.

> 'Good morning, fair maid, and whither,' says I,
> 'So early, tell me now?'
> The maid replied 'Kind sir,' she cried,
> 'I've lost my spotted cow.'

The cunning young man tells her that he has seen her cow, and persuades her to come into the woods with him to find it. Once there, naturally, the cow is forgotten as they kiss and hug:

> In the fair grove we spent the day
> And thought it passed too soon;

> At night we homeward went our way,
>   And brightly shone the moon.
> If I should cross yon flowery dell
>   Or go to view the plough,
> She comes and calls her gentle swain,
>   'I've lost my spotted cow.'

Leslie Dunkling and Gordon Wright note an amusingly different interpretation of the name. When a Spotted Cow opened at Brockham in Surrey in 1962, the owners took as inspiration the nursery rhyme which says that 'the cow jumped over the moon'; their sign showed a cow doing just that, and wearing a medal that says 'first over the moon', while a Russian Bear and American Eagle watch enviously.

See also MOTHER GEESE & CATS WITH FIDDLES, p. 46

Starving Rascal

This pub, at Amblecote near Stourbridge (Worcestershire), is another pleasing example of one which changed its name to take account of a traditional local tale. Formerly the Dudley Arms, it became the Starving Rascal in 1977 because it was reputedly haunted by the ghost of an old tramp who had come begging for food and shelter one night about a hundred years ago. The landlord refused to help him, and next morning he was found dead on the doorstep. The signboard illustrated the sad story, with the living tramp on one side and his ghost on the other.

See also GHOSTLY BARMAIDS & HAUNTED CELLARS, p. 278

Ghostly Barmaids & Haunted Cellars

A very large number of pubs, up and down the country, claim to be haunted, as any book on contemporary ghost-lore will show. However, the level of belief involved can range all the way from total to zero. At one extreme is the personal-experience account of someone who has been alarmed by uncanny sights or sounds and attributes these to a hostile ghost. At the other, there are legends which are well known in a particular community, but not taken seriously; indeed, they may be consciously exploited in order to attract customers and tourists, or to hoax outsiders. Pub lore has plenty such tales, of both types. Often they involve figures from the historical past, either a named individual, or an anonymous member of some historical group recognisable by its distinctive period costume – a Cavalier, a monk, a highwayman – or simply some anonymous Grey Lady in a vaguely old-fashioned dress.

Occasionally, where there is not merely a rumoured haunting but a well-developed tale to go with it, and the pub's name tells the story too. This is the case at the STARVING RASCAL, the WICKED LADY, the PHANTOM COACH, the Headless Woman (see QUIET WOMAN)at Duddon in Cheshire, and the BLACK DOG of Newgate. One might also take the tale of the Black Dog at Uplyme as a ghost story, interpreting the phantom hound as the ghost of the previous owner, unable to rest because he had hidden his money; this would fit well with general traditional beliefs. The Kentish village of Pluckley, which prides itself on being 'the most haunted in England', has appropriately named one of its pubs the Spectre. Usually, however, a pub's ghosts are only talked of locally; they are not famous enough in the outer world to bring it good publicity.

The tales told to account for them may draw upon historical events of national significance. In 1685, the elderly and aristocratic Dame Alice Lisle really was beheaded at Winchester, outside the building which is now the Eclipse Inn, for giving shelter to two men who had taken part in the Duke of Monmouth's rebellion. She spent her last night there, so now her ghost, it is said, is sometimes to be seen there as a quiet figure in a long grey dress, standing in the upstairs corridor. Other stories are rather more parochial. In London, the Grenadier in Wilton Row, SW1, is haunted every September by a silent figure who paces through the rooms, rattling the furniture; this is said to be a young subaltern who was beaten to death there one September by fellow soldiers who accused him of cheating at cards. Also in London, the Gatehouse in Highgate, N6, is haunted by the angry ghost of a certain Mother Marnes, said to be an old lady who was robbed and murdered in that pub; she is described as terrifying, but never appears if there are children or animals present. At the Bull at Wargrave in Berkshire it is said that an invisible woman is heard weeping; she was the landlord's wife, but when he discovered that she had a lover he drove her out, forbidding her ever to see her children again. Some stories have a touch of humour to them. The King's Head at Cuckfield in Sussex is haunted by Geranium Jane, a nineteenth-century barmaid who was seduced by her employer and became pregnant; she pestered him to marry her, so he got rid of her by dropping a pot of geraniums on her head from an upstairs window.

Reported manifestations are many and various. Perhaps the most commonly reported is a sudden inexplicable drop in temperature; doors open or shut of themselves; there are poltergeist activities, in which furniture is moved, pots and pans thrown, beer-taps turned on; footsteps are heard; figures in the dress of past eras are briefly or indistinctly seen. Such things are common to all haunted houses. More special to pubs is the quiet, contented old ghost of some long-dead customer, returning from time to time to his favourite chair in a peaceful corner; the landlord and regulars may have a friendly nickname for him – Old George, or Fred, or whatever.

Many older cities and towns now offer Ghost Walks as an after-dark entertainment for visitors, so it is worth investigating whether the ghost hunt and the pub crawl can be agreeably combined.

Sturdy's Castle

The pub of this name, at Tackley near Oxford, was formerly called the Sturdy and Castle, but neither form of the name makes much sense. In the absence of any other explanation, local opinion has decided that there were once two men, one called Sturdy and the other called Castle, who quarrelled so violently that one killed the other, and was then himself hanged for the murder on the place where the pub now stands.

Swan with Two Necks

There are several pubs of this name in England (e.g. at Armitage in Staffordshire), together with the variant Two-Necked Swan (e.g. at Great Yarmouth in Norfolk); it is first recorded in the sixteenth century, and was widely popular in the seventeenth. Although a swan pure and simple has been a common emblem in heraldry from medieval times, no two-necked version is featured there. It was therefore suggested by the eminent antiquarian Sir Joseph Banks in 1810 that the correct form of the name should be 'swan with two *nicks*', referring to the fact that swans on the Thames belonging to the Worshipful Company of Vintners are marked by having two nicks cut in their beaks – as opposed to those belonging to the Worshipful Company of Dyers, which have one nick, and those belonging to the queen, which have none. Since vintners have an obvious connection with pubs, this theory of origin is reasonably convincing.

In theory, every swan in the country belongs to the Sovereign, and has done ever since the bird was introduced in the thirteenth century; swans could not be killed without express royal permission. It was in 1473 that the Vintners and Dyers were

granted the privilege of keeping some of their own on the
Thames; this must have been
of considerable value at a
period when swans were a
luxury food at banquets. It
is still commemorated in the
annual ritual of 'swan-upping'

The Swan with Two Necks

which takes place on the Thames every July. The Royal Swan
Keeper, the equivalent official from the Vintners and the Dyers
and various assistants, take a boat at London Bridge and work
their way downstream to Henley, catching and examining every
swan and cygnet they can find (currently estimated at about six
hundred). The young birds are marked with one nick, or two, or
left unmarked, according to the markings on the parent birds;
broods of mixed parentage are split equally.

See also WHITE SWAN

Sweeney & Todd

In Reading, in Berkshire, a combined pub and restaurant called
the Sweeney & Todd proudly declares on its website that it
serves 'delicious, fresh, home made pies'. This is a clever, if
rather gruesome, joke, referring to that famous villain Sweeney
Todd, 'the Demon Barber of Fleet Street', allegedly active in
London around 1800. It is said that he would seat his customers in a tilting chair over a concealed trapdoor, and cut their
throats while shaving them. The chair and the trapdoor would
do their work, toppling the bodies into a cellar below, where
their valuables were stolen. Then they would be taken through
a tunnel to another cellar, that of a pastry-cook's shop which

belonged to Todd's accomplice, Mrs Lovett. Her meat pies were particularly delicious. It is said that when their crimes were discovered Mrs Lovett poisoned herself in prison and Todd was hanged.

Many modern popular writers and tourist guides insist that all this is really true, and that Todd was tried at the Old Bailey and hanged at Newgate on 25 January 1802, before a jubilant crowd. But this cannot be so. Legal and prison records mention no such trial (which, had it really occurred, would have been sensational), and there are no press reports of the execution. This was pointed out as long ago as 1878, when a contributor to the September issue of *Notes and Queries* stated:

> Now I happen to know, from my own personal experience, that the lower classes of London believe in the substantial truth of this story. I can trace this credulity back (by report, of course) for at least seventy years. It is never recounted without the addition that the shaver was at last detected, convicted, and suffered at Tyburn. And yet, after all, is there any foundation for the belief? I have searched in vain the various editions of the *Newgate Calendar*, the cognate *Malefactors' Register*, the Old Bailey Sessions papers, numerous collections of London legends, the late Walter Thornbury's *Old Stories Retold*, etc, but can find no trace of such a prosecution or of any crime bearing resemblance to this one, at any rate in England.

In fact, the crimes of Sweeney Todd first appeared in an anonymous serial in the magazine the *People's Periodical* in 1843, published by Edward Lloyd. The author was probably either Thomas Peckett Prest or James Rymer, both skilful writers of horrific fiction who worked for Lloyd, frequently presenting their stories as true reports. In this particular case the author was adapting a story that had first appeared in France early in the nineteenth century, relocating it from Paris to London and giving the characters English names. Other writers took up the theme, so that Sweeney Todd became a well-known figure in Victorian melodramas, boys' comics, and other popular media, and so entered the stream of traditional English lore.

Swift Nick

See HIGHWAYMEN & SMUGGLERS, p. 208, NEVISON'S LEAP

T

Tam o' Shanter

The story of Tam o' Shanter is of course a Scottish one, told in a famous comic poem by Robert Burns, and naturally almost all the pubs named after it are in Scotland, e.g. at Edinburgh, Ayr, Dumfries, and Kilmarnock. There are two, however, in England – one in Huddersfield and the other at *Tam*worth in Staffordshire, where it is obviously punning on the place name. In the poem, Tam is a farmer riding home drunk who plays the Peeping Tom when he notices a group of witches dancing wildly. He can't help cheering one whom he nicknames Cutty Sark because she is wearing a particularly short shirt or shift, and so he is discovered and must flee for his life as the angry witches chase him, led by Cutty Sark herself. He escapes, but only because he comes to a river, and witches cannot cross running water. As it is, Cutty Sark grabs his horse's tail as they gallop onto the bridge, and pulls it out by the roots.

Thieves' Kitchen

This used to be the name of a pub in Warwick Street, Worthing (West Sussex). Local people firmly believed that it commemorated smugglers, who allegedly had made a secret tunnel from the pub to the shore to bring in their contraband – a very common notion in local traditions. Unfortunately the chain which now owns it has renamed it the Vintner's Parrot, since their identifying symbol is a parrot.

See also HIGHWAYMEN & SMUGGLERS, p. 208

Thorn Bush

Most pubs called Thorn Bush or Thorn Tree are simply referring to a conspicuous tree somewhere close by, but Bryant Lillywhite records that in his time the one at Croydon in Surrey had on its signboard the image of the Holy Thorn of Glastonbury. This, according to legend, came into existence when the saintly Joseph of Arimathea, a disciple of Jesus himself who had come to Britain to spread the faith, wearily thrust his staff into the ground as he climbed a hill near Glastonbury; it miraculously took root, and became a fine thorn tree. Unlike other thorns, it blossomed on Christmas Day in honour of Christ's birth, as well as in the spring. A tree alleged to be the very one was regarded as a holy marvel in medieval times; it died long ago, but its descendants still exist in and around Glastonbury, and they really do blossom around Christmas time.

See also ANGELS & SAINTS, p. 16

Three Arrows

In most cases, this is a reference to the arms of the medieval Guild of Fletchers, craftsmen who made arrows. At Boroughbridge near York, however, it refers to a local landmark and its associated legend – a line of three tall, slender standing stones locally known as the Devil's Arrows. It is claimed that Satan, enraged at the people of the nearby town of Aldborough, stood on the crest of a hill and fired these massive 'arrows' from his bow, intending to demolish the town. Needless to say, his aim was poor, and he failed miserably.

See also QUEENS' HEADS & RED LIONS, p. 248

Three Crowns

Many of the older pubs with this name interpreted it as a straightforward historical reference to James I, the first British sovereign to unite the three crowns of England, Scotland and Ireland. This was clearly the case with the London ones illustrated in Delderfield's *British Inn Signs*; one bears a portrait of King James, and on the other the crowns are unmistakably copied from the royal crown of England. A second possible view was to see the name as alluding to the 'three kings', i.e. the Magi who brought gifts to the child Jesus (see below). Thirdly, the region of East Anglia has adopted the device of three crowns as its heraldic emblem, though it is unclear whether this first arose as a reference to the Magi, or to three royal abbesses of Ely, or (most plausibly) to the martyred St Edmund, who was at one period honoured as the patron saint of England, and whose emblem was a triple crown. Tudor writers ascribed it to a legendary prehistoric king of Britain named Belinus. Finally, and most dramatically, M. R. James in one of his scholarly ghost stories ('A Warning to the Curious', 1925) wrote of three 'holy crowns' dating from Anglo-Saxon times which had been buried near the Suffolk coast to protect the country from invaders; two had since been destroyed, but 'one's still doing its work'. Thanks to its sober and plausible details, many readers now assume that this antiquarian 'legend' which James wove into his fictional tale is authentic folklore.

See also QUEENS' HEADS & RED LIONS, p. 248

Three Feathers

See QUEENS' HEADS & RED LIONS, p. 248

Three Horseshoes

The horseshoe is in itself a common pub name, implying good luck, as has been said above (p. 137). When *three* horseshoes are specified, three explanations are possible. First, a practical one: the name could be intended as a hint to travellers to check whether their horses need to be reshod. This interpretation could be seen at Ripley in Derbyshire in the 1970s, as described by Dunkling and Wright: 'a horse squatting on its haunches and ruefully holding up a faulty shoe for inspection.' Secondly, an artistic one: objects arranged in threes make a pleasing pattern, much used in heraldry. A wide range of animals and objects occur in threes in pub names – bells, bulls' heads, crowns, fishes, swans, and wheatsheaves, to name but a few. Thirdly, superstition: throughout European folklore for many centuries three has been regarded as a powerful number, widely used in rituals of magic and in folk medicine, where it is common that specified words and actions must be repeated three times. The idea is echoed in the sayings that 'good (or bad) things come in threes', and 'third time lucky'. From this point of view, three horseshoes powerfully reinforce the luck of one. Even luckier would be the Nine Horseshoes, which Larwood and Hotten say was formerly near Bassingham in Lincolnshire.

Three Kings

This pub name, found at Twickenham and elsewhere, is normally taken as a reference to the three Magi (also called the Wise Men) who according to the Gospels were led by a star to Bethlehem (or to Nazareth), in order to worship the infant Jesus and bring him gifts of gold, frankincense and myrrh. Although the text does not call them kings, the Christian Church soon gave them this rank because of two passages in the Old Testament which were interpreted as prophecies about the birth of Jesus. One is Isa. 60:3: 'The gentiles shall come to thy light, and kings to the brightness of thy rising'; the other Psalm 72, verse 10: 'The kings of Tarshish and of the isles shall bring presents; the kings of Sheba and Seba shall offer gifts.' Medieval tradition even invented names for the three kings: Caspar, Melchior and Balthazar. They were widely honoured as saints, and the cathedral of Cologne in Germany claims to have relics of their bodies, for which reason some older pubs chose the alliterative name of Three Kings of Cologne, which some commentators have suggested was introduced to this country by the guild of mercers, who imported textiles from Cologne. Be

The Three Kings

that as it may, the fact that the Magi were famed for their long journey makes them appropriate patrons for inns that catered for travellers. They still commonly figure on Christmas cards and in carols ('We three kings from Orient are …').

A very different explanation lies behind the name of the Three Kings Inn in the village of Threekingham in Lincolnshire, where local tradition claims that the village itself had previously been called Laundon but took a new name to celebrate the deaths of three Danish Viking kings killed in a battle nearby in the year 869. The signboard, as reproduced in Eric Delderfield's *British Inn Signs*, shows this date above three crowned heads. The battle itself is historical, but the idea of three kings is more romantic than realistic.

See also ANGELS & SAINTS, p. 16

Three-Legged Mare

The name of this pub in York does not refer to a badly injured female horse, but is a grim joke – an old slang term for a three-post gallows, especially the famous one at Tyburn in London. Such gallows consisted of three posts set in a triangle and linked by three cross-beams, making a strong and stable framework from which several criminals could be hanged at once. Presumably the reason the name was chosen here is that the highwayman Dick Turpin was hanged in York in 1739, and is remembered as something of a local hero. According to contemporary accounts he died with stylish courage, bowing cheerfully to the crowds, admitting his crimes, and stepping off the ladder himself, rather than letting the hangman pull it away from under him.

To ensure that customers get the point, a half-size model gallows has been built in the pub garden.

Three Little Pigs

The story of the Three Little Pigs and their enemy the Big Bad Wolf was first printed in James Orchard Halliwell's *Popular Rhymes and Nursery Tales* (1849), and is thus one of the small handful of fairytales which is authentically English, not a translation from German, French or Danish. It has been known and loved by generations of English children, and the song 'Who's Afraid of the Big Bad Wolf?', which was composed for Walt Disney's cartoon film version in 1933, is often assumed to be a traditional nursery rhyme. Therefore this pub name, found at Crediton in Devon, joins several others drawn from children's lore.

See also MOTHER GEESE & CATS WITH FIDDLES, p. 46

Three Nuns

This name for a pub usually has the straightforward historical explanation that there is, or once was, a convent nearby, but at Mirfield in Yorkshire there is a further reference to a famous legend. There, the pub is next to Kirklees Priory, tradition-

ally the site of Robin Hood's tragic death, caused by the treachery of the Prioress. According to the chronicler Richard Grafton in 1569:

The sayd Robin Hood, being afterward troubled with sicknesse, came to a certain Nonry in Yorkshire called Kirklies

The Three Nuns

where desiryng to be let blood he was betrayed and bled to deth. After whose death the Prioresse of the same place caused him to be buried by the high way side, where he had used to rob and spoyle those that passed that way. . . And the cause why she buryed him there was for that the common passengers and trauailers [travellers] knowyng and seeyng him there buryed, might more safely and without feare take their iorneys that way, which they durst not do in the lyfe of the sayd outlawes. And at either end of the sayde Tombe was erected a crosse of stone, which is to be seene there at this present.

Various ballads of the Tudor period further emphasised the treachery of the Prioress by saying that she was a close kins-woman of Robin's, and that a knight who was her lover stabbed him while he was weakened by the blood-letting. A much later one, from the eighteenth century, added the now familiar inci-dent that as he lay dying he shot one last arrow through the window, asking to be buried where it fell. But it would seem that nowadays the people of Mirfield prefer to think well of the Prioress and her community, since Dunkling and Wright were told in the 1970s that 'Robin is said to have been tended on his deathbed by three nuns.'

Three Tuns

See QUEENS' HEADS & RED LIONS, p. 248

Three Witches

Since this is the name of a pub in Stratford-on-Avon, the refer-ence is obviously to the famous opening scene of Shakespeare's

Macbeth, with its three witches concocting their spells ('Bubble, bubble, toil and trouble, / Fire, burn, and cauldron bubble!'). But Shakespeare did not himself invent the idea of a trio of hags foretelling and possibly controlling Macbeth's fate. He found them in the book which he used as a source for Macbeth's career, Raphael Holinshed's *History of Scotland* (1577), though Holinshed did not commit himself as to what exactly the three women were:

> The common opinion was, that these three women were either the weird sisters, that is (as ye would say) the goddesses of destinie, or else some nymphs or feiries, indued with knowledge of prophecie by their necromanticall science, because euerie thing came to pass as they had spoken.

The signboard is described by Dunkling and Wright as showing 'three conical witches' hats resting on a broomstick'.

Tom Cobley (or Cobbleigh)

At least three Devon villages – Colebrook, Paignton, and Spreyton – have pubs named after this character in the famous folksong 'Widdecombe Fair', and the first two can both point to gravestones in their churchyards commemorating a Thomas Cobley who is said to be the real person alluded to in the song. At Spreyton too people claim that a man of that name was born and died in the village, and that the inn sign is his portrait. Certainly the song itself, with its list of very plausible names as a chorus, looks convincingly like a topical local joke, but what actual event inspired it must remain a mystery. All we can know is what the song itself tells: the singer, along with seven other men, borrows Tom Pearce's grey mare to ride to a fair at Widecombe-in-the-Moor; the mare lies down and dies (presumably the combined weight of the men is too much for her); Tom and the riders cry themselves to death; and now they are ghosts out on the moors. The old mare 'doth appear gashly white':

> And all the night long be heard skirling and groans,
>   All along, down along, out along lee,
> From Tom Pearce's old mare and her rattling bones,
>   With Bill Brewer, Jan Stewer,
>   Peter Gurney, Peter Davy,
>   Dan'l Widgin, Harry Hawk,
> Old Uncle Tom Cobbleigh and all,
> Old Uncle Tom Cobbleigh and all.

As the song is widely known, one can find pubs named Tom Cobbleigh far beyond the boundaries of Devon, e.g. in Leicester.

Tom o' Bedlam

There have been pubs of this name in several places – Chadwick End and Balsall (both in Warwickshire) and Redbourne in Hertfordshire, for instance. It comes from an old slang term for a madman, or for a beggar who went about half naked and deliberately terrorised people into giving him money by pretending to be dangerously mad. Shakespeare made brilliant use of the idea in *King Lear*, where Edgar disguises himself as one of the 'Bedlam beggars with roaring voices', pretends to be tormented by demons, and calls himself 'Poor Tom'. It is largely thanks to

Shakespeare that Tom o' Bedlam is remembered by later generations, but the name in fact goes back to pre-Elizabethan times, for 'Bedlam' refers to the London hospital of St Mary of Bethlehem, a priory founded in 1247 which in 1403 specialised as a lunatic asylum. The 'Toms' were originally relatively harmless inmates who were sent out into the community when the hospital became overcrowded, but who were incapable of work and so turned to begging.

Tom Thumb

There is one pub of this name in Stockport and another at Blaby near Leicester. Two explanations are possible, either of which could provide a good image for a signboard. It may commemorate a famous nineteenth-century American dwarf, 'General Tom Thumb', who was exhibited in London by the travelling showman Phineas T. Barnum, or it may refer directly to the little hero of a well-known English fairytale, 'The History of Tom Thumb'. There are references to this story in the latter part of the sixteenth century, but the oldest surviving version was printed in 1621. It tells of a woman who longed to have a child, even if it were no bigger than her husband's thumb; her wish is magically granted, and the rest of the story concerns the comic misadventures which Tom suffers because of his tiny size – he falls into a pudding, is swallowed by a cow and excreted in a cowpat, is swallowed by a fish and then vomited up, and so forth. Modern versions tone down the coarseness; some end with Tom dying heroically in combat with a spider.

See also MOTHER GEESE AND CATS WITH FIDDLES, p. 46

Tom Tiddler's Tavern

Pubs of this name can be found in Stevenage (Hertfordshire) and in London. There seems to be some reference to the old-fashioned phrase 'Tom Tiddler's Ground', meaning somewhere where it is very easy to make money, and/or somewhere where rich people congregate. This itself comes from a children's game in which one player, known as 'Tom Tiddler', guards a patch of ground and tries to prevent the others from running onto it and picking up the imaginary gold and silver coins which are supposed to lie there. These cheerful associations with wealth and fun make this an appropriate name. Leslie Dunkling and Gordon Wright point out that there was also at one time a cartoon character called Tom Tiddler.

Town Mouse

The Town Mouse in Burnley in Lancashire is probably so called because of a traditional fable about a mouse who lived in a town and his friend the country field mouse. When the field mouse invited the town mouse to come and stay with him, all he could offer him was a few grains of barley. 'Why, you live no better than an ant,' cried the town mouse. 'Come to live with me and share my abundance of good things.' The field mouse accepted gratefully, and was amazed to find what wonderful scraps of food were lying about in the human house where his friend lived – bread, cheese, flour, and fruit. But no sooner had they settled down to feed than a man came into the room, and they had to run to their hole in terror. When this had happened several times, the field mouse said: 'I see, my friend, that you eat well, but you pay for it by all this worry and

The Town Mouse

danger. I'm going home, where I can go on nibbling my barley without being scared and suspicious all the time.'

This fable is first found in the collection attributed to Aesop, a Greek of the early sixth century BC. In some of the later versions it is a cat, not a human being, whose arrival scares the mice away.

Treacle Mine

There are at least thirty villages in England which are traditionally said to possess a secret treacle mine, a few of which have named their pub after this legendary feature. Sometimes the joke implies that people of the village are so daft that they think treacle comes out of the ground; sometimes that they are so poor they live on bread and treacle only; sometimes that they are lazy scroungers; sometimes that treacle-mining is a secret and highly profitable craft, unknown to outsiders. The joke can be a taunt by outsiders, but is more often used by insiders as a mark of pride in their identity. Local people enjoy persuading children, or gullible strangers, that treacle mines really exist, and often devise complicated stories to back up their hoax.

One Treacle Mine pub, currently well known to motorists, is a very modern one, built and named in 1994; it serves to identify a major roundabout on the A13 just outside Grays in Essex. Before it opened, a competition was held to find a name for it; it was won by a man who said that, many years before, his father used to tell him of a secret treacle mine in the area then known as Nutberry Corner, more or less where the pub now stands.

In contrast, the Treacle Mine Hotel at Tadley in Hampshire lost its identity as recently as 2006, having changed ownership and been renamed the Broomsquire Hotel. This is sad, for Tadley's Treacle Mine was a common and well-loved item in village mythology, dating back at least fifty years. It was variously explained as referring to a local pig farm, or a waste-oil dump abandoned by the American Air Force at Aldermaston air base, or a large gravel pit and the quicksand it created, or an old treacle tin full of golden guineas which a little boy dug up in his back garden. An elderly ex-seaman named Joe Kelly used to entertain pub audiences with a long ballad about an alleged tragedy in this alleged mine:

> 'Twas on the third day of July
> And twelve strong men were about to die
> At the Tadley Treacle Mines.

> They were working fast without a care
> When a tunnel collapsed and buried them there
> At the Tadley Treacle Mines.

> No noise was heard above the ground
> When evening came they couldn't be found
> At Tadley Treacle Mines.

...

They buried them there that very day
And there to this day their bodies lay
At the Tadley Treacle Mines.

So gentlemen take heed I pray
And do not go to work today
At the Tadley Treacle Mines.

Though the loss of the hotel's traditional name is very regrettable, it is some consolation that the new one also embodies a local reference – 'broomsquire' was a term for Gypsies and other squatters in the New Forest who earned their living by making brooms from heath.

There is another Treacle Mine pub in Hereford, and one at Polegate in East Sussex, a few miles north of Eastbourne.
See also PUNS & OLD JOKES, p. 138

Triton

In Greek and Roman mythology tritons were minor sea-gods attendant on Neptune. Like mermaids, they were represented with a human head and torso but a fish tail (sometimes shown as forked), though they were alarming rather than seductive. Often they carried a conch, symbolising their power to summon stormy waves. The name Triton, like those of other mythological figures connected with the sea, was often given to ships, especially warships. So Triton pubs such as the ones in Liverpool and at Sledmere in Yorkshire may be only indirectly linked to myth.

Troll Inn

Trolls come in two varieties in Scandinavian folklore. In Iceland and Norway they are large, dangerous giants living among the mountains, who hurl rocks at one another and at churches, and are quite likely to catch and eat human beings; in Icelandic tales it is often said that they turn to stone if sunlight strikes them. In Denmark, however, a troll is a small, red-haired goblin, living underground in hillocks, who may be mischievous but is never a serious threat to humans. Both species are now well known in Britain through fairytales, fantasy writers, and the popularity of small 'lucky troll' figures representing the Danish variety. In Dundee there is a pub called the Troll Inn which is full of pictures and statuettes of trolls.

Trusty Servant

There are pubs of this name at Minstead in Hampshire and at Chelmsley Wood, a district of Birmingham. The former has a very curious sign, copied from a symbolic painting in Winchester College; it shows a man with a pig's snout, ass's ears, a padlock on his mouth, and the feet of a stag – the marks of a perfect, trustworthy servant, who will never speak of his master's secrets, will toil as patiently as an ass, and will run as swift as a stag to do his master's

The Trusty Servant

bidding. However, the pig's snout does hint at a more cynical meaning; does even this trusty servant eat a lot? The original painting (now lost) was the work of a Winchester scholar named Hoskyns in 1759, and the present version in the College was painted in 1809 for the jubilee of George III, which is why the figure wears Georgian costume.

Tucker's Grave

There is only one pub of this name, between Radstock in Somerset and Trowbridge in Wiltshire. Two explanations are recorded by Paul Corballis. It appears that this Tucker lived in the eighteenth century, and was refused burial in consecrated ground; some said this was because he had hanged himself in a nearby barn and was buried beside the pub, under what is now its car park, others that he used to murder customers for their money and bury the bodies there, and was subsequently hanged. Until the 1830s it was customary to bury suicides in the public roadway, and murderers too were sometimes hanged near the site of their crime and then buried at the foot of the gallows. Such lonely and unhallowed graves easily became the focus of local fears and rumours, and wicked innkeepers used also to be a favourite theme for macabre tales.

Tuck's Habit

The Tuck's Habit at Bramcote, near Nottingham, takes its name from FRIAR TUCK, the companion of ROBIN HOOD – for the Nottingham area is naturally proud of its links to that hero. The name is a double pun. Friar Tuck's *habit* is both the gown he wears as a friar and his notorious love of food and drink; while

his name puns on the verb *tuck in*, meaning 'to eat heartily'.
See also PUNS & OLD JOKES, p. 138

Tudor Rose

See QUEENS' HEADS & RED LIONS, p. 248

Turk's Head

See SARACEN'S HEAD

Turpin's Cave

See DICK TURPIN

Twa Corbies

The Twa Corbies at Cumbernauld, near Glasgow, takes its name from a fine, sinister Scottish folksong from medieval times. The singer tells how he heard two corbies – ravens – talking together, wondering where to find food. One says he knows where there is a dead knight lying in a ditch,

> And naebody kens that he lies there
> But his hawk, his hound, and his lady fair –

none of whom cares that he is dead. The hound and hawk are out hunting, the fair lady has taken a new lover, so the corbies can do as they please:

Ye'll sit on his white hause-bane [neck-bone],
And I'll pike out his bonny blue e'en;
Wi' ae lock o' his gowden hair
We'll theek [thatch] our nest when it grows bare.

The song ends with a haunting image of desolation:

O'er his white banes when they are bare
The wind sall blaw for evermair.

See also MOTHER GEESE & CATS WITH FIDDLES, p. 46

~ U ~

Ugly Duckling

Many of the fairytales of the Danish author Hans Andersen (1805–75) are the products of his own creative imagination rather than traditional lore, yet some have become so familiar that they are absorbed into the stock of stories which British children take for granted as part of our own folklore. One such is 'The Ugly Duckling', which has given its name to a pub at Haywards Heath in West Sussex. It tells of an orphaned cygnet which grows up among ducks and is mocked and rejected, because to them he seems so big and so ugly, until the day that he grows his adult plumage and is revealed to be a very fine swan indeed. Andersen meant it as a parable about writers and artists (especially himself) who are initially despised but eventually triumph, but as a fairytale it has a wide appeal. According to Dunkling and Wright, the signboard at Haywards Heath shows 'a forlorn-looking Donald Duck beside a pond'.

See also MOTHER GEESE & CATS WITH FIDDLES, p. 46

Unicorn

When pubs are named the Unicorn, as in Manchester, York, Ripon (Yorkshire), Chesterfield (Derbyshire), Malvern (Worcestershire), Abbots Langley (Hertfordshire), and a good many other places, this is because this mythical beast has an important role in heraldry as one supporter of the Royal Arms of Britain. Behind the heraldry, however, lies the medieval symbolism in which the unicorn stood for gentle innocence and purity, even for Christ himself; there was also a persistent belief that its horn was a powerful antidote to poisons. The tusks of narwhals from the Arctic seas were sold for very high prices, with the claim that they were genuine unicorn horns.

The basic unicorn legend was given in medieval bestiaries (the translation here is from T. H. White's *The Book of Beasts* (1956)):

> He is a very small animal, like a kid, excessively swift, with one horn in the middle of his forehead, and no hunter can catch him.

The Unicorn

But he can be trapped by the following stratagem. A virgin girl is led to where he lurks, and there she is sent off by herself into the wood. He soon leaps into her lap when he sees her, and embraces her, and hence he gets caught.

See also QUEENS' HEADS & RED LIONS, p. 248

V

Vale of the White Horse

There are very many White Horse pubs throughout England, generally owing their name to some heraldic association, for this animal was the emblem of the Hanoverian dynasty, and also features in the arms of many noble families and of various guilds. However, the Vale of the White Horse at Minety Station near Malmesbury in Wiltshire refers specifically to a famous and very ancient landmark, the White Horse of Uffington in Berkshire. This is a figure carved into the chalk of a steep hillside in the Berkshire Downs, and has given its name to the whole valley.

Many antiquarians speculated as to its date and purpose. In the seventeenth century John Aubrey claimed it was made by Hengest, the leader of the first Anglo-Saxon settlers; an alternative theory was put forward in 1738 by the Rev. Francis Wise, who said Alfred the Great had it cut to celebrate his victory over the Danes at Ethandune in AD 878. This patriotic interpretation was generally accepted well into the twentieth century, and no doubt accounts for the choice of pub name at Minety Station. In 1931, however, the archaeologist Stuart Piggott set out a counter-theory that it was Celtic work from about 100

BC, initiating a debate which went on until 1995, when a new scientific technique proved that the Uffington White Horse was far older than either party had imagined. It turns out that the horse had been first cut in the Bronze Age, around 1000 BC – thus confirming the poetic intuition of G. K. Chesterton, who wrote in his 'Ballad of the White Horse' (1911) that though Alfred's great battle did indeed take place in the Vale, the figure itself had existed long before his time:

> Before the gods that made the gods
>> Had seen their sunrise pass,
> The White Horse of White Horse Vale
>> Was cut out of the grass …

> For the White Horse knew England
>> When there was none to know;
> He saw the first oar break or bend,
>> Oh God, how long ago!

One can only marvel at the perseverance with which the local people kept their horse in existence for so many centuries by regularly cleaning off the grass and weeds, without which it would have become invisible within a few years. Their devotion to its maintenance is by far the oldest provable example of continuous folkloric activity in England.

See also QUEENS' HEADS & RED LIONS, p. 248

Valentine & Orson/The Valentines

The unusual name Valentine and Orson was that of a pub in Long Lane, London SE1, as recently as the 1970s, but has now been changed to the Valentines. The older name comes from a once popular romance which originated in fifteenth-century France. It tells of twin boys of noble birth, one of whom (the appropriately named Orson, 'Baby Bear') is carried off into the forest by a bear as an infant, and brought up by bears as one of themselves. The story seems to have had as much appeal to the medieval reader as that of Mowgli had for later generations; unlike the morally admirable Mowgli, however, Orson grows up to be a ferocious, barely human Wild Man of the Woods who terrorises the countryside. Eventually his twin brother Valentine, now a gallant young knight, undertakes to kill or capture the dangerous creature. Yet as soon as they meet, the instinctive ties of blood reveal themselves. Instead of killing Orson, Valentine embraces him, leads him home, and rapidly civilises him, after which the two of them embark on various knightly adventures together.

The surprising popularity of the tale may be partly due to the fact that it provided a good theme for pageantry and fairground entertainment, where a man disguised as a bear would be sure to please the crowds. It also made its way into nineteenth-century children's books, but is now hardly remembered.

The pub's new name, the Valentines, obviously refers to the association between love and St Valentine's Day, 14 February, which has been part of English folklore since the late medieval period – though in its earliest version the semi-serious belief referred to birds, not to human sweethearts. Geoffrey Chaucer, along with several other fourteenth-century poets, claimed that every year on this day birds would choose their mates, and implied that this marked the beginning of spring. The idea may well have originated in France. A few decades later, around 1440, John Lydgate wrote a love poem entitled 'A Valentine to her that Excelleth All', saying it is a custom that on Valentine's Day men should 'choose their choice by great affection'; the title of the verses proves that 'a valentine' already meant a lover's message or gift. Other sources show it also meant the person whom one chose as one's sweetheart for the day. Over the centuries the custom has developed greatly, involving gifts, letters, and cards (often anonymous or under a nickname), and now messages in newspaper columns.

St Valentine himself is said to have been a Christian priest (or possibly a bishop) martyred in Rome in the third century AD, in the time of the Emperor Claudius. There is nothing whatever in the accounts of his life and death to link him to lovers or to the mating of birds – journalists sometimes claim that while he was awaiting execution his jailer's daughter fell in love with him, but this is a quite modern romantic invention. It must have been sheer chance that the date arbitrarily chosen as the first day of spring was that of his feast – whatever the date, it was bound to be linked to some saint or other, for in the Catholic calendar every day is the feast of at least one saint – and this chance gave rise to the valentine.

There is also a Valentine pub at Gant's Hill in Ilford (Essex). *See also* THE YEAR'S MERRY ROUND, p. 310

Vulcan

In Roman mythology the god Vulcan was a smith who forged superb armour and weapons. When pubs of the nineteenth or earlier twentieth century were named after him it was usually in allusion to local furnaces and forges, though later ones may refer to the Vulcan bomber of the Second World War.

The Year's Merry Round

There is a happy symbiotic relationship between those two favourite elements in British tradition, the seasonal festival custom and the pub. The custom involves performance and draws an audience; the pub provides a venue; and both performers and audience readily buy drinks. Many customs which at the beginning of the twentieth century seemed on the point of extinction have flourished in the latter part of that century, and new ones have sprung up. The role of the pub in this revival should not be overlooked.

A welcome trend in recent years is that several pubs, such as the ASHEN FAGGOT in Northleigh in Devon and the CHEESE ROLLERS at Shurdington in Gloucestershire, have taken names from customary celebrations, whether local or widespread. It is also very fitting that Morris men (see MORRIS DANCERS) should be celebrated, for their dancing is an essential part of so many traditional events throughout the year. However, there are also many pubs which are involved in one way or another with a famous local custom, and yet – perhaps surprisingly – one would never guess this from their names and signboards.

Every January on Plough Monday, two or three hundred men representing the neighbouring villages of Haxey and Westwoodside in Lincolnshire (Humberside) struggle to capture a tightly rolled leather truncheon called the Haxey Hood and carry it into their own pub, the King's Arms and the Carpenter's Arms respectively, which are the goals. The game is rather like early forms of mass street football, as played in Tudor times; its most dramatic feature is the 'sway', a heaving mass of people like a gigantic rugby scrum, swinging to and fro and gradually nearing a goal. The game ends when the landlord of one pub or the other touches the Hood; he then becomes its guardian, keeping it behind his bar till the next year.

Padstow, in Cornwall, celebrates May Day with England's most famous processional dance featuring a HOBBY HORSE ('Obby Oss'), formed by a huge hoop of black canvas topped by a grotesque red, white and black mask and conical headdress. The event begins at midnight on May Eve, when a crowd outside the Golden Lion Inn starts a traditional song wishing luck first to the landlord, and then to other households through the town. The Oss itself emerges from its 'stable' behind the Golden Lion at ten o'clock next morning and dances all day. So close was the link with the pub that in the 1890s a rival horse was created, the Blue Ribbon or Temperance Oss (blue ribbons were the badge of the temperance movement). Both Osses now coexist, their rivalry forgotten, and dance round the maypole together at the end of the day.

The two most widespread forms of traditional public entertainment are the Morris dance and the mummers' play. Both were rural working-class customs that almost died out in the nineteenth century; both were triumphantly revived in the twentieth, though chiefly by middle-class performers for middle-class audiences. Morris dancing is a regular feature of Boxing Day, May Day and Midsummer celebrations, but can also be done on all kinds of dates and occasions; the mummers' play is more strictly seasonal, being limited to dates close to Christmas or (in certain areas only) to Easter or to All Souls (2 November). These performances need space, and were of course originally designed to attract donations of money or beer from the spectators – nowadays, money for charities. For both reasons, pub courtyards offer an excellent venue.

Currently, Londoners are keen on forging new urban festivals out of elements of old rural ones, and giving them pagan significance. Judging by Scott Wood's essay in Antony Clayton's *The Folklore of London* (2008), pubs often play a key role. Thus, on Plough Monday the Fowlers' Troop, a group including several sides of Morris dancers, undertake their own pub crawl round Royal Hill, Greenwich; on May Day they escort a JACK-IN-THE-GREEN from Southwark, Deptford or Greenwich into the City, and 'the event always involves a musical procession from pub to pub'; so does the Carshalton Straw Jack ceremony in September; and 'on Boxing Day Blackheath Morris go from pub to pub in Blackheath to dance, as do many other Morris sides in London and beyond. This marks the end of the ritual year.'

See also FLITCH OF BACON, HOODEN HORSE, MAYPOLE, RUSHCART, and SILVER BALL

W

Wansdyke

The Wansdyke, from which a pub at Odd Down, near Bath, takes its name, is a remarkably long earthwork which begins at Andover in Hampshire, crosses Wiltshire, and ends at Portishead in Somerset. It probably dates from the sixth century, and was presumably raised as a defensive boundary for some kingdom. In Anglo-Saxon times its name is recorded as *Wodnes dic*, 'Woden's dyke' (Woden being the god of war and the supposed ancestor of several dynasties of Anglo-Saxon rulers), but in later forms of English the 'd' was dropped, just as it is in the pronunciation, though not the spelling, of Wednesday, 'Woden's Day'. Many generations later, local folk-lore still insisted that the Wansdyke had a supernatural origin; in Elizabethan times the antiquary William Camden noted that people living in the area would tell how it had been made by the Devil on a Wednesday.

Water Witch

A pub on the towpath of the Basingstoke Canal at Odiham in Hampshire renamed itself the Water Witch in 1976, in honour of a narrowboat of that name which had long plied on the canal.

Presumably the underlying folkloric idea is the same as that of the Sea Witch – a woman whose spells command the winds and the waves. There is another Water Witch pub in Lancaster, similarly sited beside a canal, and this one has as its signboard the face of a handsome but fierce-looking young woman who is clearly meant to be the witch.

Wee Willie Winkie

There is a pub of this name at Middlesbrough in Yorkshire, and a shorter form, 'Wee Willie', at Dinnington near Newcastle. The reference is to a nursery rhyme for use at bedtime:

> Wee Willie Winkie runs through the town,
> Upstairs and downstairs in his night-gown,
> Rapping at the window, crying through the lock,
> 'Are the children all in bed, it's now eight o'clock?'

Like the Sandman, Willie Winkie personifies the urge to fall asleep ('wink' is here used in the older sense of 'shut one's eyes'). The lines are now generally assumed to be anonymous and traditional, and appeared as such in various English collections of nursery rhymes in the 1840s. However, they are simply adapted from the first verse of a Scottish poem by a known author, William Miller, published in 1841.

See also MOTHER GEESE & CATS WITH FIDDLES, p. 46

Whale & Cow

See PUZZLING PAIRS, p. 117

Wheatsheaf

See HARVESTERS & WHEATSHEAVES, p. 182 *and* QUEENS'
HEADS & RED LIONS, p. 248

Whiffler

There are pubs called the Whiffler(s) at Norwich and Lowestoft. This curious word was the term for men who went ahead of processions and parades to push the spectators to the side of the road, and so clear the way for the main figures. For centuries Norwich has had a large-scale annual procession; before the Reformation it was a religious event held on St George's Day, but in Protestant times it was transformed into a Midsummer civic parade, though it still kept the much loved figure of Snap the Dragon. An eighteenth-century account talks of Whifflers dressed in Tudor costume who juggled with their 'whiffles' (i.e. wooden swords) and whirled them about, keeping the crowds at a safe distance.

See also THE YEAR'S MERRY ROUND, p. 310

White Hart

'Hart' is an alternative term for a red deer stag; these do sometimes appear in albino form, but only rarely. White Hart is one of the most widespread of pub names, known since medieval times. It is derived from a heraldic source, the favourite badge of

Richard II being a white hart with a gold crown worn as a collar round its neck, and a gold chain hanging from it. Therefore, in order to be historically correct, the sign should show the animal in this way.

Behind Richard's choice of this badge lies a legend going back through medieval sources to classical antiquity, telling how some king or hero pursued and captured a white stag or hart, tamed it, and set a collar of gold round its neck; in Ancient Greece this story was told of Alexander the Great, in Rome of Julius Caesar, in France and Germany of Charlemagne. (The sign of the White Hart at Old Woking, Surrey, shows Alexander the Great putting a gold collar on the noble creature.) In Arthurian romances too, knights set off in pursuit of white stags which, it is implied, are fairy beasts, but which they do not catch; instead, the strange creatures lead them to further adventures. Such animals also feature in religious legends. It is said that King David of Scotland went hunting on Holy Rood Day, despite a priest's warning that he should respect the holy feast. While chasing a huge white hart (or stag) he was thrown from his horse; the hart turned and attacked him, but David, with a hasty prayer, grasped its antlers, which miraculously turned into a crucifix. The beast then vanished.

White deer do occur fairly frequently in nature, but the notion that they are in some way sacred, or enchanted, or simply ominous has persisted for many centuries. At this present time (February 2008), there is a young white stag somewhere in the Scottish Highlands whose whereabouts are kept secret to protect him from poachers. Reporting this, a *Times* journalist writes that 'from time immemorial' a white deer has been regarded as 'a messenger from the afterlife, a mystical creature which chilled the blood'; that to encounter one will bring about a profound change in one's life; also, that those who kill one bring a curse on themselves. Similarly, in the Erzgebirge mountains in Saxony (eastern Germany) in November 2006, some local hunters refused to shoot a white buck because of a belief that if anyone kills a white deer he (or one of his family) will be doomed to die within a year. Legend claims that Archduke Ferdinand shot a white stag in the autumn of 1913, and that it was because of the curse that he was assassinated at Sarajevo, triggering the First World War.

See also QUEENS' HEADS & RED LIONS, p. 248

White Heather

The White Heather Roadhouse at Kirkcaldy has taken its name from one of the most widely publicised symbols of Scotland, especially Highland Scotland. In her letters and diaries, Queen Victoria referred several times to the belief that a sprig of white heather brings good luck, and it was no doubt her enthusiasm for all things Scottish which made this well known south of the Border. Ideally, of course, it ought to be a natural sprig of true heather, growing wild and found by mere chance, but the 'white heather' now sold in large quantities to tourists is a commercially grown variety of ling.

White Horse

See VALE OF THE WHITE HORSE

White Lady

The White Lady at Shardlow (near Derby) is so called because of a local tale of a ghostly woman in a long white dress who is said to haunt the area. Nameless White Ladies of vaguely medieval appearance are a common form of ghost in British lore. Those that appear out of doors are quite often associated with ponds or streams, which has led some writers to suggest that they are a relatively modern development from older beliefs about minor nature goddesses.

See also GHOSTLY BARMAIDS & HAUNTED CELLARS, p. 278

White Swan

This, like SWAN WITH TWO NECKS, Black Swan and plain Swan, is a widespread, popular and picturesque name and does not normally have any folklore significance. But the White Swan at Dunstable in Bedfordshire, though a relatively modern name, has a remarkable link to a famous medieval legend from the Continent. Originally the pub was called the Two Black Boys (and it may be that this was dropped in order to avoid racist implications), but its new name alludes to a delight-ful medieval jewel which was found by archaeologists in 1965 during excavations at Dunstable Priory. It is a small gold brooch representing a swan with white enamelled feathers, black enamelled eyes

The White Swan

and feet, a gold crown worn like a collar round its neck, and a gold chain. It dates from the late fourteenth or early fifteenth century and is in the British Museum. A swan with these embellishments was the heraldic badge of the Stafford family, who were dukes of Buckingham, and also of Henry VI, who is known to have visited Dunstable in 1495; both this king and the Staffords wore it as a sign of their claim to be descended from the celebrated Crusader Godfrey de Bouillon in the eleventh century, and through him from his supposed grandfather, the legendary Swan Knight.

The tale of the Swan Knight was immensely popular in medieval France, Flanders, and Germany, and there were English versions too; it is set either in Flanders or in the Rhine valley, and is generally told as the 'explanation' of the origins of the powerful dynasty of the dukes of Brabant, the family of Godfrey (Godefroi) de Bouillon. It begins when a young prince named Orient finds a mysterious naked girl called Beatrix beside a fountain, and marries her, to the fury of his mother, the queen. Later he goes off to war, leaving her pregnant. She gives birth to seven babies, each with a silver chain round its neck. The wicked queen says such a birth is unnatural; she accuses Beatrix of having had sexual intercourse with a dog, and orders the babies to be killed, but they are rescued and reared by a hermit. Some years later, the queen learns that they are alive and sends men to murder them, but instead the assassins steal the chains off their necks, whereupon they turn into swans – all but one, Helias, who was not there when the villains came. Later still, the truth is revealed, Beatrix is vindicated, and five of the six silver chains are recovered, whereupon five of the six swans resume human shape, though the sixth cannot. The focus of the tale now shifts to Helias, who sets off on his adventures in a boat drawn by his brother the swan, and who is therefore known as the Swan Knight. He keeps his real name secret. Eventually he hears of the plight of a widowed Duchess of Bouillon whose lands are about to be seized by a false claimant. He defeats the claimant in single combat, and weds the duchess's daughter, thus founding the dynasty of the dukes of Brabant. In some versions, the swan is disenchanted at this point, and also becomes the ancestor of famous aristocratic lines. Usually, however, the tale ends sadly, for Helias's wife insists on knowing who he really is, though he has warned her that if she does he will be forced by magic powers to leave her. As soon as he speaks his name, the swan returns, towing the little boat, Helias steps aboard, and disappears for ever. A variant of this story is the basis for Wagner's opera *Lohengrin*.

Whittington & Cat

See DICK WHITTINGTON

Whittington Stone

See DICK WHITTINGTON

Who'd Have Thought It?

See PUNS & OLD JOKES, p. 138

Why Not

See PUNS & OLD JOKES, p. 138

Wicked Lady

Near Wheathampton in Hertfordshire, alongside the road leading from the village of Markyate Street to Sandridge, there is a common known as Nomansland, on which stands a pub which since 1967 has been called the Wicked Lady, though previously it was the Park Inn. The new name was taken from that of a highly popular film made in 1945 and starring Margaret Lockwood and James Mason, but the film (and the novel on which it was based) drew upon on a local legend which already existed, and was first printed in John Cussans's *History of Hertfordshire* (1870–81). According to this, it was the ghost of 'Wicked Lady Ferrers' which caused the ancient mansion of the Ferrers family at Markyate Cell to be burnt down in 1840, after she had haunted the place for several generations. Cussans writes:

> It is said, that in the disguise of male attire, and mounted on a coal-black horse with white forefeet, she robbed travellers on the highway, but at length was fatally wounded at No Mans Land, when so engaged. She was found lying dead outside a door leading by a secret staircase to the chamber where she changed her dress.

He also records that after the fire local workmen who were demolishing the ruins refused to open this door, so great was their fear of Lady Ferrers's ghost, and that many of them swore they had seen her swinging on the branch of a sycamore near the house – at the foot of which, supposedly, a large amount of treasure was buried. Augustus Hare, a Victorian writer who took a keen interest in the paranormal, recorded in his journal in November 1894 that the current owner of Markyate Cell regularly saw the ghost:

> Mr Adey, who lives there now, meets her on the stairs and wishes her Goodnight. Once seeing her with arms outstretched in a doorway he called to his wife who was outside 'Now we've got her'. And then they rushed upon her from both sides, but caught nothing.

It is still claimed in local tradition that she can be seen in her highwayman's garb galloping along various roads and lanes in the area.

It is not known whether there is any historical core to the legend, nor who exactly this 'Wicked Lady Ferrers' could have been, especially since the family at Markyate Cell had no title; those who believe in the tale generally identify her as an Elizabeth Ferrers who died in 1659. The film adds a good deal of romantic love interest to the basic tale of disguise and adventure, and says nothing about a ghost.

See also HIGHWAYMEN & SMUGGLERS, p. 208

Widow's Son

In Devons Road in Bromley-by-Bow, London E3, there is a pub which has been called the Widow's Son since at least 1851; it is sometimes also known as the Bun House. It is famous for the clusters of very dry hot cross buns hanging in nets from the ceiling; a new one is added every year on Good Friday, usually by some sailor, for this was originally a docklands area. A fire some years ago destroyed many of the older ones, and those that were saved are heavily charred. It is a condition of the lease that whoever runs the pub must keep the custom going, though it is not known in what year it began.

There is a tale to explain this. It is said that before the pub was built there was a cottage on the same site, in which there lived a widow and her only son, whom she dearly loved. The boy became a sailor, and when he set out on his first voyage he told his mother not to fret – he would be sure to be home for Easter, and she must have a hot cross bun ready for him. So she did, but when Easter came round her son had not come home. She kept the bun hanging from a beam in her kitchen, and waited. The next year she did the same, and the next, and the next … The boy never returned, and the collection of buns went on growing. When the widow died, her cottage was pulled down and the buns transferred to the newly built pub. According to some accounts, her name was Mrs Hart, and she died in 1813. Currently, the pub sign shows the departing lad turning for a last look at his home.

It is a striking story, but unlikely to be true, since the custom it purports to explain was a common one in the eighteenth and nineteenth centuries. Many women would make a hard-baked bun or small loaf on Good Friday and keep it all year 'for luck', hanging it from the kitchen ceiling so that it stayed dry. It would be taken down the following Good Friday, and replaced by another. Some people believed this would prevent the house catching fire; others, especially along the coast, that it would protect members of the household from shipwreck – an idea which could have inspired the story of the Widow's Son.

See also THE YEAR'S MERRY ROUND, p. 310

Wild Man

Wild Men appear quite often in medieval art and literature. They were thought of as large, strong semi-human savages living in deep forests, and were represented as armed with a club, and either covered in shaggy hair or naked, apart from girdles and garlands of leaves. In the latter guise, they could also be called Green Men. Court masques and civic pageants often included performers costumed as Wild Men, and they were also represented in heraldry, usually as supporters of the main coat of arms. Symbolically, they stood for the uncontrolled, potentially violent aspects of 'nature', contrasted with chivalry and civilisation, but in pageantry and art the implication is that their savagery has been tamed.

The Distillers' Company was one institution which had them on its coat of arms, which was why the Wild Man became a name used by inns, though it was never as popular as the GREEN MAN. However, according to the seventeenth-century writer John Bagford, it was appropriate, because inns sold 'intoxicating liquor which berefts [drinkers] of their senses'. In this context, the Wild Man was represented in the same way as a Green Man: a robust, club-wielding giant, with a garland of green leaves on his head and more leaves around

The Wild Man

his loins. A fine modern rendering of this image can be seen at the Woodstock Arms in Oxford, where two leafy giants flank a coat of arms, though since the pub's name is heraldic the question whether they are 'green' or 'wild' remains open. In the eighteenth and nineteenth centuries there were also versions where the Wild Man wore feathers, not leaves; in which case the allusion was to the supposedly savage 'Red Indians' and the tobacco trade.

This historical background being largely forgotten nowadays, there are very few Wild Man pubs left, and those that do keep the name sometimes produce new explanations for it. One such is in Bedford Street, Norwich; its signboard used to show the conventional feathered savage, but currently shows a baby boy, together with a she-bear. This refers to a real person, an imbecile boy found living wild in the forests near Hanover in Germany in 1724, who was given to George I as a curiosity, and brought by him to England. He was kept in London for a while, but later entrusted to the care of a farmer at Haxter End in Hertfordshire. He used to run away, and once got as far as Norwich, where he was imprisoned as a vagrant; he almost died when the prison caught fire, but was rescued, identified, and returned to Haxter End. He died at Northchurch, aged about seventy. Norwich people, however, insist that he was locked in the cellar of the building which is now the pub but was at that time a lunatic asylum, and died when it caught fire. According to C. M. Tennant's semi-fictional book *Peter the Wild Boy* (1938), he had been reared by bears; hence the new signboard. It is said that his ghost now haunts the pub.

See also QUEENS' HEADS & RED LIONS, p. 248

Windwhistle Inn

See HIGHWAYMEN & SMUGGLERS, p. 208

Winged Horse

See PEGASUS

Wishing Well

This is quite a common pub name, which can be found in Reading, Nottingham, Milton Keynes, various parts of London, and elsewhere. It is possible that in some cases the idea is simply to convey a message of friendly welcome ('We wish you well'), but there is likely also to be some implication of good luck, since most people are aware of the custom of throwing a coin into a well, pool, or fountain to obtain a wish. This custom is demonstrably old, being simply the modern equivalent of the pins, bent coins, and other offerings thrown into holy wells by medieval pilgrims as they prayed, or, earlier still, the various objects left by worshippers at sacred springs in pagan times.

Witch Ball

One might easily think that the term 'witch ball', found as a pub name at Thame in Oxfordshire, refers to the crystal ball so often used by fortune-tellers for scrying, but it does not. A witch ball was a hollow glass ball coated with very glossy paint in brilliant colours (red, blue, silver or gold), like an outsize Christmas tree bauble. They were first made in the eighteenth century, and were very popular in the nineteenth. Such balls were hung in cottage windows, there being a belief that any witch intending to cast the Evil Eye on the house would inevitably glance first at the glittering object, which would reflect her gaze outwards, and so turn aside its power.

Wizard's Inn

This pub at Nether Alderley, near Macclesfield (Cheshire), takes its name from the famous legend of the Wizard of Alderley Edge, this being a picturesque rocky outcrop pitted with quarries and honeycombed with the tunnels of ancient mine workings. There was once a farmer from Mobberley who was taking a white mare to Macclesfield, hoping to sell her at the market there. As he passed through the woods by Alderley Edge he was stopped by an old, white-bearded man who offered to buy her. Thinking he would get a better price at market, the farmer refused. 'You will find no buyer today,' said the old man. Which proved true. But that evening, as the disappointed farmer was heading home, the wizard was there again, at the same spot. This time he showed the farmer great iron gates among the rocks, and ordered him to follow (bringing the mare too) into the depths of the hill. There he saw a host of warriors lying asleep in a cavern, all but one having a white horse sleeping beside him; the wizard explained that they would arise one day to join in some fearsome battle when the fate of England itself hung in the balance. The farmer was glad now to sell his mare for a purse of gold. As he left the hill the iron gates clanged shut, and nobody has ever found them since.

The tale goes back at least to the eighteenth century; in several later versions the wizard is said to be Merlin, and the sleeping warriors King Arthur and his knights. It was retold by Alan Garner in *The Weirdstone of Brisingamen* (1960).

Woden

The name of the Woden Inn at Wednesbury (near Birmingham) is a tribute to the town's own remarkable name, for Wednesbury comes from *Wodnes burgh*, 'the stronghold of Woden', who was the chief god of the pagan Anglo-Saxons, and from whom several of their royal dynasties claimed descent. The same change of vowel can be seen in Wednesday, which also comes from this god's name. Only scraps of information about him can be got from English sources in Christian times, but much is known about his Icelandic counterpart Odin, the god of war, of death, and of magic wisdom.

Wookey Hole

At Wookey, near Wells in Somerset, is the Wookey Hole pub, which takes its name from a very famous landmark, an extensive and picturesque cave notable for the weird shapes of some of the rock formations and stalactites inside it. Thomas Percy in his *Reliques of Ancient English Poetry* (1765) gives a good account of how it impressed visitors in the days before modern access and lighting:

Wookey Hole is a noted cavern in Somersetshire, which has given birth to as many wild fanciful stories as the Sybil's Cave in Italy. Through a very narrow entrance, it opens into a very large vault, the roof whereof, either on account of its height, or the thickness of the gloom, cannot be discovered by the light of torches. It goes winding a great way under the ground, is crossed by a stream of very cold water, and is all horrid with broken pieces of rock; many of these are evident petrifactions which, on account of their singular forms, have given rise to the fables alluded to in this poem.

The poem he then quotes, written in 1748 by 'the ingenious Dr Harrington of Bath', tells how a wicked witch came to live in 'this dreary dismal cell / Which seemed and was ycleped Hell', accompanied by nine demons, plus owls and wolves.

> Her haggard face was foul to see,
> Her mouth unmeet a mouth to be,
>   Her eyes of deadly leer;
> She nought devis'd but neighbour's ill,
> She wreak'd on all her wayward will,
>   And marr'd all goodly cheer.

She plagued the neighbourhood until a learned cleric from Glastonbury arrived, armed with holy water:

> He chauntede out his godlie booke,
> He crost the water, blest the brooke,
>   Then – pater noster done –
> The ghastly hag he sprinkled o'er;
> When lo! Where stood a hag before,
>   Now stood a ghastly stone.

Other eighteenth-century versions give the credit for this exorcism to a cleric from Oxford, not Glastonbury, but all agree that the figure of the petrified witch is still to be seen, as are various of her possessions. The story has been featured in virtually every guidebook to Somerset from that day to this.

The basis for the tale is the undoubted resemblance of one of the stalactites to a woman. This is already mentioned in the writings of William Worcestre in 1480. He gives a detailed account of the caves and pools, the stalactites, a rock at the entrance called 'the Porter'('one must ask leave from the Porter, to enter the hall of Wookey'), and then, in an inner cave, 'the figure of a woman clothed and spinning with what is called in English a distaff held beneath her girdle'. However, he says nothing about her being a witch.

There seems to have been a belief, at one time, that Wookey Hole would be a suitable place in which to imprison a troublesome ghost, though admittedly less effective than the Red Sea. An anonymous poem from the early nineteenth century explores this idea, though rather flippantly:

> To lay the lorn spirit, you o'er it must pray,
> And command it, at length, to be gone far away,
> And in Wookey's deep hole
> To be under control
> For the space of seven years and a day.
>
> If then it return, you must pray and command
> By midnight,
> By moonlight,
> By death's ebon wand,
> That to Cheddar cliffs now it departeth in peace,
> And another seven years its sore troubling will cease.

If it return still,
As, I warn you, it will,
To the Red Sea for ever
Command it; and never
Or noise more or sound
In the house will be found.

World Turned Upside Down

This is a curious phrase, with many applications. It occurs twice in the Bible, once in an Old Testament text generally taken to foretell the destruction of the world at Doomsday (Isa. 24:1, 'The Lord maketh the earth empty, and maketh it waste, and turneth it upside down'); and once in the Acts of the Apostles (17:6), where people opposing the preaching of Paul and Silas complain that 'these men have turned the world upside down', which gives it a revolutionary flavour. But in popular usage it more usually referred to situations where the natural order of things is turned topsy-turvy in quite ridiculous ways. This was a favourite theme for visual jokes in medieval manuscripts and church carvings, often involving situations where the power relationship between men and animals, or between different species of animal, is reversed – hares roasting a huntsman, mice hanging a cat, geese hanging a fox, a fox riding a hound, and so forth.

Faced with this pub name, some sign-painters chose the simple literalism of a globe with the poles and continents reversed, while others continued the tradition of medieval animal jokes. One at Reading in 1980, for instance, had on one side of the sign a hay wagon with a horse inside it, pulled by a man; on the other, a man fleeing from a hare which holds a gun. Leslie Dunkling and Gordon Wright, in their *Pub Names of Britain*, mention a pub in London's New Kent Road (SE1) which took first one option, then the other. At one time its sign showed 'a man walking at the South Pole', but it was later changed to one (which they illustrate) which has 'on one side an enormous fish which has just caught a man, and on the other side a football with legs about to boot a man between two goalposts'. This too has now been removed.

See also PUNS & OLD JOKES, p. 138

World's End

This name was sometimes chosen for inns and pubs which stand (or originally stood) in an isolated spot some way beyond the boundaries of a village or town. In Edinburgh, however, the World's End has a more precise historical and local reference. It is built over part of an old fortification, the Flodden Wall, which was hastily erected round the city to protect it after that disastrous battle; for city-dwellers, the line of the wall marked the 'end' of their world.

The name is still popular, since it lends itself to more dramatic interpretations, some of which take 'end' in a geographical sense, while others see it as referring to Doomsday, the end of time and of the universe. The World's End in Camden High Street (London NW1, formerly the Mother Redcap) first chose the geographical option. Exploiting the medieval notion that the world is a mere disc, with a rim to it, it showed a Viking-style sailing ship just about to be swept over this rim into the void. Currently its sign, painted in a rather surrealist style, offers a dramatic scene of cosmic destruction, symbolised by an eclipsed sun, a cracked ladder, a paved floor wrenched by an earthquake. An eclipsed sun can also be seen at the World's

End in King's Road, Chelsea (London sw10), and a sailing ship teetering on the edge of the world's disc at Pudsey in Yorkshire. The most extreme example of this theme can be found in William Hogarth's last painting, *Finis: Or the Tail Piece*. Father Time himself lies dying in a landscape strewn with symbols of death, near a tumbledown inn called the World's End, whose signboard shows the globe cracking and bursting into flame.

In contrast, the World's End at Knaresborough in Yorkshire has chosen a purely local reference. Its sign shows a bridge collapsing into a river – which is a puzzle to outsiders, since it alludes to a prophecy attributed to the town's famous witch, Mother Shipton. She is said to have declared that if Knaresborough bridge should fall for the third time into the river Nidd (it had already done so twice), this would be a sign that Doomsday had come.

Whatever explanation is offered, this pub name also offers the opportunity for a joke. The would-be customer can always boast that he'd go to the world's end for a drink.

Wyvern

There are pubs named the Wyvern in Sheffield, at Lee-on-Solent (Hampshire), at Church Cookham (Somerset), and elsewhere. In heraldry, a wyvern is a two-legged winged dragon, as opposed to the more common four-legged species, and one can assume that it was originally adopted into the repertoire of inn signs from the coat of arms of some landowning family.

See also QUEENS' HEADS & RED LIONS, p. 248

Index